GACE Middle Grades
014 Science
Teacher Certification Exam

By: Sharon A. Wynne, M.S.

XAMonline, INC.
Boston

To obtain permission(s) to use the material from this work for any purpose including workshops or seminars, please submit a written request to:

XAMonline, Inc.
21 Orient Avenue
Melrose, MA 02176
Toll Free 1-800-301-4647
Email: info@xamonline.com
Web www.xamonline.com

Library of Congress Cataloging-in-Publication Data

Wynne, Sharon A.
GACE Middle Grades Science 014: Teacher Certification / Sharon A. Wynne.
ISBN 978-1-64239-036-0
      1. GACE Middle Grades Science 014.   2. Study Guides.   3. GACE
      4. Teachers' Certification & Licensure.   5. Careers

Disclaimer:
The opinions expressed in this publication are the sole works of XAMonline and were created independently from the National Education Association, Educational Testing Service, or any State Department of Education, National Evaluation Systems or other testing affiliates.

Between the time of publication and printing, state specific standards as well as testing formats and website information may change that is not included in part or in whole within this product. Sample test questions are developed by XAMonline and reflect similar content as on real tests; however, they are not former tests. XAMonline assembles content that aligns with state standards but makes no claims nor guarantees teacher candidates a passing score. Numerical scores are determined by testing companies such as NES or ETS and then are compared with individual state standards. A passing score varies from state to state.

Printed in the United States of America   œ-1

GACE: Middle Grades Science 014
ISBN: 978-1-64239-036-0

Table of Contents

DOMAIN I.   EARTH SCIENCE

COMPETENCY 1.0   **UNDERSTAND CURRENT SCIENTIFIC VIEWS OF THE UNIVERSE** 1

Skill 1.1   Demonstrating knowledge of the development of theories about the formation of the universe and the solar system 1

Skill 1.2   Demonstrating knowledge of characteristics and general locations of objects in the solar system and universe 2

Skill 1.3   Recognizing the effects of gravity on the motion of objects in the solar system 5

Skill 1.4   Analyzing the motion of objects in the sky in terms of relative position 6

Skill 1.5   Recognizing the effects of the orientations, positions, and movements of the Earth, Moon, and Sun 6

Skill 1.6   Identifying the methods and types of technology used to observe and collect data about the solar system and universe 7

COMPETENCY 2.0   **UNDERSTAND THE CHARACTERISTICS AND DISTRIBUTION OF WATER AND ITS ROLE IN THE EARTH'S PROCESSES** 9

Skill 2.1   Identifying the properties of water in its different physical states 9

Skill 2.2   Analyzing the water cycle and its relationship to various atmospheric conditions 10

Skill 2.3   Identifying major reservoirs of water on the Earth and their distribution 11

Skill 2.4   Demonstrating knowledge of the composition, location, and subsurface topography of the world's oceans 12

Skill 2.5   Identifying the causes and effects of waves, currents, and tides ... 15

Skill 2.6   Demonstrating knowledge of freshwater resources 16

COMPETENCY 3.0   UNDERSTAND CHARACTERISTICS OF THE ATMOSPHERE AND OF CLIMATE AND WEATHER 17

Skill 3.1   Identifying the basic composition, structure, and properties of the atmosphere 17

Skill 3.2   Analyzing the significance of changes in weather variables 18

Skill 3.3   Recognizing the effects of large bodies of water, large land areas, and differences in elevation on weather and climate 19

Skill 3.4   Demonstrating knowledge of weather patterns and the causes and effects of local and regional weather events 20

Skill 3.5   Analyzing global weather and climate patterns 21

Skill 3.6   Recognizing the methods and types of technology used to observe, measure, and predict climate and weather 21

COMPETENCY 4.0   UNDERSTAND CHARACTERISTICS OF THE EARTH AND PROCESSES THAT HAVE SHAPED ITS SURFACE 23

Skill 4.1   Demonstrating knowledge of the Earth's structure and composition 23

Skill 4.2   Classifying rocks and minerals based on their process of formation and characteristics 24

Skill 4.3   Identifying the characteristics of soil and analyzing how it forms... 25

Skill 4.4   Analyzing constructive and destructive processes that form and change major geological features 26

Skill 4.5   Demonstrating knowledge of the theory of plate tectonics and evidence that supports the theory 31

Skill 4.6   Recognizing characteristics of fossils and how they show evidence of the changing surface and climate of the earth 33

COMPETENCY 5.0   **UNDERSTAND THE TYPES AND USES OF THE EARTH'S NATURAL RESOURCES** 34

Skill 5.1   Identifying types, characteristics, and uses of renewable and nonrenewable resources 34

Skill 5.2   Recognizing the Sun as the major source of energy on the Earth's surface and analyzing its relationship to wind and water energy ... 35

Skill 5.3   Identifying the effects of natural events and human activities on the Earth's natural resources 36

Skill 5.4   Demonstrating knowledge of methods for conserving and protecting natural resources 38

DOMAIN II.   **LIFE SCIENCE**

COMPETENCY 6.0   **UNDERSTAND THE DIVERSITY OF LIVING ORGANISMS AND THEIR CLASSIFICATION** 39

Skill 6.1   Identifying criteria used to classify organisms based upon a six-kingdom system 39

Skill 6.2   Recognizing the distinguishing characteristics of different groups of organisms 41

Skill 6.3   Recognizing the features of dichotomous keys and their development and use 42

COMPETENCY 7.0   **UNDERSTAND THE STRUCTURE AND FUNCTION OF LIVING SYSTEMS** 43

Skill 7.1   Identifying characteristics of prokaryotic and eukaryotic cells 43

Skill 7.2   Comparing and contrasting the structures and functions of plant and animal cells 46

Skill 7.3   Demonstrating knowledge of the relationship between cell structures and their functions 46

Skill 7.4   Recognizing basic characteristics of living things 48

Skill 7.5   Demonstrating knowledge of the characteristics of plant structures and the functional relationships that connect them 48

Skill 7.6   Demonstrating knowledge of cells, tissues, organs, and organ systems in animals and the functional relationships that connect them 50

Skill 7.7   Recognizing the characteristics and functions of major organ systems in the human body 50

COMPETENCY 8.0   UNDERSTAND THE PRINCIPLES AND PROCESSES OF THE INHERITANCE OF BIOLOGICAL TRAITS 60

Skill 8.1   Recognizing the role of DNA and RNA in the transmission of genetic information 60

Skill 8.2   Demonstrating knowledge of the roles of genes and chromosomes in the transfer of biological traits between generations 64

Skill 8.3   Differentiating sexual and asexual reproduction in organisms 66

Skill 8.4   Demonstrating knowledge of the basic principles of inheritance and Mendel's laws 68

Skill 8.5   Solving problems involving the probability of inheriting a specific trait 68

Skill 8.6   Identifying applications of genetic engineering technology 71

COMPETENCY 9.0   UNDERSTAND THE DEPENDENCE OF ORGANISMS ON ONE ANOTHER AND UNDERSTAND THE FLOW OF ENERGY AND MATTER IN ECOSYSTEMS 73

Skill 9.1   Identifying the roles of producers, consumers, and decomposers in ecosystems 73

Skill 9.2   Demonstrating knowledge of the flow of energy and matter through a food web, food chain, or ecosystem 73

Skill 9.3   Evaluating how changes in environmental conditions can affect the survival of individuals or entire species 75

Skill 9.4   Recognizing the types and characteristics of relationships between organisms 76

Skill 9.5   Demonstrating knowledge of harmful and beneficial microorganisms 77

Skill 9.6   Identifying characteristics of the earth's major terrestrial biomes and aquatic communities 77

COMPETENCY 10.0   UNDERSTAND THE THEORY OF EVOLUTION AND THE ROLE OF NATURAL SELECTION 79

Skill 10.1   Recognizing the roles of variation and natural selection in the process of evolution 79

Skill 10.2   Recognizing evidence for the evolution of species 79

Skill 10.3   Identifying and comparing features and behaviors of organisms that allow them to survive or reproduce more effectively than organisms that do not have those features or behaviors 80

Skill 10.4   Demonstrating knowledge of factors that affect the evolution of species 81

DOMAIN III.   PHYSICAL SCIENCE

COMPETENCY 11.0   UNDERSTAND THE NATURE OF MATTER AND ITS CLASSIFICATION 83

Skill 11.1   Demonstrating knowledge of the difference between pure substances and mixtures 83

Skill 11.2   Identifying the component parts of a substance 86

Skill 11.3   Distinguishing between physical and chemical properties of matter 88

Skill 11.4   Identifying the characteristics of ionic and covalent chemical bonds and their influence on the chemical and physical properties of a substance 88

Skill 11.5   Demonstrating knowledge of the organization of the Periodic Table and its relationship to the properties of matter 89

Skill 11.6   Identifying chemical symbols and interpreting formulas 93

COMPETENCY 12.0   UNDERSTAND CHANGES IN MATTER 95

Skill 12.1   Identifying physical, chemical, and nuclear changes in matter and examples of those changes in everyday life 95

Skill 12.2   Applying knowledge of the law of conservation of matter to the analysis of physical changes and chemical changes....................96

Skill 12.3   Recognizing the characteristics of physical states of matter.........98

Skill 12.4   Identifying the properties of solutions..99

Skill 12.5   Analyzing factors that affect rates of physical changes and chemical reactions...101

COMPETENCY 13.0   UNDERSTAND PRINCIPLES AND CONCEPTS RELATED TO ENERGY   103

Skill 13.1   Comparing the characteristics of different forms of energy.........103

Skill 13.2   Applying knowledge of the law of conservation of energy to the analysis of physical and chemical changes................................105

Skill 13.3   Recognizing the relationship between potential energy and kinetic energy...106

Skill 13.4   Demonstrating knowledge of energy transformations and the processes by which energy is transferred.................................107

Skill 13.5   Interpreting diagrams that illustrate changes in the physical states of matter...108

Skill 13.6   Applying knowledge of the kinetic molecular model to the analysis of the properties and behaviors of matter as solids, liquids, gases, and plasmas...109

COMPETENCY 14.0   UNDERSTAND THE RELATIONSHIPS AMONG FORCE, MASS, AND MOTION OF OBJECTS...........111

Skill 14.1   Distinguishing between the mass and weight of an object..........111

Skill 14.2   Identifying characteristics of forces that act on objects...............111

Skill 14.3   Determining the relationship between the velocity and acceleration of an object...112

Skill 14.4   Solving quantitative problems involving force, mass, and motion of objects...113

Skill 14.5   Demonstrating knowledge of Newton's three laws of motion and their applications to everyday situations.....................................114

Skill 14.6   Applying knowledge of the concepts of work and power to the analysis of everyday activities 115

Skill 14.7   Demonstrating knowledge of types and characteristics of simple machines and their effect on work 116

COMPETENCY 15.0   UNDERSTAND THE PROPERTIES OF WAVES, SOUND, AND LIGHT 117

Skill 15.1   Recognizing the characteristics of mechanical waves.................117

Skill 15.2   Demonstrating knowledge of the properties of sound in everyday phenomena 118

Skill 15.3   Recognizing how the behavior of waves is affected by the medium through which the waves are passing...118

Skill 15.4   Recognizing characteristics of the electromagnetic spectrum 119

Skill 15.5   Identifying the effect of mirrors, lenses, and prisms on the behavior of light...119

Skill 15.6   Demonstrating knowledge of the relationship between the properties of waves and how they are perceived by humans 122

COMPETENCY 16.0   UNDERSTAND ELECTRICITY AND MAGNETISM ... 123

Skill 16.1   Recognizing the characteristics of static electricity.....................123

Skill 16.2   Demonstrating knowledge of the components of an electric circuit and their functions 124

Skill 16.3   Comparing series and parallel circuits.......................................125

Skill 16.4   Identifying the properties of magnets and the characteristics of magnetic fields 126

Skill 16.5   Demonstrating knowledge of the relationship between moving electric charges and magnetic fields and applications of electromagnetism in everyday life 127

DOMAIN IV.		CHARACTERISTICS OF SCIENCE

COMPETENCY 17.0 UNDERSTAND THE CHARACTERISTICS OF SCIENTIFIC KNOWLEDGE AND THE PROCESS OF SCIENTIFIC INQUIRY..129

Skill 17.1   Demonstrating knowledge of the nature, purpose, and characteristics of science and the limitations of science in terms of the kinds of questions that can be answered............................129

Skill 17.2   Recognizing the dynamic nature of scientific knowledge through the continual testing, revision, and occasional rejection of existing theories..130

Skill 17.3   Determining an appropriate scientific hypothesis or investigative design for addressing a given problem......................................130

Skill 17.4   Identifying the characteristics and uses of various types of scientific investigations..131

Skill 17.5   Demonstrating knowledge of the principles and procedures for designing and carrying out scientific investigations 132

Skill 17.6   Recognizing the importance of and strategies for avoiding bias in scientific investigations 133

COMPETENCY 18.0   UNDERSTAND SCIENTIFIC TOOLS, INSTRUMENTS, MATERIALS, AND SAFETY PRACTICES.................134

Skill 18.1   Recognizing procedures for the safe and proper use of scientific tools, instruments, chemicals, and other materials in investigations..134

Skill 18.2   Selecting and using appropriate tools and international system (SI) units for measuring objects or substances 136

Skill 18.3   Identifying potential safety hazards associated with scientific equipment, materials, procedures, and settings 136

Skill 18.4   Demonstrating knowledge of procedures for the ethical use and care of living organisms in scientific research 137

Skill 18.5   Recognizing appropriate protocols for maintaining safety and for responding to emergencies during classroom laboratory activities..138

COMPETENCY 19.0   UNDERSTAND SKILLS AND PROCEDURES FOR
ANALYZING DATA AND COMMUNICATING
SCIENCE 140

Skill 19.1   Recognizing the concepts of precision, accuracy, and error and
identifying potential sources of error in gathering and recording data
.... 140

Skill 19.2   Applying appropriate mathematical concepts and computational
skills to analyze data 141

Skill 19.3   Identifying methods and criteria for organizing data to aid in the
analysis of data 141

Skill 19.4   Recognizing that there may be more than one way to interpret a
given set of findings 142

Skill 19.5   Demonstrating knowledge of the use of data to support or
challenge scientific arguments and claims 142

Skill 19.6   Identifying appropriate methods for communicating the outcomes of
scientific investigations 142

Skill 19.7   Demonstrating familiarity with effective resources and strategies for
reading to gain information about science-related topics and
developing subject-area vocabulary 143

Skill 19.8   Demonstrating knowledge of conventions and strategies for
scientific writing 144

COMPETENCY 20.0   UNDERSTAND THE UNIFYING CONCEPTS OF
SCIENCE AND TECHNOLOGY 145

Skill 20.1   Demonstrating knowledge of the unifying concepts of science and
technology 145

Skill 20.2   Recognizing the characteristics of systems, how the components of
a system interact, and how different systems interact 146

Skill 20.3   Identifying types and characteristics of models used in science and
technology, including the advantages and limitations of models . 147

Sample Test...149

Answer Key 175

Rigor Table 176

Sample Questions with Rationale 177

Great Study and Testing Tips!

What to study in order to prepare for the subject assessments is the focus of this study guide but equally important is *how* you study.

You can increase your chances of truly mastering the information by taking some simple, but effective steps.

Study Tips:

1. <u>Some foods aid the learning process</u>. Foods such as milk, nuts, seeds, rice, and oats help your study efforts by releasing natural memory enhancers called CCKs (*cholecystokinin*) composed of *tryptopha*n, *choline*, and *phenylalanine*. All of these chemicals enhance the neurotransmitters associated with memory. Before studying, try a light, protein-rich meal of eggs, turkey, and fish. All of these foods release the memory enhancing chemicals. The better the connections, the more you comprehend.

Likewise, before you take a test, stick to a light snack of energy boosting and relaxing foods. A glass of milk, a piece of fruit, or some peanuts all release various memory-boosting chemicals and help you to relax and focus on the subject at hand.

2. <u>Learn to take great notes</u>. A by-product of our modern culture is that we have grown accustomed to getting our information in short doses (i.e. TV news sound bites or USA Today style newspaper articles.)

Consequently, we've subconsciously trained ourselves to assimilate information better in <u>neat little packages</u>. If your notes are scrawled all over the paper, it fragments the flow of the information. Strive for clarity. Newspapers use a standard format to achieve clarity. Your notes can be much clearer through use of proper formatting. A very effective format is called the *"Cornell Method."*

Take a sheet of loose-leaf lined notebook paper and draw a line all the way down the paper about 1-2" from the left-hand edge.

Draw another line across the width of the paper about 1-2" up from the bottom. Repeat this process on the reverse side of the page.

Look at the highly effective result. You have ample room for notes, a left hand margin for special emphasis items or inserting supplementary data from the textbook, a large area at the bottom for a brief summary, and a little rectangular space for just about anything you want.

3. Get the concept then the details. Too often we focus on the details and don't gather an understanding of the concept. However, if you simply memorize only dates, places, or names, you may well miss the whole point of the subject.

A key way to understand things is to put them in your own words. If you are working from a textbook, automatically summarize each paragraph in your mind. If you are outlining text, don't simply copy the author's words.

Rephrase them in your own words. You remember your own thoughts and words much better than someone else's, and subconsciously tend to associate the important details to the core concepts.

4. Ask Why? Pull apart written material paragraph by paragraph and don't forget the captions under the illustrations.

Example: If the heading is "Stream Erosion", flip it around to read "Why do streams erode?" Then answer the questions.

If you train your mind to think in a series of questions and answers, not only will you learn more, but it also helps to lessen the test anxiety because you are used to answering questions.

5. Read for reinforcement and future needs. Even if you only have 10 minutes, put your notes or a book in your hand. Your mind is similar to a computer; you have to input data in order to have it processed. *By reading, you are creating the neural connections for future retrieval.* The more times you read something, the more you reinforce the learning of ideas.

Even if you don't fully understand something on the first pass, *your mind stores much of the material for later recall.*

6. Relax to learn so go into exile. Our bodies respond to an inner clock called biorhythms. Burning the midnight oil works well for some people, but not everyone.

If possible, set aside a particular place to study that is free of distractions. Shut off the television, cell phone, and pager and exile your friends and family during your study period.

If you really are bothered by silence, try background music. Light classical music at a low volume has been shown to aid in concentration over other types. Music that evokes pleasant emotions without lyrics is highly suggested. Try just about anything by Mozart. It relaxes you.

7. **<u>Use arrows not highlighters</u>.** At best, it's difficult to read a page full of yellow, pink, blue, and green streaks. Try staring at a neon sign for a while and you'll soon see that the horde of colors obscure the message.

A quick note, a brief dash of color, an underline, and an arrow pointing to a particular passage is much clearer than a horde of highlighted words.

8. **<u>Budget your study time</u>.** Although you shouldn't ignore any of the material, *allocate your available study time in the same ratio that topics may appear on the test.*

Testing Tips:

1. <u>Get smart, play dumb</u>. Don't read anything into the question. Don't make an assumption that the test writer is looking for something else than what is asked. Stick to the question as written and don't read extra things into it.

2. <u>Read the question and all the choices *twice* before answering the question</u>. You may miss something by not carefully reading, and then re-reading both the question and the answers.

If you really don't have a clue as to the right answer, leave it blank on the first time through. Go on to the other questions, as they may provide a clue as to how to answer the skipped questions.

If later on, you still can't answer the skipped ones . . . ***Guess.*** The only penalty for guessing is that you *might* get it wrong. Only one thing is certain; if you don't put anything down, you will get it wrong!

3. <u>Turn the question into a statement</u>. Look at the way the questions are worded. The syntax of the question usually provides a clue. Does it seem more familiar as a statement rather than as a question? Does it sound strange?

By turning a question into a statement, you may be able to spot if an answer sounds right, and it may also trigger memories of material you have read.

4. <u>Look for hidden clues</u>. It's actually very difficult to compose multiple-foil (choice) questions without giving away part of the answer in the options presented.

In most multiple-choice questions you can often readily eliminate one or two of the potential answers. This leaves you with only two real possibilities and automatically your odds go to Fifty-Fifty for very little work.

5. <u>Trust your instincts</u>. For every fact that you have read, you subconsciously retain something of that knowledge. On questions that you aren't really certain about, go with your basic instincts. **Your first impression on how to answer a question is usually correct.**

6. <u>Mark your answers directly on the test booklet</u>. Don't bother trying to fill in the optical scan sheet on the first pass through the test.

Just be very careful not to miss-mark your answers when you eventually transcribe them to the scan sheet.

7. <u>Watch the clock!</u> You have a set amount of time to answer the questions. Don't get bogged down trying to answer a single question at the expense of 10 questions you can more readily answer.

COMPETENCY 1.0   UNDERSTAND CURRENT SCIENTIFIC VIEWS OF THE UNIVERSE

Skill 1.1   Demonstrate knowledge of the development of theories about the formation of the universe and the solar system

The two main hypotheses of the origin of the solar system are the tidal hypothesis and the condensation hypothesis.

The tidal hypothesis proposes that the solar system began with a near collision of the sun and a large star. Some astronomers believe that as these two stars passed each other, the great gravitational pull of the large star extracted hot gases out of the sun. The mass from the hot gases started to orbit the sun, which began to cool and then condensed into the nine planets (few astronomers support this example).

The condensation hypothesis proposes that the solar system began with rotating clouds of dust and gas. Condensation occurred in the center forming the sun, and the smaller parts of the cloud formed the nine planets (this example is widely accepted by many astronomers).

The two main theories to explain the origins of the universe include the Big Bang Theory and the Steady-State Theory.

The Big Bang Theory has been widely accepted by many astronomers. It states that the universe originated from a magnificent explosion spreading mass, matter, and energy into space. The galaxies formed from this material as it cooled during the next half-billion years.

The Steady-State Theory is the least accepted theory. It states that the universe is continuously being renewed. Galaxies move outward and new galaxies replace the older galaxies Astronomers have not found any evidence to support this theory.

The future of the universe is hypothesized with the Oscillating Universe Hypothesis. It states that the universe will oscillate or expand and contract. Galaxies will move away from one another and will eventually slow down and stop. Then, a gradual moving toward each other will again activate the explosion or The Big Bang theory.

Skill 1.2   Demonstrate knowledge of characteristics and general location of objects in the solar system and universe

There are eight planets in our solar system; Mercury, Venus, Earth, Mars, Jupiter, Saturn, Uranus, and Neptune. These eight planets are divided into two groups based on distance from the sun. The inner planets include: Mercury, Venus, Earth, and Mars. The outer planets include: Jupiter, Saturn, Uranus, and Neptune.

Planets

Mercury – is the closest planet to the sun. Its surface has craters and rocks. The atmosphere is composed of hydrogen, helium, and sodium. Mercury was named after the Roman messenger god.

Venus - has a slow rotation when compared to Earth. Venus and Uranus rotate in opposite directions from the other planets. This opposite rotation is called retrograde rotation. The surface of Venus is not visible due to extensive cloud cover. The atmosphere is composed mostly of carbon dioxide. Sulfuric acid droplets in the dense cloud cover give Venus its distinctive yellow appearance. Venus has a greater greenhouse effect than observed on Earth. The dense clouds combined with carbon dioxide traps heat. Venus was named after the Roman goddess of love.

Earth - considered a water planet with 70% of its surface covered by water. Gravity holds the masses of water in place. The different temperatures observed on Earth allow for the different states of water to exist; solid, liquid or gas. The atmosphere is composed mainly of oxygen and nitrogen. Earth is the only planet that is known to support life.

Mars – has a surface that contains numerous craters, active and extinct volcanoes, ridges, and valleys with extremely deep fractures. Iron oxide found in the dusty soil makes the surface seem rust colored and the skies seem pink in color. The atmosphere is composed of carbon dioxide, nitrogen, argon, oxygen, and water vapor. Mars has polar regions with ice caps composed of water. Mars has two satellites. Mars was named after the Roman war god.

Jupiter – is largest planet in the solar system. Jupiter has 16 moons. The atmosphere is composed of hydrogen, helium, methane, and ammonia. There are white colored bands of clouds indicating rising gas and dark colored bands of clouds indicating descending gases, which are caused by heat resulting from the energy of Jupiter's core. Jupiter has a Great Red Spot that is thought to be a hurricane type cloud. Jupiter has a strong magnetic field.

Saturn – is the second largest planet in the solar system. Saturn has beautiful rings of ice, rock, and dust particles circling it. Saturn's atmosphere is composed of hydrogen, helium, methane, and ammonia. Saturn has 20 plus satellites. Saturn was named after the Roman god of agriculture.

Uranus – is the second largest planet in the solar system with retrograde revolution. Uranus is a gaseous planet and it has 10 dark rings and 15 satellites. Its atmosphere is composed of hydrogen, helium, and methane. Uranus was named after the Greek god of the heavens.

Neptune – is a gaseous planet with an atmosphere consisting of hydrogen, helium, and methane. Neptune has 3 rings and 2 satellites. Neptune was named after the Roman sea god because its atmosphere has the same color as the sea.

Notes about Pluto – Until very recently, Pluto was considered the ninth and smallest planet in our solar system. In the summer of 2006 its category shifted as a new classification scheme for planets was proposed. Therefore, Pluto was down-graded from a planet to a celestial body. Pluto's atmosphere probably contains methane, ammonia, and frozen water. Pluto has 1 satellite. Pluto revolves around the sun every 250 years. Pluto was named after the Roman god of the underworld.

Comets, asteroids, and meteors

Astronomers believe that the rocky fragments known as asteroids may be the remains from the birth of the solar system that never formed into a planet. Asteroids are found in the region between Mars and Jupiter.

Comets are masses of frozen gases, cosmic dust, and small rocky particles. Astronomers think that most comets originate in a dense comet cloud beyond Pluto. A comet consists of a nucleus, a coma, and a tail. A comet's tail always points away from the sun. The most famous comet, Halley's Comet, is named after the person whom first discovered it in 240 B.C. It returns to the skies near Earth every 75 to 76 years.

Meteoroids are composed of particles of rock and metal of various sizes. When a meteoroid travels through the Earth's atmosphere, friction causes its surface to heat up and it begins to burn. Once a meteoroid begins to fall through the Earth's atmosphere and burns, it is called a meteor or a "shooting star." Meteorites are meteors that strike the Earth's surface. A physical example of the impact of a meteorite on the Earth's surface can be seen in Arizona; the Barringer Crater is a large meteor crater. There are many meteor craters found throughout the world.

Astronomers use groups or patterns of stars, called constellations, as reference points to locate stars in the sky. Familiar constellations include Ursa Major (also known as the big bear) and Ursa Minor (known as the little bear). The Big Dipper is found within the Ursa Major. The Little Dipper is found within Ursa Minor, a smaller constellation,.

As the Earth revolves, different constellations are visible in the sky. The pattern of constellations change with the seasons as well. In addition, there are seasonal changes in the constellations based upon where the Earth is in relation to the Sun.

Magnitude stars are the 21 brightest stars that can be seen from Earth; these are the first stars that appear in the sky at night. In the Northern Hemisphere, 15 magnitudes stars can be commonly observed.

A vast collection of stars is defined as a galaxy. Galaxies are classified as irregular, elliptical, and spiral. An irregular galaxy has no real structured appearance; most are in their early stages of life. Elliptical galaxies are smooth ellipses, containing little dust and gas, but composed of millions or trillions of stars. Spiral galaxies are disk-shaped and have extending arms that rotate around its dense center. Earth's galaxy is found in the Milky Way and it is a spiral galaxy.

Parts of the Sun include the core, the inner portion of the Sun where fusion takes place, the photosphere, considered the surface of the Sun which produces sunspots (cool, dark areas that can be seen on its surface), the chromosphere, hydrogen gas causes this portion to be red in color, and solar flares (sudden brightness of the chromosphere) and solar prominences (gases that shoot outward from the chromosphere) are found here, and the corona, the transparent area of Sun visible only during a total eclipse.

The Sun is considered the nearest star to Earth that produces solar energy. Solar energy is the process of nuclear fusion, in which hydrogen gas is converted to helium gas. Energy flows from the Sun's core to the surface, then radiation escapes into space. Solar radiation is energy traveling from the Sun that radiates into space. Solar flares produce excited protons and electrons that shoot outward from the chromosphere at great speeds reaching Earth. These particles disturb radio reception and also affect the magnetic field on Earth.

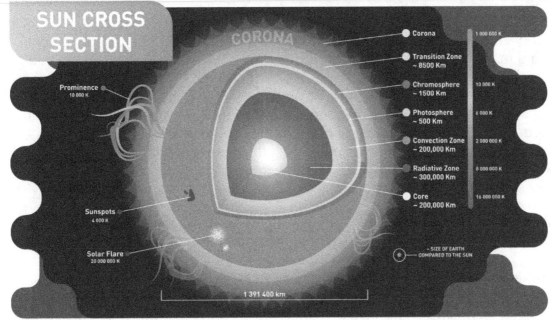

VectorMine/Shutterstock.com

Terms related to deep space

A pulsar is defined as a variable radio source that emits signals in very short, regular bursts. Pulsars are believed to be rotating neutron stars.

A quasar is defined as an object that photographs like a star but has an extremely large redshift and a variable energy output. Quasars are believed to be the active core of very distant galaxies.

Black holes are defined as an object that has collapsed to such a degree that light can not escape from its surface- light is trapped by the intense gravitational field.

Skill 1.3 Recognize the effects of gravity on the motion of objects in the solar system

The mass of any celestial object may be determined by using Newton's laws of motion and his law of gravity.

For example, to determine the mass of the Sun, use the following formula:

$$M = \frac{4\pi^2}{G} = \frac{a^3}{P^2}$$

where M = the mass of the Sun, G = a constant measured in laboratory experiments, a = the distance of a celestial body in orbit around the Sun from the Sun, and P = the period of the body's orbit.

In our solar system, measurable objects range in mass from the largest, the Sun, to the smallest, a near-Earth asteroid. (This does not take into account objects with a mass less than 10^{21} kg.)

In order for two bodies to interact gravitationally, they must have significant mass. When two bodies in the solar system interact gravitationally, they orbit about a fixed point (the center of mass of the two bodies). This point lies on an imaginary line between the bodies, joining them such that the distances to each body multiplied by each body's mass are equal. The orbits of these bodies will vary slightly over time because of the gravitational interactions.

Skill 1.4   Analyze the motion of objects in the sky in terms of relative position

Bodies in the sky seem to move, because the Earth orbits the Sun and rotates on its own axis,. While other bodies may be moving as well, the Earth's spin is continuous, and the result is that distant objects appear to move in a predictable manner. For example, we can expect to see certain planets or stars in specific locations at certain times of the year and can chart their progress across the sky.

Skill 1.5   Recognize the effects of the orientations, positions, and movements of the Earth, Moon, and Sun

The tilt of the Earth's axis allows for the seasonal changes of Summer, Spring, Autumn, and Winter. As Earth revolves around the Sun, the angle of the Earth's axis changes relative to the Sun. This change results in different amounts of sunlight being received by any one spot throughout the year. We recognize these changes as seasonal variations. The Summer solstice occurs when the North Pole is tilted toward the Sun on June 21 or 22, providing increased daylight hours for the Northern Hemisphere and shorter daylight hours for the Southern Hemisphere. Winter solstice occurs when the South Pole is tilted toward the Sun on December 21 or 22, providing shorter daylight hours in the Northern Hemisphere and longer daylight hours in the Southern Hemisphere. The Spring or Vernal Equinox occurs on March 20 or 21, when the direct energy from the Sun falls on the equator providing equal lengths of day and night hours in both hemispheres. The Autumn Equinox occurs on September 22 or 23, again providing equal amounts of day and night hours in both hemispheres.

Eclipses are defined as the passing of one object into the shadow of another object. A Lunar eclipse occurs when the Moon travels through the shadow of the Earth. A Solar eclipse occurs when the Moon positions itself between the Sun and Earth.

From Earth, the lighted half of the Moon can only be seen when the Moon is opposite the Sun. The Moon is totally dark when it is located in the direction of the Sun. The appearances of full dark and full light are divided into four groups or quarters These quarters are designated as (1) new moon, (2) first quarter, (3) full moon, and (4) third quarter.

Tides are changes in the level of the ocean caused by the varying gravitational pull of the Moon as it orbits the Earth. The Moon's gravitational force coexists with that of the Earth. This interaction produces a common center of gravity between the Earth and the Moon. This center is called the barycenter. As the barycenter rotates around the Earth, it causes both high tides and low tides. Neap tides are low tides that occur twice a month when the Sun, Earth, and Moon are positioned at right angles to one another. Spring tides are abnormally high tides that occur twice a month when the Sun, Earth, and Moon are aligned or positioned in a straight line.

Skill 1.6   Identify the methods and types of technology used to observe and collect data about the solar system and universe

Knowledge of telescope types

Galileo Galilei was the first person to use telescopes to observe the solar system. He invented the first refracting telescope. A refracting telescope uses lenses to bend light rays to focus an image.

Sir Isaac Newton invented the reflecting telescope using mirrors to gather light rays on a curved mirror which produces a small, focused image.

The world's largest telescope is located in Mauna Kea, Hawaii. It uses multiple mirrors to gather light rays.

The Hubble Space telescope uses a single-reflector mirror. It provides an opportunity for astronomers to observe objects seven times farther away than, and even those objects that are 50 times fainter than, any other telescope on Earth. There are future plans to make repairs and install new mirrors and other equipment on the Hubble Space telescope.

Refracting and reflecting telescopes are considered optical telescopes since they gather visible light and focus it to produce images. A different type of telescope that collects invisible radio waves created by the Sun and stars is called a radio telescope.

Radio telescopes consists of a reflector or dish with special receivers. The reflector collects radio waves that are created by the Sun and stars. There are many advantages when using a radio telescope; they can receive signals 24 hours a day, can operate in any kind of weather, and dust particles or clouds do not interfere with its performance. The most impressive aspect of the radio telescope is its ability to detect objects from such great distances in space.

The world's largest radio telescope is located in Arecibo, Puerto Rico and has a collecting dish antenna greater than 300 meters in diameter.

Use spectral analysis to identify or infer features of stars or star systems

The spectroscope is a device, or an attachment for telescopes, that is used to separate white light into a series of different colors according to wavelengths. This series of colors of light is called a spectrum. A spectrograph can photograph a spectrum. Wavelengths of light have distinctive colors. The color red has the longest wavelength and violet has the shortest wavelength. Wavelengths are arranged to form an electromagnetic spectrum and range from very long radio waves to very short gamma rays. Visible light covers a small portion of the electromagnetic spectrum. Spectroscopes observe the spectra, temperatures, pressures, and also the movement of stars. The movements of stars indicate if they are moving toward or away from Earth.

If a star is moving towards Earth, light waves compress and the wavelengths of light seem shorter. This will cause the entire spectrum to move towards the blue or violet end of the spectrum. This spectral shift to the blue or violet spectrum is observed on the electromagnetic spectrum.

If a star is moving away from Earth, light waves expand and the wavelengths of light seem longer. This will cause the entire spectrum to move towards the red end of the spectrum. This spectral shift to the red spectrum is observed on the electromagnetic spectrum.

Knowledge of astronomical measurement

The three formulas astronomers use for calculating distances in space are the AU or astronomical unit, the LY or Light year, and the parsec. It is important to remember that these formulas are measured in distances, not time.

The distance between the Earth and the sun is about 150×10^6 km. This distance is known as an astronomical unit or AU. This formula is used to measure distances within the solar system, it is not used to measure time.

The distance light travels in one year is a light year or 9.5×10^{12} km. This formula is used to measure distances in space, it does not measure time.

Large distances are measured in parsecs. One parsec equals 3.26 light-years, not time.

There are approximately 63,000 AU's in one light year or,

$$9.5 \times 10^{12} \text{ km} / 150 \times 10^6 \text{ km} = 6.3 \times 10^4 \text{ AU}$$

COMPETENCY 2.0   UNDERSTAND THE CHARACTERISTICS AND DISTRIBUTION OF WATER AND ITS ROLE IN THE EARTH'S PROCESSES.

Skill 2.1   Identify the properties of water in its different physical states

The unique properties of water are partially responsible for the development of life on Earth. Many of the unique qualities of water stem from the hydrogen bonds that form between the molecules. Hydrogen bonds are particularly strong dipole-dipole interactions that form between the H-atom of one molecule and an F, O, or N atom of an adjacent molecule. The partial positive charge on the hydrogen atom is attracted to the partial negative charge on the electron pair of the other atom. The hydrogen bond between two water molecules is shown as the dashed line below:

Note that hydrogen bonding occurs because of the high polarity of the H-O bonds in water. Let's examine how this effect contributes to several of water's unique properties.

1.   Density change during freezing
Hydrogen bonds govern the shape of the crystals that form when water freezes. Thus, relatively large spaces of air are present between the water molecules. Since these spaces do not exist when the water is in liquid form, ice is less dense and will float on liquid water.

2.   High specific heat/ high heat of vaporization
A molecule the size of water would typically have a fairly low specific heat and heat of vaporization. That is, very little energy would be required to trigger a phase change or to heat the water by a given amount. However, extra energy is required to break the network of hydrogen bonds, meaning water has surprisingly high values for both specific heat and heat of vaporization.

3.   High surface tension/strong cohesion
Another effect of hydrogen bonding is that water molecules are extremely attracted to one another, as shown in the diagram above. This makes water highly cohesive and produces high surface tension on both droplets of water and large bodies of water. This same phenomenon is responsible for capillary action.

Skill 2.2   Analyze the water cycle and its relationship to various atmospheric conditions

Water that falls to Earth in any form (hail rain, sleet, or snow) is called precipitation. Precipitation is part of a continuous process in which water at the Earth's surface evaporates, condenses into clouds, and returns to Earth. This process is termed the water cycle. The water located below the surface is called groundwater.

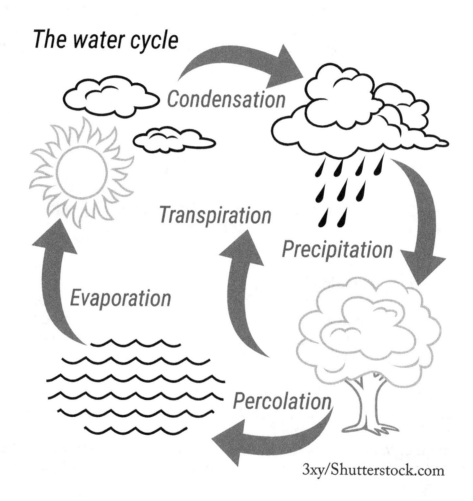

3xy/Shutterstock.com

Altitude's impacts upon climatic conditions are primarily temperature and precipitation related. As altitude increases, climatic conditions become increasingly drier and colder. Solar radiation becomes more severe as altitude increases while the effects of convection forces are minimized. Climatic changes as a function of latitude follow a similar pattern (as a reference, latitude moves either north or south from the equator). The climate becomes colder and drier as the distance from the equator increases. Proximity to land or water masses produces climatic conditions based upon the available moisture. Dry and arid climates prevail where moisture is scarce; lush tropical climates prevail where moisture is abundant. Climate depends upon the specific combination of conditions making up an area's environment. Man impacts all environments by producing pollutants in earth, air, and water. It follows then, that man is a major player in world climatic conditions.

Skill 2.3   Identify major reservoirs of water on the Earth (i.e., glaciers, lakes, groundwater, oceans) and their distribution

Precipitation that soaks into the ground through small pores or openings becomes groundwater. Gravity causes groundwater to move through interconnected porous rock formations from higher to lower elevations. The upper surface of the zone saturated with groundwater is the water table. A swamp is an area where the water table is at the surface. Sometimes the land dips below the water table and these areas fill with water forming lakes, ponds, or streams. Spring water is groundwater that flows out from underground to the surface. .

Permeable rocks filled with water are called aquifers. When a layer of permeable rock is trapped between two layers of impermeable rock, an aquifer is formed. Groundwater fills the pore spaces in the permeable rock. Layers of limestone are common aquifers. Groundwater provides drinking water for 53% of the population in the United States and is collected in reservoirs.

Precipitation that is collected in running waterbeds becomes a river. A river undergoes changes as it flows and erodes the land, passing through different stages of development. There are three main stages in the lifecycle of a river: youth, maturity, and old age.

During the youth stage, a river flows rapidly down mountains and hills. It carries large quantities of coarse-grained sediments. The river cuts and erodes a deep, narrow, V-shaped channel. The Colorado River is an example of a young river. A mature river is slow flowing and has less cutting power than a young river. A mature river begins to form curved, S-shaped channels called meanders.

When it fills with sediment, the slope of a river channel becomes almost flat as the water flows very slowly. It is said to be in old age. The lower part of the Mississippi River is in this stage.

Glaciers are huge, frozen masses of solid slow-moving ice. A time period in which glaciers advance over a large portion of a continent is called an ice age. A glacier moves or flows over land in response to gravity. Glaciers form among high mountains and in other cold regions. There are two main types of glaciers: valley glaciers and continental glaciers. Erosion by valley glaciers is characterized by U-shaped erosion; this type of erosion produces sharp-peaked mountains such as the Matterhorn in Switzerland. When continental glaciers ride over mountains in their paths, the erosion generally leaves smoothed, rounded mountains and ridges.

Skill 2.4   Demonstrate knowledge of the composition, location, and subsurface topography of the world's oceans

Seventy percent of the Earth's surface is covered with saltwater, which is called the hydrosphere. The approximate mass of the Earth's saltwater is 1.4×10^{24} grams. The ocean waters continuously circulate among different parts of the hydrosphere. There are seven major oceans: the North Atlantic Ocean, South Atlantic Ocean, North Pacific Ocean, South Pacific Ocean, Indian Ocean, Arctic Ocean, and the Antarctic Ocean.

Pure water is a combination of the elements hydrogen and oxygen. These two elements make up about 96.5% of ocean water. The remaining portion is made up of dissolved solids. The concentration of these dissolved solids determines the water's salinity.

Salinity is measured by the grams of dissolved salts in 1,000 grams of sea water. The average salinity of ocean water is about 3.5%. In other words, one kilogram of sea water contains about 35 grams of salt. Sodium Chloride or salt (NaCl) is the most abundant of the dissolved salts. The dissolved salts also include smaller quantities of magnesium chloride, magnesium and calcium sulfates, and traces of several other salt elements. Salinity varies throughout the world's water bodies and also varies by depth of the water. Salinity is low near the mouths of rivers, where the ocean mixes with fresh water, and salinity is high in areas with high evaporation rates.

The temperature of the ocean water varies with different latitudes and with ocean depths. The temperature of ocean water is almost constant to depths of 90 meters (m). The temperature of surface water will drop rapidly from 28° C at the equator to -2° C at the Poles. The freezing point of sea water is lower than the freezing point of pure water. Pure water freezes at 0° C. The dissolved salts in the sea water keep sea water at a freezing point of -2° C. The freezing point of water varies by salinity.

The ocean can be divided into three temperature zones. The surface layer consists of relatively warm water and exhibits most of the wave action present. The area where the wind and waves churn and mix the water is called the mixed layer. This is the layer where most living creatures are found due to abundant sunlight and warmth. The second layer is called the thermocline and it becomes increasingly cold as its depth increases. This change is due to the lack of energy from sunlight. The layer below the thermocline continues to the deep dark, very cold, and semi-barren ocean floor.

Oozes - the name given to the sediment that contains at least 30% plant or animal shell fragments. Ooze contains calcium carbonate.

Deposits that form directly from sea water in the place where they are found are called: Authigenic deposits. Manganese nodules are deposits found over large areas of the ocean floor.

Causes for the formation of ocean floor features

The study of the movement of the Earth's surface is called Plate Tectonics. Major plate separation lines lie along the ocean floors. As these plates separate, molten rock rises, continuously forming new oceanic crust and creating new and taller mountain ridges under the ocean. The Mid-Atlantic Range, which divides the Atlantic Ocean basin into two nearly equal parts, shows evidence from mapping of these deep-ocean floor changes.

Seamounts are formed by underwater volcanoes. Seamounts and volcanic islands are found in long chains on the ocean floor. They are formed when the movement of an oceanic plate positions a plate section over a stationary hot spot located deep in the mantle. Magma rising from the hot spot punches through the plate and forms a volcano. The Hawaiian Islands are examples of volcanic island chains.

Magma that rises to produce a curving chain of volcanic islands is called an island arc. An example of an island arc is the Lesser Antilles chain in the Caribbean Sea.

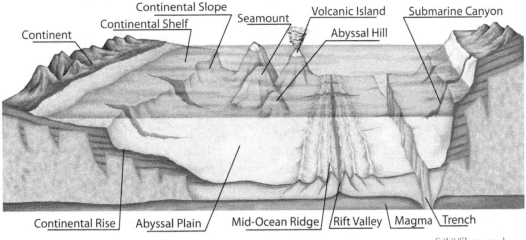

Stihii/Shutterstock.com

Seafloor

The ocean floor has many of the same features that are found on land. The ocean floor has higher mountains than are present on land, extensive plains, and deeper canyons than are present on land. Oceanographers have named different parts of the ocean floor according to their structure.

The continental shelf is the sloping part of the continent that is covered with water extending from the shoreline to the continental slope.

The continental slope is the steeply sloping area that connects the continental shelf and the deep-ocean floor.

The continental rise is the gently sloping surface at the base of the continental slope.

The abyssal plains are the flat, level parts of the ocean floor.

A seamount is an undersea volcano peak that is at least 1000 m above the ocean floor.

Guyot - A submerged, flat-topped seamount.

Mid ocean-ridges are continuous undersea mountain chains that are found mostly in the middle portions of the oceans.

Ocean trenches are long, elongated narrow troughs or depressions formed where ocean floors collide with another section of ocean floor or continent. The deepest trench in the Pacific Ocean is the Marianas Trench which is about 11 km deep.

Shorelines

The shoreline is the boundary where land and sea meet. Shorelines mark the average position of sea level, which is the average height of the sea without consideration of tides and waves. Shorelines are classified according to the way they were formed. The three types of shorelines are: submerged, emergent, and neutral. When the sea has risen, or the land has sunk, a submerged shoreline is created. An emergent shoreline occurs when sea falls or the land rises. A neutral shoreline does not show the features of a submerged or an emergent shoreline. A neutral shoreline is usually observed as a flat, broad beach. A stack is an island of resistant rock left after weaker rock is worn away by waves and currents. Waves approaching the beach at a slight angle create a current of water that flows parallel to the shore. This longshore current carries loose sediment almost like a river of sand. A spit is formed when a weak longshore current drops its load of sand as it turns into a bay.

Rip currents are narrow currents that flow seaward at a right angle to the shoreline. These currents are very dangerous to swimmers. Most of the beach sands are composed of grains of resistant material like quartz and orthoclase, but coral and/or basalt are found in some locations. Many beaches have rock fragments that are too large to be classified as sand.

Skill 2.5   Identify the causes and effects of waves, currents, and tides

The movement of ocean water is caused by the wind, the Sun's heat energy, the Earth's rotation, the Moon's gravitational pull on Earth, and by underwater earthquakes. Most ocean waves are caused by the impact of winds. Wind blowing over the surface of the ocean transfers energy (friction) to the water and causes waves to form. Waves are also formed by a seismic activity on the ocean floor. A wave formed by an earthquake is called a seismic sea wave. These powerful waves can be very destructive, with wave heights increasing to 30 m or more near the shore. The crest of a wave is its highest point. The trough of a wave is its lowest point. The distance from wave top to wave top is the wavelength. The wave period is the time between the passing of two successive waves.

World weather patterns are greatly influenced by ocean surface currents in the upper layer of the ocean. These currents continuously move along the ocean surface in specific directions. Ocean currents that flow deep below the surface are called sub-surface currents. These currents are influenced by such factors as the location of landmasses in the current's path and the Earth's rotation.

Surface currents are caused by winds and classified by temperature. Cold currents originate in the Polar regions and flow through surrounding water that is measurably warmer. Those currents with a higher temperature than the surrounding water are called warm currents and can be found near the equator. These currents follow swirling routes around the ocean basins and the equator. The Gulf Stream and the California Current are the two main surface currents that flow along the coastlines of the United States. The Gulf Stream is a warm current in the Atlantic Ocean that carries warm water from the equator to the northern parts of the Atlantic Ocean. Benjamin Franklin studied and named the Gulf Stream. The California Current is a cold currant that originates in the Arctic regions and flows southward along the west coast of the United States.

Differences in water density also create ocean currents. Water found near the bottom of oceans is the coldest and the densest. Water tends to flow from a denser area to a less dense area. The currents that flow because of a difference in the density of the ocean water are called density currents. Water with a higher salinity is denser than water with a lower salinity. Water that has salinity different from the surrounding water may form a density current.

Tides are changes in the level of the ocean caused by the varying gravitational pull of the Moon as it orbits the Earth. This interaction produces a common center of gravity between the Earth and the Moon. Neap tides are low tides that occur twice a month when the Sun, Earth, and Moon are positioned at right angles to one another. Spring tides are abnormally high tides that occur twice a month when the Sun, Earth, and Moon are aligned or positioned in a straight line. The Bay of Fundy in Nova Scotia experiences the largest difference in sea height in the world. Comparing when the tide is highest and lowest, the difference is 45 feet.

Skill 2.6   Demonstrate knowledge of freshwater resources

The upper surface of the zone saturated with groundwater is the water table. A swamp is an area where the water table is at the surface. Sometimes the land dips below the water table and these areas fill with water forming lakes, ponds, or streams.

Permeable rocks filled with water are called aquifers. When a layer of permeable rock is trapped between two layers of impermeable rock, an aquifer is formed. Groundwater fills the pore spaces in the permeable rock. Layers of limestone are common aquifers. Groundwater may be collected in reservoirs.

Groundwater provides drinking water for 53% of the population in the United States. Much groundwater is clean enough to drink without any type of treatment. Impurities in the water are filtered out by the rocks and soil through which it flows. However, many groundwater sources are becoming contaminated. Septic tanks, broken pipes, agriculture fertilizers, garbage dumps, rainwater runoff, and leaking underground tanks all pollute groundwater. Toxic chemicals from farmland mix with groundwater. Removal of large volumes of groundwater can cause the collapse of soil and rock underground, causing the ground to sink. Along shorelines, excessive depletion of underground water supplies allows the intrusion of salt water into the fresh water field. The groundwater supply becomes undrinkable.

COMPETENCY 3.0   **UNDERSTAND CHARACTERISTICS OF THE ATMOSPHERE AND OF CLIMATE AND WEATHER.**

Skill 3.1   **Identify the basic composition, structure, and properties of the atmosphere**

Dry air is composed of three basic components: dry gas, water vapor, and solid particles (dust from soil, etc.).

The most abundant dry gases in the atmosphere are:

(N_2)	Nitrogen	78.09 %	makes up about 4/5 of gases in atmosphere
(O_2)	Oxygen	20.95 %	
(AR)	Argon	0.93 %	
(CO_2)	Carbon Dioxide	0.03 %	

The atmosphere is divided into four main layers based on temperature. These layers are labeled Troposphere, Stratosphere, Mesosphere, and Thermosphere.

Troposphere - this layer is the closest to the Earth's surface and all weather phenomena occurs here, as it is the layer with the most water vapor and dust., Air temperature decreases with increasing altitude. The average thickness of the Troposphere is 7 miles (11 km).

Stratosphere - this layer contains very little water and rarely contains clouds. The Ozone layer is located in the upper portions of the stratosphere. Air temperature is fairly constant, but does increase somewhat with height due to the absorption of solar energy and ultra violet rays from the ozone layer.

Mesosphere - air temperature decreases with height in this layer. It is the coldest layer with temperatures in the range of -100^0 C at the top.

Thermosphere - extends upward into space. Oxygen molecules in this layer absorb energy from the Sun, causing temperatures to increase with height. The lower part of the thermosphere is called the Ionosphere. Here, charged particles or ions and free electrons can be found. When gases in the Ionosphere are excited by solar radiation, the gases give off light and glow in the sky. These glowing lights are called the Aurora Borealis in the Northern Hemisphere and Aurora Australis in Southern Hemisphere. The upper portion of the Thermosphere is called the Exosphere. Gas molecules are very far apart in this layer. Layers of Exosphere are also known as the Van Allen Belts and are held together by Earth's magnetic field.

Skill 3.2   Analyze the significance of changes in weather variables (e.g., clouds, humidity, wind speed)

Air masses moving toward, or away from, the Earth's surface are called air currents. Air moving parallel to Earth's surface is called wind. Weather conditions are generated by winds and air currents carrying large amounts of heat and moisture from one part of the atmosphere to another. Wind speeds are measured by instruments called anemometers.

The wind belts in each hemisphere consist of convection cells that encircle Earth like belts. There are three major wind belts on Earth: (1) trade winds, (2) prevailing westerlies, and (3) polar easterlies. Wind belt formation depends on the differences in air pressures that develop in the doldrums, the horse latitudes, and the polar regions. The Doldrums surround the equator. Within this belt heated air usually rises straight up into Earth's atmosphere. The Horse latitudes are regions of high barometric pressure with calm and light winds. The Polar regions contain cold, dense air that sinks to the Earth's surface.

Winds caused by local temperature changes include sea breezes and land breezes.

Sea breezes are caused by the unequal heating of the land and an adjacent, large body of water. Land heats up faster than water. The movement of cool ocean air toward the land is called a sea breeze. Sea breezes usually begin blowing about mid-morning; ending about sunset.

A breeze that blows from the land to the ocean or a large lake is called a land breeze.

Monsoons are huge wind systems that cover large geographic areas and that reverse direction seasonally. The monsoons of India and Asia are examples of these seasonal winds. They alternate wet and dry seasons. As denser, cooler air over the ocean moves inland, a steady seasonal wind called a summer or wet monsoon is produced.

Cloud types

Cirrus clouds - White and feathery, high in sky

Cumulus – thick, white, fluffy

Stratus – layers of clouds cover most of the sky

Nimbus – heavy, dark clouds that represent thunderstorm clouds

Variation on the clouds mentioned above

Cumulo-nimbus

Strato-nimbus

The air temperature at which water vapor begins to condense is called the dew point.

Relative humidity is the actual amount of water vapor in a certain volume of air compared to the maximum amount of water vapor this air could hold at a given temperature.

Skill 3.3   Recognize the effects of large bodies of water, large land areas, and differences in elevation on weather and climate

World weather patterns are greatly influenced by ocean surface currents in the upper layer of the ocean. These currents continuously move along the ocean surface in specific directions. Ocean currents that flow deep below the surface are called sub-surface currents. These currents are influenced by such factors as the location of landmasses in the current's path and the Earth's rotation.

Tropical rain forests covered much of the world millions of years ago. Climatic changes currently limit this biome to about six percent of the Earth's land surface. Rain forests are found in South America, Africa, New Guinea, Malaysia, Burma, and Indonesia. The moist conditions and constant heat provide for a great growing environment. Fifty percent of all the species in the world are found in the rain forests. Only about one percent of the available sunlight reaches the forest floor. The climate is hot and humid; therefore the landform is a jungle.

Desert biome – Hot like the rainforest but relatively little moisture. Sand accounts for 15 percent of desert terrain. Most deserts are bare rock or pebbles and gravel areas. The landform requires no moisture.

Tundra – Geologic time of the Ice Age has reports of a small number of mankind living at the poles. The Indians, Aleuts, and Eskimos had little effect on the tundra's ecosystem. The climate is extremely cold. Moss and lichens exist in this fragile environment of polar ice. More and more scientists are fearful that the polar caps are melting, which would not only change the landform and vegetation at the poles but also shift the water levels worldwide.

Taiga – Mild climate that is neither extremely hot nor cold and has a hardy type of lumber such as birch, aspen, poplars, and/or willows. In the niche created by the cool shade of the large trees there are a great variety of plants. They include lots of mosses, lichens, and ferns. The landform is often laced with rivers and streams. The soils of the taiga thaw out completely each summer and are the home to lots of tiny invertebrates and vertebrates. These microscopic organisms help break down the leaves and evergreen needles on the forest floor, enriching the soil. The recycled nutrients are then available for use by the taiga's trees to continue growing and producing for yet another season.

Grasslands – Grasslands have different names in different parts of the world. In North America they are called prairies, in Asia, steppes, in Africa and Australia, savannas and on and on. Grasses have deep root systems. Therefore the climate would have to be mild to support it. For thousands of years the growth cycle of the grasslands has created very rich top soil. Farming has converted much of the grasslands into crop-growing areas. Only 11% of the Earth is suitable for farming. Grasses are pollinated by wind. The animals of this region tend to be fast and have mottled colors to blend in with the dry grass.

Skill 3.4 Demonstrate knowledge of weather patterns and the causes and effects of local and regional weather events (e.g., thunderstorms, hurricanes)

A thunderstorm is a brief, local storm produced by the rapid upward movement of warm, moist air within a cumulo-nimbus cloud. Thunderstorms always produce lightning and thunder accompanied by strong wind gusts and heavy rain or hail.

A severe storm with swirling winds that may reach speeds of hundreds of kilometers per hour is called a tornado. Such a storm is also referred to as a "twister". The sky is covered by large cumulo-nimbus clouds and violent thunderstorms; a funnel-shaped swirling cloud may extend downward from a cumulonimbus cloud and reach the ground. Tornadoes are narrow storms that leave a narrow path of destruction on the ground.

A swirling, funnel-shaped cloud that extends downward and touches a body of water is called a waterspout.

Hurricanes are storms that develop when warm, moist air carried by trade winds rotates around a low-pressure "eye". A large, rotating, low-pressure system accompanied by heavy precipitation and strong winds is called a tropical cyclone (better known as a hurricane). In the Pacific region, a hurricane is called a typhoon.

Storms that occur only in the winter are known as blizzards or ice storms. A blizzard is a storm with strong winds, blowing snow and frigid temperatures. An ice storm consists of falling rain that freezes when it strikes the ground, covering everything with a layer of ice.

Skill 3.5   Analyze global weather and climate patterns

The term 'local weather' includes hourly and daily changes in the atmosphere of a region. When we refer to climate we are discussing the average weather for a region over a period of time. Two primary factors discussed in reference to local weather are temperature and precipitation. Climate varies from one place to another because of unequal heating of the Earth's surface. This varied heating of the surface is the result of the unequal distribution of land masses, oceans, and polar ice caps. Differences in area surface temperatures result in pressure gradients. A hot surface heats the air above it and the air expands, which then lowers the air pressure. The result is creation of wind. This simple system can combine or collide with other simple systems to create complex systems and severe weather. A large scale example is a hurricane, while a small scale example is a coastal breeze.

El Niño refers to a sequence of changes in the ocean and atmospheric circulation across the Pacific Ocean. The water around the equator is unusually hot every two to seven years. Trade winds normally blowing east to west across the equatorial latitudes pile warm water into the western Pacific. A huge mass of heavy thunderstorms usually forms in the area and produces vast currents of rising air that displace heat poleward. This helps create the strong mid-latitude jet streams. The world's climate patterns are disrupted by the change in location of the massive cluster of thunderstorms. The West coast of America experienced a wet winter. Sacramento, California recorded 103 days of rain.

Skill 3.6   Recognize the methods and types of technology used to observe, measure, and predict climate and weather

Weather instruments that forecast weather include the aneroid barometer and the mercury barometer. They measure air pressure. The air exerts varying pressures on a metal diaphragm that reads air pressure. The mercury barometer operates when atmospheric pressure pushes on a pool (of mercury) in a glass tube. The level of mercury in the tube rises with higher barometric pressures.

Relative humidity is measured by two kinds of weather instruments, the psychrometer and the hair gygrometer. Relative humidity simply indicates the amount of moisture in the air. Relative humidity is defined as a ratio of existing amounts of water vapor and moisture in the air when compared to the maximum amount of moisture that the air can hold at the same given pressure and temperature. Relative humidity is stated as a percentage. For example the relative humidity can be 100%.

If you were to analyze relative humidity from data, an example might be:

Ex: If a parcel of air is saturated (meaning it now holds all the moisture it can hold at a given temperature), then the relative humidity is 100%.

Lesson Plans for teachers to analyze data and predict weather can be found at:

http://www.srh.weather.gov/srh/jetstream/synoptic/ll_analyze.htm

Meteorologists use an anemometer to measure wind speed and a wind vane to measure wind direction.

COMPETENCY 4.0   UNDERSTAND CHARACTERISTICS OF THE
                  EARTH AND PROCESSES THAT HAVE SHAPED
                  ITS SURFACE.

Skill 4.1   Demonstrate knowledge of the Earth's structure and composition

The interior of the Earth is divided into three chemically distinct layers. From the center to the surface, these layers are: the core, the mantle, and the crust. Much of what we know about the inner structure of the Earth has been inferred from various data. Subsequently, there is still some uncertainty about the composition and conditions in the Earth's interior

.
Core
The outer core of the Earth begins about 3000 km beneath the surface and is a liquid, though far more viscous than that of the mantle. Even deeper, approximately 5000 kilometers beneath the surface, is the solid inner core. The inner core has a radius of about 1200 km. Temperatures in the core exceed 4000°C. Scientists agree that the core is extremely dense. This conclusion is based on the fact that the Earth is known to have an average density of 5515 kg/m^3 even though the material close to the surface has an average density of only 3000 kg/m^3. It is hypothesized that when the Earth was forming, the densest material sank to the middle of the planet. Thus, it is not surprising that the Earth's core is believed to be 80% iron. In fact, there is some speculation that the entire inner core is a single iron crystal, while the outer core is a mix of liquid iron and nickel.

Mantle
The Earth's mantle begins about 35 km beneath the surface and stretches all the way to 3000 km beneath the surface, where the outer core begins. Since the mantle stretches so far into the Earth's center, its temperature varies widely; near the boundary with the crust it is approximately 1000°C, while near the outer core it may reach nearly 4000°C. Within the mantle there are silicate rocks, which are rich in iron and magnesium. The silicate rocks exist as solids, but the high heat means they are ductile enough to "flow" over long time scales. In general, the mantle is semi-solid/plastic and the viscosity varies as pressures and temperatures change at varying depths.

Crust

It is not clear how long the Earth has actually had a solid crust. Most rocks are less than 100 million years, though some are 4.4 billion years old. The crust of the Earth is the outermost layer and continues down for between 5 and 70 km beneath the surface. Thin areas generally exist under ocean basins (oceanic crust) and thicker crust underlies the continents (continental crust). Oceanic crust is composed largely of iron magnesium silicate rocks, while continental crust is less dense and consists mainly of sodium potassium aluminum silicate rocks. The crust is the least dense layer of the Earth and is rich in those materials that "floated" during Earth's formation. Additionally, some heavier elements that bound to lighter materials are present in the crust.

Interactions between the Layers

It is not the case that these layers exist as separate entities with little interaction between them. For instance, it is generally believed that swirling of the iron-rich liquid in the outer core results in the Earth's magnetic field, which is readily apparent on the surface. Heat also moves out from the core to the mantle and crust. The core still retains heat from the formation of the Earth and additional heat is generated by the decay of radioactive isotopes. While most of the heat in our atmosphere comes from sun, radiant heat from the core does warm oceans and other large bodies of water.

There is also a great deal of interaction between the mantle and the crust. The slow convection of rocks in the mantle is responsible for the shifting of tectonic plates on the crust. Matter can also move between the layers as occurs during the rock cycle. Within the rock cycle, igneous rocks are formed when magma escapes from the mantle as lava during volcanic eruptions. Rocks may also be forced back into the mantle, where the high heat and pressure recreate them as metamorphic rocks.

Skill 4.2 Classify rocks and minerals based on their process of formation and characteristics

The three major subdivisions of rocks are sedimentary, metamorphic, and igneous.

Lithification of sedimentary rocks

When fluid sediments are transformed into solid sedimentary rocks the process is known as lithification. One very common process affecting sediments is compaction, where the weights of overlying materials compress and compact the deeper sediments. The compaction process leads to cementation. Cementation is when sediments are converted to sedimentary rock.

Factors in crystallization of igneous rocks

Igneous rocks can be classified according to their texture, their composition, and the way they were formed.

Molten rock is called magma. When molten rock pours out onto the surface of Earth, it is called lava.

As magma cools, the elements and compounds begin to form crystals. The slower the magma cools, the larger the crystals grow. Rocks with large crystals are said to have a coarse-grained texture. Granite is an example of a coarse grained rock. Rocks that cool rapidly, before any crystals can form, have a glassy texture such as obsidian, also commonly known as volcanic glass.

Metamorphic rocks are formed by high temperatures and great pressures. The process by which the rocks undergo these changes is called metamorphism. The outcome of metamorphic changes include deformation by extreme heat and pressure, compaction, destruction of the original characteristics of the parent rock, bending and folding while in a plastic stage, and the emergence of completely new and different minerals due to chemical reactions with heated water and dissolved minerals.

Metamorphic rocks are classified into two groups. These are foliated (leaflike) rocks and unfoliated rocks. Foliated rocks consist of compressed, parallel bands of minerals, which give the rocks a striped appearance. Examples of such rocks include slate, schist, and gneiss. Unfoliated rocks are not banded and examples include quartzite, marble, and anthracite rocks. Minerals are natural, non-living solids with a definite chemical composition and a crystalline structure. Ores are minerals or rock deposits that can be mined for a profit. Rocks are Earth materials made of one or more minerals. Rock Facies is a rock group that differs from comparable rocks (as in composition, age, or fossil content).

Characteristics by which minerals are classified

Minerals must adhere to five criteria. They must be non-living, formed in nature, solid in form, their atoms forming a crystalline pattern, and its chemical composition is fixed within narrow limits. There are over 3,000 minerals in Earth's crust. Minerals are classified by composition. The major groups of minerals are silicates, carbonates, oxides, sulfides, sulfates, and halides. The largest group of minerals is the silicates. Silicates are made of silicon, oxygen, and one or more other elements.

Skill 4.3 Identify the characteristics of soil and analyze how it forms

Soils are composed of particles of sand, clay, various minerals, tiny living organisms, and humus, plus the decayed remains of plants and animals. Soils are divided into three classes according to their texture. These classes are sandy soils, clay soils, and loamy soils. Sandy soils are gritty, and their particles do not bind together firmly. Sandy soils are porous - water passes through them rapidly. Sandy soils do not hold much water.

Clay soils are smooth and greasy, their particles bind together firmly. Clay soils are moist and usually do not allow water to pass through easily.

Loamy soils feel somewhat like velvet and their particles clump together. Loamy soils are made up of sand, clay, and silt. Loamy soils hold water but some water can pass through.

Soils are grouped into three major types based upon their composition. These are pedalfers, pedocals, and laterites. Pedalfers form in the humid, temperate climate of the eastern United States. Pedalfer soils contain large amounts of iron oxide and aluminum-rich clays, making the soil a brown to reddish brown color. This soil supports forest type vegetation. Pedocals are found in the western United States where the climate is dry and temperate. These soils are rich in calcium carbonate This type of soil supports grasslands and brush vegetation. Laterites are found where the climate is wet and tropical. Large amounts of water flow through the soil. Laterites are red-orange soils rich in iron and aluminum oxides. There is little humus and this soil is not very fertile.

Skill 4.4   Analyze constructive and destructive processes that form and change major geological features (e.g., tectonic movements, erosion, deposition)

Orogeny is the term given to mountains built naturally.

A mountain is terrain that has been raised high above the surrounding landscape by volcanic action, or by some form of tectonic plate collisions. The plate collisions could be intercontinental or ocean floor collisions with a continental crust (subduction). The physical composition of mountains would include igneous, metamorphic, or sedimentary rocks; some may have rock layers that are tilted or distorted by plate collision forces.

There are many different types of mountains. The physical attributes of a mountain range depend upon the angle at which plate movement thrust layers of rock to the surface. Many mountains (Adirondacks, Southern Rockies) were formed along high angle faults.

Folded mountains (Alps, Himalayas) are produced by the folding of rock layers during their formation. The Himalayas are the highest mountains in the world. Mount Everest rises almost 9 km above sea level. The Himalayas were formed when India collided with Asia. The movement which created this collision is still in process at the rate of a few centimeters per year.

Fault-block mountains (e.g. Utah, Arizona, and New Mexico) are created when plate movement produces tension forces instead of compression forces. The area under tension produces normal faults. Rock along these faults is displaced upward.

Dome mountains are formed as magma tries to push up through the crust but fails to break the surface. Dome mountains resemble a huge blister on the Earth's surface.

Upwarped mountains (Black Hills of South Dakota) are created in association with a broad arching of the crust. They can also be formed by rock thrust upward along high angle faults.

Volcanic mountains are built by successive deposits of volcanic materials.

Volcanism is the term given to the movement of magma through the crust and its emergence as lava onto the Earth's surface.

An active volcano is one that is presently erupting or building to an eruption. A dormant volcano is one that is in-between eruptions but still shows signs of internal activity that might lead to an eruption in the future. An extinct volcano is said to be no longer capable of erupting. Most of the world's active volcanoes are found along the rim of the Pacific Ocean, which is also a major earthquake zone. This curving belt of active faults and volcanoes is often called the Ring of Fire.

The world's best known volcanic mountains are Mount Etna in Italy and Mount Kilimanjaro in Africa. The Hawaiian Islands are actually the tops of a chain of volcanic mountains that rise from the ocean floor.

There are three types of volcanic mountains: shield volcanoes, cinder cones, and composite volcanoes.

Shield Volcanoes are associated with quiet eruptions. Lava emerges from the vent or opening in the crater and flows freely out over the Earth's surface until it cools and hardens into a layer of igneous rock. Repeated lava flows build this type of volcano into the largest volcanic mountains. Mauna Loa, found in Hawaii, is the largest volcano on Earth.

Cinder Cone Volcanoes are associated with explosive eruptions as lava is hurled high into the air in a spray of various sized droplets. These droplets cool and harden into cinders and particles of ash before falling to the ground. The ash and cinder pile up around the vent to form a steep, cone-shaped hill called the cinder cone. Cinder cone volcanoes are relatively small but may form quite rapidly.

Composite Volcanoes are described as being built by both lava flows and layers of ash and cinders. Mount Fuji in Japan, Mount St. Helens in Washington, USA, and Mount Vesuvius in Italy are all famous Composite Volcanoes.

Mechanisms of producing mountains

Mountains are produced by different types of mountain-building processes. Most major mountain ranges are formed by the processes of folding and faulting.

Folded Mountains are produced by the folding of rock layers. Crustal movements may press horizontal layers of sedimentary rock together from the sides, squeezing them into wavelike folds. Up-folded sections of rock are called anticlines; down-folded sections of rock are called synclines. The Appalachian Mountains are an example of folded mountains with long ridges and valleys in a series of anticlines and synclines formed by folded rock layers.

Faults are fractures in the Earth's crust which have been created by either tension or compression forces transmitted through the crust. These forces are produced by the movement of separate blocks of crust.

Faults are categorized on the basis of the relative movement between the blocks on both sides of the fault plane. The movement can be horizontal, vertical, or oblique.

A dip-slip fault occurs when the movement of the plates is vertical and opposite. The displacement is in the direction of the inclination, or dip, of the fault. Dip-slip faults are classified as normal faults when the rock above the fault plane moves down relative to the rock below.

Reverse faults are created when the rock above the fault plane moves up relative to the rock below. Reverse faults having a very low angle to the horizontal are also referred to as thrust faults.

Faults in which the dominant displacement is horizontal movement along the trend or strike (length) of the fault, are called strike-slip faults. When a large strike-slip fault is associated with plate boundaries it is called a transform fault. The San Andreas Fault in California is a well-known transform fault. Faults that have both vertical and horizontal movement are called oblique-slip faults.

When lava cools, igneous rock is formed. This formation can occur either above ground or below ground. Intrusive rock includes any igneous rock that was formed below the Earth's surface. Batholiths are the largest structures of intrusive type rock and are composed of near granite materials; they are the core of the Sierra Nevada Mountains. Extrusive rock includes any igneous rock that was formed at the Earth's surface.

Dikes are old lava tubes formed when magma entered a vertical fracture and hardened. Sometimes magma squeezes between two rock layers and hardens into a thin horizontal sheet called a sill. A laccolith is formed in much the same way as a sill, but the magma that creates a laccolith is very thick and does not flow easily. It pools and forces the overlying strata, thus creating an obvious surface dome.

A caldera is normally formed by the collapse of the top of a volcano. This collapse can be caused by a massive explosion that destroys the cone and empties most, if not all, of the magma chamber below the volcano. The cone collapses into the empty magma chamber forming a caldera.

An inactive volcano may have magma solidified in its pipe. This structure, called a volcanic neck, is resistant to erosion and today may be the only visible evidence of the presence of an active volcano in the past.

When lava cools, igneous rock is formed. This formation can occur either above ground or below ground.

Glaciation

A continental glacier covered a large part of North America during the most recent ice age. Evidence of this glacial coverage remains as abrasive grooves, large boulders from northern environments dropped in southerly locations, glacial troughs created by the rounding out of steep valleys by glacial scouring, and the remains of glacial sources called cirques, which were created by frost wedging the rock at the bottom of the glacier. Remains of plants and animals found in warm climates have been discovered in the moraines and out wash plains. This supports the theory that there were periods of warmth during past ice ages.

The Ice Age began about 2-3 million years ago. This age saw the advancement and retreat of glacial ice over millions of years. Theories relating to the origin of glacial activity include Plate Tectonics, where it can be demonstrated that some continental masses, now in temperate climates, were at one time blanketed by ice and snow. Another theory involves changes in the Earth's orbit around the Sun, changes in the angle of the Earth's axis, and the wobbling of the Earth's axis. Support for the validity of this theory has come from deep ocean research that indicates a correlation between climatic sensitive micro-organisms and the changes in the Earth's orbital status.

About 12,000 years ago, a vast sheet of ice covered a large part of the northern United States. This huge, frozen mass had moved southward from the northern regions of Canada as several large bodies of slow-moving ice, or glaciers. A time period in which glaciers advance over a large portion of a continent is called an ice age. A glacier is a large mass of ice that moves or flows over the land in response to gravity. Glaciers form among high mountains and in other cold regions.

There are two main types of glaciers: valley glaciers and continental glaciers. Erosion by valley glaciers is characterized by U-shaped erosion. They produce sharp peaked mountains such as the Matterhorn in Switzerland. Erosion by continental glaciers often rides over mountains in their paths leaving behind smoothed, rounded mountains and ridges.

Erosion is the inclusion and transportation of surface materials by another moveable material, usually water, wind, or ice. The most important cause of erosion is running water. Streams, rivers, tides and such are constantly at work removing weathered fragments of bedrock and carrying them away from their original location.

A stream erodes bedrock by the grinding action of the sand, pebbles and other rock fragments. This grinding against each other is called abrasion.

Streams also erode rocks by dissolving or absorbing their minerals. Limestone and marble are readily dissolved by streams.

Weathering causes the gradual wearing down of rocks, at or near the Earth's surface. Weathering breaks down these rocks into smaller and smaller pieces. There are two types of weathering: physical weathering and chemical weathering. Physical weathering is the process by which rocks are broken down into smaller fragments without undergoing any change in chemical composition. Physical weathering is mainly caused by the freezing of water, the expansion of rock, and the activities of plants and animals. [Chemical weathering?]

Frost wedging is the cycle of daytime thawing and refreezing at night. This cycle causes large rock masses, especially the rocks exposed on mountain tops, to be broken into smaller pieces.

The peeling away of the outer layers of a rock is called exfoliation. Rounded mountain tops are called exfoliation domes and have been formed in this way.

Chemical weathering is the breaking down of rocks through changes in their chemical composition. An example would be the change of feldspar in granite to clay. Water, oxygen, and carbon dioxide are the main agents of chemical weathering. When water and carbon dioxide combine chemically, they produce a weak acid that breaks down rocks.

Skill 4.5   Demonstrate knowledge of the theory of plate tectonics and evidence that supports the theory

Data obtained from many sources led scientists to develop the theory of plate tectonics. This theory is the most current model that explains not only the movement of the continents, but also the changes in the Earth's crust caused by internal forces.

Plates are rigid blocks of Earth's crust and upper mantle. These rigid, solid blocks make up the lithosphere. The Earth's lithosphere is broken into nine large sections and several small ones. These moving slabs are called plates. The major plates are named after the continents they are transporting. The plates float on and move with a layer of hot, plastic-like rock in the upper mantle. Geologists believe that the heat currents circulating within the mantle cause this plastic zone of rock to slowly flow, carrying along the overlying crustal plates.

Movement of these crustal plates creates areas where the plates diverge as well as areas where the plates converge. In the Mid-Atlantic there is a major area of divergence. Currents of hot mantle rock rise and separate at this point of divergence creating new oceanic crust at the rate of 2 to 10 centimeters per year. Convergence is when the oceanic crust collides with either another oceanic plate or a continental plate. The oceanic crust sinks, forming an enormous trench and generating volcanic activity. Convergence also includes continent to continent plate collisions. When two plates slide past one another a transform fault is created.

These movements produce many major features of the Earth's surface, such as mountain ranges, volcanoes, and earthquake zones. Most of these features are located at plate boundaries, where the plates interact by spreading apart, pressing together, or sliding past each other. These movements are very slow, averaging only a few centimeters a year.

Boundaries form between spreading plates where the crust is forced apart in a process called rifting. Rifting generally occurs at mid-ocean ridges. Rifting can also take place within a continent, splitting the continent into smaller landmasses that drift away from each other, thereby forming an ocean basin (like the Red Sea) between them. As seafloor spreading takes place, new material is added to the inner edges of the separating plates. In this way, the plates grow larger, and the ocean basin widens. This is the process that broke up the super-continent Pangaea and created the Atlantic Ocean.

CONTINENTAL DRIFT

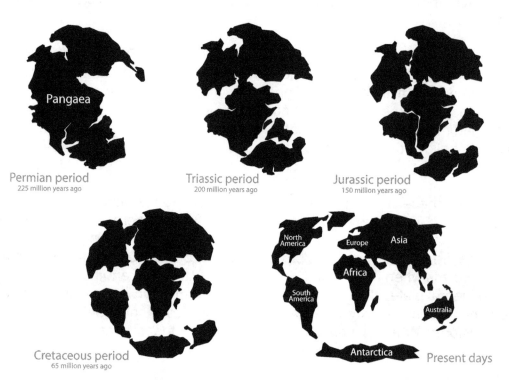

Tinkivinki/Shutterstock.com

Boundaries between plates that are colliding are zones of intense crustal activity. When a plate of oceanic crust collides with a plate of continental crust, the more dense oceanic plate slides under the lighter continental plate and plunges into the mantle. This process is called subduction, and the site where it takes place is called a subduction zone. A subduction zone is usually seen on the sea-floor as a deep depression called a trench.

The crustal movement which is characterized by plates sliding sideways past each other produces a plate boundary characterized by major faults that are capable of unleashing powerful earthquakes. The San Andreas Fault forms such a boundary between the Pacific Plate and the North American Plate.

Skill 4.6   Recognize characteristics of fossils and how they show evidence of the changing surface and climate of the earth

A fossil is the remains or trace of an ancient organism that has been preserved naturally in the Earth's crust. Sedimentary rocks are usually rich sources of fossil remains. Those fossils found in layers of sediment were embedded in the slowly forming sedimentary rock strata. The oldest fossils known are the traces of 3.5 billion year old bacteria found in sedimentary rocks. Few fossils are found in metamorphic rock and virtually none are found in igneous rocks. The magma is so hot that any organism trapped in the magma is destroyed.

The fossil remains of a woolly mammoth embedded in ice were found by a group of Russian explorers. However, the best-preserved animal remains have been discovered in natural tar pits. When an animal accidentally fell into the tar, it became trapped, sinking to the bottom. Preserved bones of the saber-toothed cat have been found in tar pits.

Prehistoric insects have been found trapped in ancient amber (fossil resin) that was excreted by some extinct species of pine trees.

Fossil molds are the hollow spaces in a rock previously occupied by bones or shells. A fossil cast is a fossil mold that fills with sediments or minerals that later harden, forming a cast.

Fossil tracks are the imprints in hardened mud left behind by birds or animals.

COMPETENCY 5.0   UNDERSTAND THE TYPES AND USES OF THE EARTH'S NATURAL RESOURCES.

Skill 5.1   Identify types, characteristics, and uses of renewable and nonrenewable resources

A renewable resource is one that can be replaced naturally. Living renewable resources would be plants and animals. Plants are renewable because they grow and reproduce. Sometimes renewal of the resource doesn't keep up with the demand. Such is the case with trees. Since the housing industry uses lumber for frames and homebuilding, they are often cut down faster than new trees can grow. Tree farms use special methods that allow trees to grow faster.

A second renewable resource is animals. They renew by the process of reproduction. Some wild animals need protection. As the population of humans increases resources are used faster. Cattle are used for their hides and for food. Some animals, such as deer, are killed for sport. Each state has an environmental protection agency with divisions of forest management and wildlife management.

Non-living renewable resources would be water, air, and soil. Water is renewed in a natural cycle called the water cycle. Air is a mixture of gases. Oxygen is given off by plants and taken in by animals that in turn expel the carbon dioxide that plants require. Soil is another renewable resource. Fertile soil is rich in minerals. When plants grow they remove the minerals and make the soil less fertile. Chemical treatments are one way or renewing the composition. It is also accomplished naturally when the plants decay back into the soil. The plant material is used to make compost to mix with the soil.

Nonrenewable resources are not easily replaced in a timely fashion. Minerals are nonrenewable resources. Quartz, mica, salt and sulfur are some examples. Mining depletes these resources so that society may benefit by glass from quartz and electronic equipment from mica. Salt has many uses. Sulfur is used in medicine, fertilizers, paper, and matches.

Metals are among the most widely used nonrenewable resources. Metals must be separated from the ore. Iron is our most important ore. Gold, silver, and copper are often found in a more pure form called native metals.

Skill 5.2 **Recognize the Sun as the major source of energy on the Earth's surface and analyze its relationship to wind and water energy**

The vast majority of energy on the Earth's surface is derived from sunlight. However, sunlight is attenuated by the Earth's atmosphere, so that not all solar energy reaches the planet's surface. Specifically, about 1300 watts are delivered per square meter of Earth, but only about 1000 watts actually reach the surface.

It is easy for us to understand how sunlight warms the land and water on the surface of the Earth. We are similarly familiar with the capture of sunlight by solar cells, which then can be used for heating or electricity. However, it is important to understand that sunlight is the basis for many of our other sources of power. This is because sunlight is used to drive photosynthesis, which is the major method by which carbon is fixed by living things. The energy harnessed by plants is used to fuel all heterotrophs further up the food chain. When these life forms (plant or animal) die, they may ultimately be converted to fossil fuels. Thus the petroleum, oil, and other fossil fuels we use as major power sources all originally derived their energy from sunlight.

The Sun and the energy it transfers to the Earth also influence the movement of air and water (i.e., the winds and ocean currents). This is a result of the fact that different areas of the Earth's surface receive varying amounts of energy from the sunlight. The movements of warmer and cooler masses of air or water are the source of wind and water currents. Note that this means that wind and hydrologic energy also have their origin in energy from the Sun.

Finally, it is important to recognize that the Sun is a star with its own strong and ever changing magnetic field. These changes in the field are responsible for solar activity such as sunspots, solar flares, and solar wind. These changes in turn affect Earth's climate and sometimes increase or decrease the solar energy that reaches the entire Earth or certain areas of it. Fluctuations in solar cycles can also lead to especially low or high temperatures. For instance, during the 17th and 18th centuries there was a period in which very few sunspots were seen. This lasted for about 70 years and coincided with the "Little Ice Age" in Europe, an era of unusually cold temperatures throughout the continent. It is not only the extended period of changes in solar activity that affect climate and weather on Earth. It has been observed that stratospheric winds near the equator blow in different directions depending on changes in the solar cycle.

Skill 5.3   Identify the effects of natural events and human activities on the Earth's natural resources

Pollutants are impurities in air and water that may be harmful to life. All forms of pollution have both local and global economic, aesthetic, and medical consequences. Air, land, and water pollution directly and indirectly affect human health. Pollution negatively influences the local and global economy by increasing medical costs, increasing pollution treatment costs (e.g. water and soil clean up), and decreasing agricultural yields. Finally, all types of pollution decrease natural beauty and diminish enjoyment of nature and the outdoors.

Air pollution, possibly the most damaging form of pollution, has both local and global consequences. Air pollution results largely from the burning of fuels. Major sources of air pollution include transportation, industrial processes, heat and power generation, and the burning of solid waste. At the local level, air pollution negatively affects quality of life by increasing medical problems and decreasing comfort and enjoyment of outdoor activities. Air pollution can cause medical problems ranging from simple throat or eye irritations to asthma and lung cancer. Globally, air pollution threatens the Earth's ozone layer and may cause global warming. Ozone depletion and global warming increase the risk of health problems (e.g. skin cancer) and threaten the Earth's ecological balance and biodiversity. Possible solutions to air pollution are government controls on fuel types, industry combustion standards, and the development and use of alternative, cleaner sources of energy.

Land pollution is the destruction of the Earth's surface resulting from improper industrial and urban waste disposal, damaging agricultural practices, and mining and mineral exploitation. Land pollution greatly effects aesthetic appeal and human health. At the local level, improper waste disposal threatens the health of people living in the effected areas. Waste accumulation attracts pests and creates unsightly, dirty living conditions. Globally, damage and depletion of the soil by improper agricultural practices has great economic consequences. Overuse of pesticides and herbicides and depletion of soil nutrients causes long-term damage to the soil, leading to decreased crop yield in the future. Close regulation of waste disposal and agricultural practices is the most effective strategy for the prevention of land pollution.

Water pollution, perhaps the most prevalent form of pollution, greatly effects human health and the economy. The agricultural industry is the leading contributor to water pollution. Rain runoff carrying pesticides, herbicides, and fertilizer readily pollutes oceans, lakes, and rivers. Also contributing to water pollution are industrial effluents, sewage, and domestic waste. Water pollution negatively affects the economy because clean up and treatment of polluted water is very costly. Spills from barges carrying large quantities of oil pollute beaches and harm fish. In addition, consumption of polluted water causes health problems and increases associated medical costs. Finally, polluted water disrupts aquatic ecosystems, decreasing the availability of fish and other aquatic resources. Like air and land pollution, limiting water pollution requires strict governmental control. Proper oversight requires the implementation and enforcement of environmental standards regulating agricultural and industrial discharge into bodies of water.

All acids contain hydrogen. Acidic substances from factory and car exhausts dissolve in rain water forming acid rain. Acid rain forms predominantly from pollutant oxides in the air (usually nitrogen-based NO_x or sulfur-based SO_x), which become hydrated into their acids (nitric or sulfuric acid). When the rain falls onto stone, the acids react with metallic compounds and gradually wear the stone away.

Radioactivity is the breaking down of atomic nuclei by releasing particles or electromagnetic radiation. Radioactive nuclei give off radiation in the form of streams of particles or energy. Alpha particles are positively charged particles consisting of two protons and two neutrons. It is the slowest form of radiation. It can be halted by paper. Beta particles are electrons. It is produced when a neutron in the nucleus breaks up into a proton and an electron. The proton remains inside the nucleus, increasing its atomic number by one. But the electron is given off. They can be stopped by aluminum. Gamma rays are electromagnetic waves with extremely short wavelengths. They have no mass. They have no charge and consequently they are not deflected by an electric field. Gamma rays travel at the speed of light. It takes a thick block of lead to stop their flow. Uranium is the source of radiation and therefore is radioactive. Marie Curie discovered the elements radium and polonium, which actually release more radiation than uranium.

The major concern with radioactivity is in the case of a nuclear disaster. Medical misuse is also a threat. Radioactivity ionizes the air it travels through. It is strong enough to kill cancer cells and dangerous enough to cause illness or even death. Gamma rays can penetrate the body and damage cells. Protective clothing is needed when working with gamma rays. Electricity from nuclear energy uses the fuel-like uranium 235. The devastation of the Russian nuclear power plant disaster has evacuated entire regions. The damage to land and food sources will last for hundreds of years.

Skill 5.4   Demonstrate knowledge of methods for conserving and protecting natural resources

Stewardship is the responsible management of resources entrusted to one. Since human presence and activity has such a drastic impact on the environment, humans are the stewards of the Earth. In other words, it is the responsibility of humans to balance their needs as a population with the needs of the environment and all of the Earth's living creatures and resources. Stewardship requires the regulation of human activity to prevent, reduce, and mitigate environmental degradation. An important aspect of stewardship is the preservation of resources and ecosystems for future generations of humans. Finally, the concept of stewardship often, but not necessarily, draws from religious, theological, or spiritual thought and principles.

Strategies for the management of renewable resources focuses on balancing the immediate demand for resources with long-term sustainability. In addition, renewable resource management attempts to optimize the quality of the resources. For example, scientists may attempt to manage the amount of timber harvested from a forest, balancing the human need for wood with the future viability of the forest as a source of wood. Scientists attempt to increase timber production by fertilizing, manipulating trees genetically, and managing pests and density. Similar strategies exist for the management and optimization of water sources, air quality, and other plants and animals.

The main concerns in nonrenewable resource management are conservation, allocation, and environmental mitigation. Policy makers, corporations, and governments must determine how to use and distribute scarce resources. Decision makers must balance the immediate demand for resources with the need for resources in the future. This determination is often the cause of conflict and disagreement. Finally, scientists attempt to minimize and mitigate the environmental damage caused by resource extraction. Scientists devise methods of harvesting and using resources that do not unnecessarily impact the environment. After the extraction of resources from a location, scientists devise plans and methods to restore the environment to as close to its original state as is possible.

COMPETENCY 6.0   UNDERSTAND THE DIVERSITY OF LIVING ORGANISMS AND THEIR CLASSIFICATION.

Skill 6.1   Identify criteria used to classify organisms based upon a six-kingdom system

The six kingdom system consists of the following kingdoms:
1.   Eubacteria
2.   Archaebacteria
3.   Protista
4.   Fungi
5.   Plantae
6.   Animalia

The following is a comprehensive list of the majors kingdoms and divisions.

Kingdom Monera – This kingdom consists of bacteria and blue-green algae, prokaryotes and other organisms having no true nucleus; all are unicellular.

Bacteria are classified according to their morphology (shape). Bacilli are rod shaped, cocci are round, and spirillia are spiral shaped. The gram stain is a staining procedure used to identify bacteria. Gram positive bacteria pick up the stain and turn purple. Gram negative bacteria do not pick up the stain and are pink in color.

Kingdom Protista - eukaryotic, unicellular, some are photosynthetic and others are consumers. Microbiologists use methods of locomotion, reproduction, and how the organism obtains its food to classify protista.

Methods of locomotion - Flagellates have a flagellum, ciliates have cilia, and ameboids move through use of pseudopodia.

Methods of reproduction - binary fission is simply dividing in half. It is asexual reproduction. All new organisms are clones of the parent. Sexual modes provide more diversity. Bacteria can reproduce sexually through conjugation, where genetic material is exchanged.

Methods of obtaining nutrition - photosynthetic organisms, or producers, convert sunlight into chemical energy, consumers (heterotrophs) eat other living things. Saprophytes are consumers that live off dead or decaying material.

Kingdom Fungi - eukaryotic, multicellular, absorptive consumers, contain a chitin cell wall.

Plants

NONVASCULAR PLANTS - small in size, do not require vascular tissue (xylem and phloem) because individual cells are close to their environment. The nonvascular plants have no true leaves, stems, or roots.

Division Bryophyta - mosses and liverworts, these plants have a dominant gametophyte generation. They possess rhizoids, which are root-like structures. Moisture in their environment is required for reproduction and absorption.

VASCULAR PLANTS - the development of vascular tissue enabled these plants to grow in size. Xylem and phloem allows for the transport of water and minerals up to the top of the plant, as well as transport food manufactured in the leaves to the bottom of the plant. All vascular plants have a dominant sporophyte generation.

Division Lycophyta - club mosses; these plants reproduce with spores and require water for reproduction.

Division Sphenophyta - horsetails; also reproduce with spores. These plants have small, needle-like leaves and rhizoids. Require moisture for reproduction.

Division Pterophyta - ferns; reproduce with spores and flagellated sperm. These plants have a true stem and need moisture for reproduction.

Gymnosperms - The word means "naked seed". These were the first plants to evolve with seeds, which made them less dependent on water to assist in reproduction. Their seeds could travel by wind. Pollen from the male was also easily carried by the wind. Gymnosperms have cones that protect their seeds.

Division Cycadophyta - cycads; these plants look like palms with cones.

Division Ghetophyta - desert dwellers.

Division Coniferophyta - pines; these plants have needles and cones.

Division Ginkgophyta - the Ginkgo is the only member of this division.

Angiosperms (Division Anthophyta) - Angiosperms are the largest group in the plant kingdom. They are the flowering plants and produce true seeds for reproduction.

Animals are further divided into five subcategories, whose characteristics are outlined in skill 6.2.

Skill 6.2   Recognize the distinguishing characteristics of different groups of organisms

Annelida - the segmented worms; the first with specialized tissue. The circulatory system is more advanced in these worms and is a closed system with blood vessels. The nephridia are their excretory organs. They are hermaphrodidic and each worm fertilizes the other upon mating. They support themselves with a hydrostatic skeleton and have circular and longitudinal muscles for movement.

Mollusca - clam, octopus; the soft bodied animals. These animals have a muscular foot for movement. They breathe through gills and most are able to make a shell for protection from predators. They have an open circulatory system, with sinuses bathing the body regions.

Arthropoda - insects, crustaceans and spiders; this is the largest group of the animal kingdom. Phylum arthropoda accounts for about 85% of all the animal species. Animals in the arthropoda phylum possess an exoskeleton made of chitin. They must molt to grow. Insects, for example, go through four stages of development. They begin as an egg, hatch into a larva, form a pupa, then emerge as an adult. Arthropods breathe through gills, trachae, or book lungs. Movement varies, with members being able to swim, fly, and/or crawl. There is a division of labor among the appendages (legs, antennae, etc). This is an extremely successful phylum with members occupying diverse habitats.

Echinodermata - sea urchins and starfish; these animals have spiny skin. Their habitat is marine. They have tube feet for locomotion and feeding.

Chordata - all animals with a notocord or a backbone. The classes in this phylum include Agnatha (jawless fish), Chondrichthyes (cartilage fish), Osteichthyes (bony fish), Amphibia (frogs and toads; gills which are replaced by lungs during development), Reptilia (snakes, lizards; the first to lay eggs with a protective covering), Aves (birds; warm-blooded with wings consisting of a particular shape and composition designed for flight), and Mammalia (animals with body hair that bear their young alive, possess mammary glands that produce milk, and are warm-blooded).

Skill 6.3   Recognize the features of dichotomous keys and their development and use

A dichotomous key is a biological tool for identifying unknown organisms. It is constructed of a series of couplets, each consisting of two statements describing characteristics of a particular organism or group of organisms. A choice between the statements is made that bet fits the organism in question. The statements typically begin with broad characteristics and become narrower as more choices are needed.

Example A - Numerical key

1   Seeds round – soybeans
1   Seeds oblong – 2
2.   Seeds white – northern beans
2.   Seeds black – black beans

Example B - Alphabetical key

A. Seeds oblong – B
B. Seeds white – northern beans
B. Seeds black – black beans
A. Seeds round - soybeans

COMPETENCY 7.0   **UNDERSTAND THE STRUCTURE AND FUNCTION OF LIVING SYSTEMS**

Skill 7.1   Identify characteristics of prokaryotic and eukaryotic cells

The cell is the basic unit of all living things. There are two types of cells. Prokaryotic cells consist only of bacteria and blue-green algae. Bacteria were most likely the first cells and date back to 3.5 billion years ago in the fossil record. The important things that put these cells in their own group are:

1. They have no defined nucleus or nuclear membrane. The DNA and ribosomes float freely within the cell.

2. They have a thick cell wall. This is for protection, to give shape, and to keep the cell from bursting.

3. The cell walls contain amino sugars (glycoproteins). Penicillin works by disrupting the cell wall, which is bad for the bacteria, but will not harm the host.

4. Some have a capsule made of polysaccharides which make the bacteria sticky (like on your teeth).

5. Some have pili, which is a protein strand. This also allows for attachment of the bacteria and may be used for sexual reproduction called conjugation.

6. Some have flagella for movement.

Eukaryotic cells are found in protists, fungi, plants, and animals. Some features of eukaryotic cells include:

1. They are usually larger than prokaryotic cells.

2. They contain many organelles, which are membrane bound areas for specific cell functions.

3. They contain a cytoskeleton which provides a protein framework for the cell.

4. They contain cytoplasm to support the organelles and contain the ions and molecules necessary for cell function.

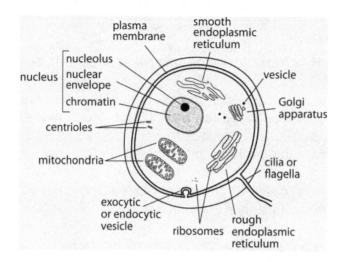

1. Nucleus - The brain of the cell. The nucleus contains:

chromosomes- DNA, RNA, and proteins tightly coiled to conserve space while providing a large surface area.
chromatin - loose structure of chromosomes. Chromosomes are called chromatin when the cell is not dividing.
nucleoli - where ribosomes are made. These are seen as dark spots in the nucleus.
nuclear membrane - contains pores which let RNA out of the nucleus. The nuclear membrane is continuous with the endoplasmic reticulum which allows the membrane to expand or shrink if needed.

2. Ribosomes - the site of protein synthesis. Ribosomes may be free floating in the cytoplasm or attached to the endoplasmic reticulum. There may be up to a half a million ribosomes in a cell, depending on how much protein is made by the cell.

3. Endoplasmic Reticulum (ER) - These are folded and provide a large surface area. They are the "roadway" of the cell and allow for transport of materials through and out of the cell. The lumen of the endoplasmic reticulum helps to keep materials out of the cytoplasm and headed in the right direction. The endoplasmic reticulum is capable of building new membrane material. There are two types of ER:

Smooth Endoplasmic Reticulum - contains no ribosomes on its surface.

Rough Endoplasmic Reticulum - contains ribosomes on its surface. This form of ER is abundant in cells that make many proteins, like in the pancreas, which produces many digestive enzymes.

4. Golgi Complex or Golgi Apparatus - This structure is stacked which helps to increase its surface area. The Golgi Complex functions to sort, modify, and package molecules that are made in other parts of the cells. These molecules are either sent out of the cell or to other organelles within the cell.

5. Lysosomes - found mainly in animal cells. These contain digestive enzymes that break down food, substances not needed, viruses, damaged cell components, and eventually the cell itself. It is believed that lysosomes are responsible for the aging process.

6. Mitochondria - large organelles that make ATP to supply energy to the cell. Muscle cells have many mitochondria because they use a great deal of energy. The folds inside the mitochondria are called cristae. They provide a large surface area where the reactions of cellular respiration occur. Mitochondria have their own DNA and are capable of reproducing themselves if the demand for energy is increased.

7. Plastids - found in photosynthetic organisms only. They are similar to the mitochondria because of their double membrane structure. They also have their own DNA and can reproduce if the need for the increased capture of sunlight becomes necessary. There are several types of plastids:

> Chloroplasts - green, function in photosynthesis. They are capable of trapping sunlight.
> Chromoplasts - make and store yellow and orange pigments; they provide color to leaves, flowers and fruits.
> Amyloplasts - store starch and are used as a food reserve. They are abundant in roots (like potatoes).

8. Cell Wall - found in plant cells only, it is composed of cellulose and fibers. It is thick enough for support and protection, yet porous enough to allow water and dissolved substances to enter. Cell walls are cemented to each other.

9. Vacuoles - hold stored food and pigments. Vacuoles are very large in plants, which allows them to fill with water to provide turgor pressure. Lack of turgor pressure causes a plant to wilt.

10. Cytoskeleton - composed of protein filaments attached to the plasma membrane and organelles. They provide a framework for the cell and aid in cell movement. They constantly change shape and move about. Three types of fibers make up the cytoskeleton:

Microtubules - largest of the three makes up cilia and flagella for locomotion. Flagella grow from a basal body. Some examples are sperm cells and tracheal cilia. Centrioles are also composed of microtubules. They form the spindle fibers that pull the cell apart into two cells during cell division. Centrioles are not found in the cells of higher plants.

Intermediate Filaments - they are smaller than microtubules but larger than microfilaments. They help the cell to keep its shape.

Microfilaments - smallest of the three, they are made of actin and small amounts of myosin (like in muscle cells). They function in cell movement like cytoplasmic streaming, endocytosis, and ameboid movement. This structure pinches the two cells apart after cell division, forming two cells.

Skill 7.2   Compare and contrast the structures and functions of plant and animal cells

Animal cells – begin a discussion of the nucleus as a round body inside the cell. It controls the cell's activities. The nuclear membrane contains threadlike structures called chromosomes. The genes are units that control cell activities found in the nucleus. The cytoplasm has many structures in it. Vacuoles contain the food for the cell. Other vacuoles contain waste materials.

Plant cells – have cell walls. A cell wall differs from a cell membrane. The cell membrane is very thin and is a part of the cell. The cell wall is thick and is a nonliving part of the cell. They are little bundles of chlorophyll. The structure of the cell is often related to the cell's function. Root hair cells differ from flower stamens or leaf epidermal cells. They all have different functions.

Skill 7.3   Demonstrate knowledge of the relationship between cell structures and their functions

The function of different systems in all organisms, from bacteria to humans, dictates system structure. The basic principle that "form follows function" applies to all organismal systems. We will discuss a few examples to illustrate this principle. Keep in mind that we can relate the structure and function of all organismal systems.

Mitochondria, subcellular organelles present in eukaryotic cells, provide energy for cell functions. Much of the energy-generating activity takes place in the mitochondrial membrane. To maximize this activity, the mitochondrial membrane has many folds to pack a relatively large amount of membrane into a small space.

Bacterial cells maintain a high surface area to volume ratio to maximize contact with the environment and allow for exchange of nutrients and waste products. Bacterial cells achieve this high ratio by maintaining a small internal volume by cell division.

The cardiovascular system of animals has many specialized structures that help achieve the function of delivering blood to all parts of the body. The heart has four chambers for the delivery and reception of blood. The blood vessels vary in size to accommodate the necessary volume of blood. For example, vessels near the heart are large to accommodate large amounts of blood and vessels in the extremities are very small to limit the amount of blood delivered.

Animals use muscles to convert the chemical energy of ATP into mechanical work. A muscle is composed of bundles of specialized cells capable of creating movement through a combination of contraction and relaxation. Muscle fibers are grouped according to where they are found (skeletal muscle, smooth muscle, and cardiac muscle). A skeletal muscle fiber is not a single cell, but is commonly thought of as the unit of a muscle and is composed of myofibrils. Smooth muscle, including the human heart, is composed of individual cells each containing thick (myosin) and thin (actin) filaments that slide against each other to produce contraction of the cell.

All cells exhibit a voltage difference across the cell membrane. Nerve cells and muscle cells are excitable. Their cell membrane can produce electrochemical impulses and conduct them along the membrane. The nerve cell may be divided into three main parts: the cell body or soma, short processes called the dendrites, and a single long nerve fiber, the axon. The body of a nerve cell is similar to that of other cells in that it includes the nucleus, mitochondria, endoplasmic reticulum, ribosomes, and other organelles. The dendrites receive impulses from other cells and transfer them to the cell body. The effect of these impulses may be excitatory or inhibitory. The long nerve fiber, the axon, transfers the signal from the cell body to another nerve or to a muscle cell.

The guard cells control the stomata (openings for gas exchange) found in the epidermis of a leaf. These plant cells are regulated by the environmental conditions of light, CO_2 concentration, and water availability. When the guard cells are activated, potassium pumps actively transport K+ (potassium) into the guard cells, resulting in a high concentration of K+ in the cells. As a result, water enters the cells by osmosis. This causes the guard cells to swell. When the stoma is open CO_2 can diffuse into the leaf and enter the Calvin Cycle. The oxygen produced in photosynthesis diffuses out of the open stoma. Water vapor also escapes from the stoma by the process of transpiration.

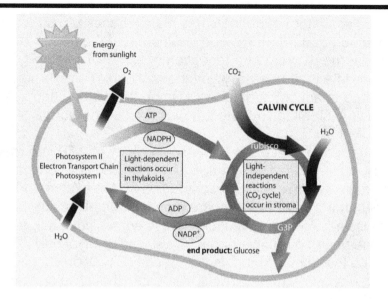

Finally, the structure of the skeletal systems of different animals varies based on the animal's method of movement. For example, the honeycombed structure of bird bones provides a lightweight skeleton of great strength to accommodate flight. The bones of the human skeletal system are dense, strong, and aligned in such a way as to allow walking on two legs in an upright position.

Skill 7.4   Recognize basic characteristics of living things (e.g., reproducing, obtaining nutrients)

Several characteristics have been described to identify living versus non-living substance.

> 1. Living things are made of cells; they grow, are capable of reproduction and respond to stimuli.

> 2. Living things must adapt to environmental changes or perish.

> 3. Living things carry on metabolic processes. They use and make energy.

Skill 7.5   Demonstrate knowledge of the characteristics of plant structures (e.g., roots, stems, leaves) and the functional relationships that connect them

Plant Tissues - specialization of tissue enabled plants to grow larger. Be familiar with the following tissues and their functions.

Xylem - transports water.

Phloem - transports food (glucose).

Cortex - storage of food and water.

Epidermis – protection.

Endodermis - controls movement between the cortex and the cell interior.

Pericycle - meristematic tissue which can divide when necessary.

Pith - storage in stems.

Sclerenchyma and collenchyma - support in stems.

Stomata - openings on the underside of leaves. They let carbon dioxide in and water out (transpiration).

Guard cells - control the size of the stomata. If the plant has to conserve water, the stomates will close.

Palisade mesophyll - contain chloroplasts in leaves. Site of photosynthesis.

Spongy mesophyll - open spaces in the leaf that allows for gas circulation.

Seed coat - protective covering on a seed.
Cotyledon - small seed leaf that emerges when the seed germinates.

Endosperm - food supply in the seed.

Apical meristem - this is an area of cell division allowing for growth.

Flowers are the reproductive organs of the plant. Know the following functions and locations:

Pedicel - supports the weight of the flower.

Receptacle - holds the floral organs at the base of the flower.

Sepals – green, leaf like parts that cover the flower prior to blooming.

Petals - contain coloration by pigments to attract insects to assist in pollination.

Anther - male part that produces pollen.

Filament - supports the anther; the filament and anther make up the stamen.

Stigma - female part that holds pollen grains.

Style - tube that leads to the ovary (female).

Ovary - contains the ovules; the stigma, style, and ovary make up the carpel.

Skill 7.6 Demonstrate knowledge of cells, tissues, organs, and organ systems in animals and the functional relationships that connect them

The organization of living systems builds on levels from small to increasingly more large and complex. All aspects, whether it be a cell or an ecosystem have the same requirements to sustain life. Life is organized from simple to complex in the following way:

Organelles make up cells which make up tissues which make up organs. Groups of organs make up organ systems. Organ systems work together to provide life for the organism.

Skill 7.7 Recognize the characteristics and functions of major organ systems in the human body

Skeletal System - The skeletal system functions in support. Vertebrates have an endoskeleton, with muscles attached to bones. Skeletal proportions are controlled by area to volume relationships. Body size and shape is limited due to the forces of gravity. Surface area is increased to improve efficiency in all organ systems.

The axial skeleton consists of the bones of the skull and vertebrae. The appendicular skeleton consists of the bones of the legs, arms, tail, and shoulder girdle. Bone is a connective tissue. Parts of the bone include compact bone which gives strength, spongy bone which contains red marrow to make blood cells, yellow marrow in the center of long bones to store fat cells, and the periosteum which is the protective covering on the outside of the bone. A joint is defined as a place where two bones meet. Whereas, joints enable movement, Ligaments attach bone to bone, and tendons attach bones to muscles.

Muscular System - function is for movement. There are three types of muscle tissue. Skeletal muscle is voluntary. These muscles are attached to bones. Smooth muscle is involuntary. It is found in organs and enables functions such as digestion and respiration. Cardiac muscle is a specialized type of smooth muscle and is found in the heart. Muscles can only contract; therefore they work in antagonistic pairs to allow back and forth movement. Muscle fibers are made of groups of myofibrils which are made of groups of sarcomeres. Actin and myosin are proteins which make up the sarcomere.

Physiology of muscle contraction - A nerve impulse strikes a muscle fiber. This causes calcium ions to flood the sarcomere. Calcium ions allow ATP to expend energy. The myosin fibers creep along the actin, causing the muscle to contract.

Once the nerve impulse has passed, calcium is pumped out and the contraction ends.

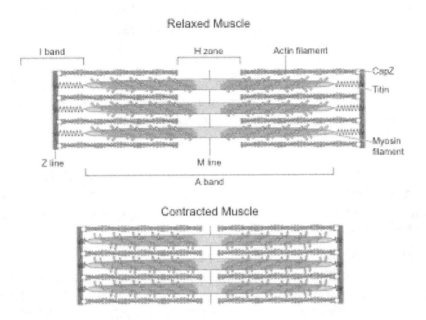

Nervous System - The neuron is the basic unit of the nervous system. It consists of an axon, which carries impulses away from the cell body, the dendrite, which carries impulses toward the cell body, and the cell body, which contains the nucleus. Synapses are spaces between neurons. Chemicals called neurotransmitters are found close to the synapses. The myelin sheath, composed of Schwann cells, covers the neurons and provides insulation.

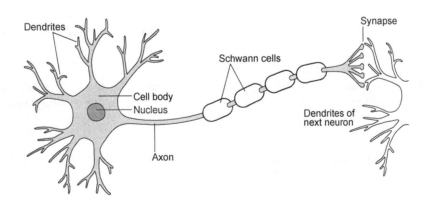

Physiology of the nerve impulse - Nerve action depends on depolarization and an imbalance of electrical charges across the neuron. A polarized nerve has a positive charge outside of the neuron. A depolarized nerve has a negative charge outside of the neuron. Neurotransmitters turn off the sodium pump which results in depolarization of the membrane. This wave of depolarization (as it moves from neuron to neuron) carries an electrical impulse. This is actually a wave of opening and closing gates that allows for the flow of ions across the synapse. Nerves have an action potential. There is a threshold of the level of chemicals that must be met or exceeded in order for muscles to respond. This is called the "all or   none" response.

The reflex arc is the simplest nerve response. The brain is bypassed. When a stimulus (like touching a hot stove) occurs, sensors in the hand send the message directly to the spinal cord. This stimulates motor neurons that contract the muscles to move the hand.

Voluntary nerve responses involve the brain. Receptor cells send the message to sensory neurons which lead to association neurons. The message is taken to the brain. Motor neurons are stimulated and the message is transmitted to effector cells which cause the end effect.

Organization of the Nervous System - The somatic nervous system is controlled consciously. It consists of the central nervous system (brain and spinal cord) and the peripheral nervous system (nerves that extend from the spinal cord to the muscles). The autonomic nervous system is unconsciously controlled by the hypothalamus of the brain. Smooth muscles, the heart and digestion are some processes controlled by the autonomic nervous system. It works in opposition. The sympathetic nervous system works opposite of the parasympathetic nervous system. For example, if the sympathetic nervous system stimulates an action, the parasympathetic nervous system would end that action.

Neurotransmitters - these are chemicals released by exocytosis. Some neurotransmitters stimulate while others inhibit action.

Acetylcholine - the most common neurotransmitter; it controls muscle contraction and heartbeat. The enzyme acetylcholinesterase breaks it down, ending the transmission.

Epinephrine - responsible for the "fight or flight" reaction. It causes an increase in heart rate and blood flow to prepare the body for action. It is also called adrenaline.

Endorphins and enkephalins - these are natural pain killers and are released during serious injury and childbirth.

Digestive System - The function of the digestive system is to break food down and absorb it into the blood stream where it can be delivered to all cells of the body for use in cellular respiration. The teeth and saliva begin digestion by breaking down food into smaller pieces and lubricating it so that it can be swallowed. The lips, cheeks, and tongue form a bolus (ball) of food. It is carried down the pharynx by the process of peristalsis (wave like contractions) and enters the stomach through the cardiac sphincter which then closes to keep food from going back up. In the stomach, pepsinogen and hydrochloric acid form pepsin, the enzyme that breaks down proteins. The food is broken down further by this chemical action and is churned into chyme. The pyloric sphincter muscle opens to allow the food to enter the small intestine. Most nutrient absorption occurs in the small intestine. Its large surface area, accomplished by its length and protrusions called villi and microvilli, allow for a great absorptive surface into the bloodstream. Chyme is neutralized after leaving the acidic stomach to allow the proper function of any enzymes encountered. Any food left after the trip through the small intestine enters the large intestine. The large intestine functions to reabsorb water and produce vitamin K. The feces, or remaining waste, are passed out through the anus.

Accessory organs - although not part of the digestive tract, these organs function in the production of necessary enzymes and bile. The pancreas makes many enzymes to break down food in the small intestine. The liver makes bile which breaks down and emulsifies fatty acids.

Respiratory System - This system functions in the gas exchange of needed oxygen and carbon dioxide waste. It delivers oxygen to the bloodstream and collects carbon dioxide for release out of the body. Air enters the mouth and nose, where it is warmed, moistened, and filtered of dust and particles. Cilia in the trachea trap unwanted material in mucus which can be expelled. The trachea splits into two bronchial tubes and the bronchial tubes divide into smaller bronchioles in the lungs. The internal surface of the lung is composed of alveoli, which are thin walled air sacs. These allow for a large surface area for gas exchange. The alveoli are lined with capillaries. Oxygen diffuses into the bloodstream and carbon dioxide diffuses out to be exhaled by the lungs. The oxygenated blood is carried to the heart and delivered to all parts of the body.

The thoracic cavity holds the lungs. A muscle, the diaphragm, below the lungs is an adaptation that makes inhalation possible. As the volume of the thoracic cavity increases, the diaphragm muscle flattens out and inhalation occurs. When the diaphragm relaxes, exhalation occurs.

Circulatory System- The function of the circulatory system is to carry oxygenated blood and nutrients to all cells of the body and return carbon dioxide waste to be expelled from the lungs. Be familiar with the parts of the heart and the path blood takes from the heart to the lungs, through the body and back to the heart. In short, unoxygenated blood enters the heart through the inferior and superior vena cava. The first chamber it encounters is the right atrium. It goes through the tricuspid valve to the right ventricle to the pulmonary arteries and then to the lungs where it is oxygenated. It returns to the heart through the pulmonary vein into the left atrium. It travels through the bicuspid valve to the left ventricle where it is pumped to all parts of the body through the aorta.

Sinoatrial node (SA node) - the pacemaker of the heart. Located on the right atrium, it is responsible for contraction of the right and left atrium.

Atrioventricular node (AV node) - located on the left ventricle, it is responsible for contraction of the ventricles.

Blood vessels include arteries, arterioles, capillaries, venules, and veins.

arteries - lead away from the heart. All arteries carry oxygenated blood except the pulmonary artery going to the lungs. Arteries are under high pressure.

arterioles - arteries branch off to form smaller arterioles.

capillaries - arterioles branch off to form tiny capillaries that reach every cell. Blood moves slowest here due to the small size; only one red blood cell may pass at a time to allow for diffusion of gases into and out of cells. Nutrients are also absorbed by the cells from the capillaries.

venules - capillaries combine to form larger venules. The vessels are now carrying waste products from the cells.

veins - venules combine to form larger veins, leading back to the heart. Veins and venules have thinner walls than arteries because they are not under as much pressure. Veins contain valves to prevent the backward flow of blood due to gravity.

Components of blood

plasma – 60% of the blood is plasma. It contains salts called electrolytes, nutrients and waste. It is the liquid part of blood.

erythrocytes - also called red blood cells; they contain hemoglobin which carries oxygen molecules.

leukocytes - also called white blood cells. White blood cells are larger than red cells. They are phagocytic and can engulf invaders. White blood cells are not confined to the blood vessels and can enter the interstitial fluid between cells.

platelets - assist in blood clotting. Platelets are made in the bone marrow.

Blood clotting - the neurotransmitter that initiates blood vessel constriction following an injury is called serotonin. A material called prothrombin is converted to thrombin with the help of thromboplastin. The thrombin is then used to convert fibrinogen to fibrin which traps red blood cells to form a scab and stop blood flow.

Lymphatic System (Immune System)- uses both nonspecific and specific mechanisms to defend the body.

Nonspecific defense mechanisms – They do not target specific pathogens, but are a whole body response. Results of nonspecific mechanisms are seen as symptoms of an infection. These mechanisms include the skin, mucous membranes, and cells of the blood and lymph (ie: white blood cells, macrophages). Fever is a result of an increase of white blood cells. Pyrogens are released by white blood cells which set the body's thermostat to a higher temperature. This inhibits the growth of microorganisms. It also increases metabolism to increase phagocytosis and body repair.

Specific defense mechanisms - They recognize foreign material and respond by destroying the invader. These mechanisms are specific and diverse. They are able to recognize individual pathogens. They also have recognition of foreign material versus the self. Memory of the invaders provides immunity upon further exposure.

antigen - any foreign particle that invades the body.

antibody - manufactured by the body, they recognize and latch onto antigens, hopefully destroying them.

immunity - this is the body's ability to recognize and destroy an antigen before it causes harm. Active immunity develops after recovery from an infectious disease (chicken pox) or after a vaccination (mumps, measles, rubella). Passive immunity may be passed from one individual to another. It is not permanent. A good example is the immunities passed from mother to nursing child.

Excretory System- The function of the excretory system is to rid the body of nitrogenous wastes in the form of urea. The functional unit of excretion is the nephron, which make up the kidneys. Antidiuretic hormone (ADH) which is made in the hypothalamus and stored in the pituitary, is released when differences in osmotic balance occur. This will cause more water to be reabsorbed. As the blood becomes more dilute, ADH release ends.

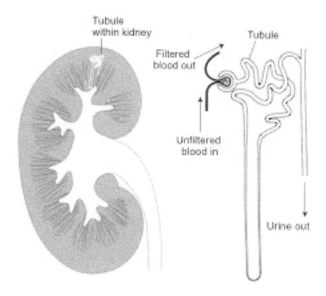

The Bowman's capsule contains the glomerulus, a tightly packed group of capillaries. The glomerulus is under high pressure. Waste and fluids leak out due to pressure. Filtration is not selective in this area. Selective secretion by active and passive transport occur in the proximal convoluted tubule. Unwanted molecules are secreted into the filtrate. Selective secretion also occurs in the loop of Henle. Salt is actively pumped out of the tube and much water is lost due to the hyperosmosity of the inner part (medulla) of the kidney. As the fluid enters the distal convoluted tubule, more water is reabsorbed. Urine forms in the collecting duct which leads to the ureter, then to the bladder where it is stored. Urine is passed from the bladder through the urethra. The amount of water reabsorbed back into the body is dependent upon how much water or fluids an individual has consumed. Urine can be very dilute or very concentrated if dehydration is present.

Endocrine System - The function of the endocrine system is to manufacture proteins called hormones. Hormones are released into the bloodstream and are carried to a target tissue where they stimulate an action. Hormones may build up over time to cause their effect, as in puberty or the menstrual cycle.

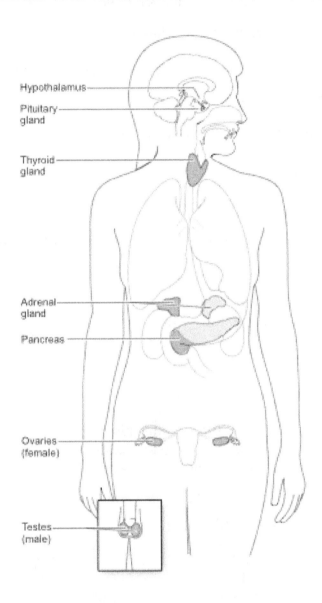

Hormone activation - Hormones are specific and fit receptors on the target tissue's cell surface. The receptor activates an enzyme which converts ATP to cyclic AMP. Cyclic AMP (cAMP) is a second messenger from the cell membrane to the nucleus. The genes found in the nucleus turn on or off to cause a specific response.

There are two classes of hormones. Steroid hormones come from cholesterol. Steroid hormones cause sexual characteristics and mating behavior. Hormones include estrogen and progesterone in females and testosterone in males.

Peptide hormones are made in the pituitary, adrenal glands on the kidneys, and the pancreas. They include the following:

Follicle stimulating hormone (FSH) - production of sperm or egg cells

Luteinizing hormone (LH) - functions in ovulation

Luteotropic hormone (LTH) - assists in production of progesterone

Growth hormone (GH) - stimulates growth

Antidiuretic hormone (ADH) - assists in retention of water

Oxytocin - stimulates labor contractions at birth and let-down of milk

Melatonin - regulates circadian rhythms and seasonal changes

Epinephrine (adrenalin) - causes fight or flight reaction of the nervous system

Thyroxin - increases metabolic rate

Calcitonin - removes calcium from the blood

Insulin - decreases glucose level in blood

Glucagon - increases glucose level in blood

Although you probably won't be tested on individual hormones, be aware that hormones work on a feedback system. The increase or decrease in one hormone may cause the increase or decrease in another.

Reproductive System- Sexual reproduction greatly increases diversity due to the many combinations possible through meiosis and fertilization. Gametogenesis is the production of the sperm and egg cells. Spermatogenesis begins at puberty in the male. One spermatozoa produces four sperm. The sperm mature in the seminiferous tubules located in the testes. Oogenesis, the production of egg cells, is usually complete by the birth of a female. Egg cells are not released until menstruation begins at puberty. Meiosis forms one ovum with all the cytoplasm and three polar bodies which are reabsorbed by the body. The ovum are stored in the ovaries and released each month from puberty to menopause.

Path of the sperm - sperm are stored in the seminiferous tubules in the testes where they mature. Mature sperm are found in the epididymis located on top of the testes. After ejaculation, the sperm travels up the vas deferens where they mix with semen made in the prostate and seminal vesicles and travel out the urethra.

Path of the egg - eggs are stored in the ovaries. Ovulation releases the egg into the fallopian tubes which are ciliated to move the egg along. Fertilization normally occurs in the fallopian tube. If pregnancy does not occur, the egg passes through the uterus and is expelled through the vagina during menstruation. Levels of progesterone and estrogen stimulate menstruation and are affected by the implantation of a fertilized egg so menstruation does not occur.

Pregnancy - if fertilization occurs, the zygote implants in the uterus in about two to three days. Implantation promotes secretion of human chorionic gonadotrophin (HCG). This is what is detected in pregnancy tests. The HCG keeps the level of progesterone elevated to maintain the uterine lining in order to feed the developing embryo until the umbilical cord forms. Labor is initiated by oxytocin which causes labor contractions and dilation of the cervix. Prolactin and oxytocin cause the production of milk.

COMPETENCY 8.0   **UNDERSTAND THE PRINCIPLES AND PROCESSES OF THE INHERITANCE OF BIOLOGICAL TRAITS**

Skill 8.1   **Recognize the role of DNA and RNA in the transmission of genetic information**

The modern definition of a gene is that of a unit of genetic information. DNA makes up genes which in turn make up the chromosomes. DNA is wound tightly around proteins in order to conserve space. The DNA/protein combination makes up the chromosome. DNA controls the synthesis of proteins, thereby controlling the total cell activity. DNA is capable of making copies of itself.

Review of DNA structure:

1.   Made of nucleotides, which are each made of a five carbon sugar, phosphate group, and nitrogen base (either adenine, guanine, cytosine, or thymine).

2. Consist of a sugar/phosphate backbone which is covalently bonded. The bases are joined down the center of the molecule and are attached by hydrogen bonds which are easily broken during replication.

3. The amount of adenine equals the amount of thymine, and the amount of cytosine equals the amount of guanine.

4. The shape is that of a twisted ladder called a double helix. The sugar/phosphates make up the sides of the ladder and the base pairs make up the rungs of the ladder.

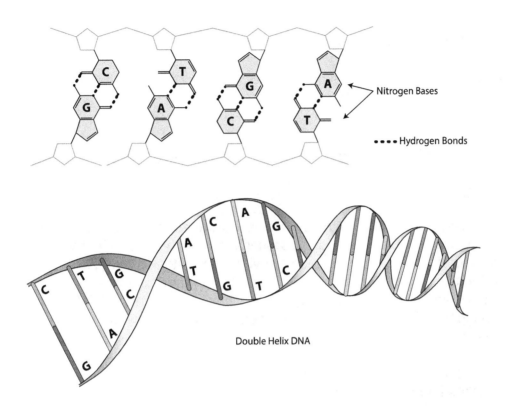

Double Helix DNA

DNA Replication

Enzymes control each step of the replication of DNA. The molecule untwists. The hydrogen bonds between the bases break and serve as a pattern for replication. Free nucleotides found inside the nucleus join on to form a new strand. Two new identical pieces of DNA are formed. This is a very accurate process. There is only one mistake for every billion nucleotides added. This is because there are enzymes (polymerases) present that proofread the molecule. In eukaryotes, replication occurs in many places along the DNA at once. The molecule may open up at many places like a broken zipper. In prokaryotic circular plasmids, replication begins at a point on the plasmid and goes in both directions until it meets itself.

Base pairing rules are important in determining the sequence of the new strand of DNA. For example, say our original strand of DNA had the sequence as follows:

    1. A T C G G C A A T A G C

This may be called our sense strand as it contains a sequence that makes sense or codes for something. The complementary strand (or other side of the ladder) would follow base pairing rules (A bonds with T and C bonds with G) and would read:

2. T A G C C G T T A T C G

When the molecule opens up and nucleotides join on, the base pairing rules create two new identical strands of DNA:

1. A T C G G C A A T A G C   and   A T C G G C A A T A G C
    T A G C C G T T A T C G   2. T A G C C G T T A T C G

Protein Synthesis

It is necessary for cells to manufacture new proteins for growth and repair of the organism. Protein Synthesis is the process that allows the DNA code to be read and carried out of the nucleus into the cytoplasm in the form of RNA. This is where the ribosomes are found, which are the sites of protein synthesis. The protein is then assembled according to the instructions on the DNA. There are several types of RNA. Familiarize yourself with where they are found and their function.

Messenger RNA - (mRNA) copies the code from DNA in the nucleus and takes it to the ribosomes in the cytoplasm.

Transfer RNA - (tRNA) free floating in the cytoplasm. Its job is to carry and position amino acids for assembly on the ribosome.

Ribosomal RNA - (rRNA) found in the ribosomes. They make a place for the proteins to be made. Much research is being done currently on rRNA and it is believed to have many important functions.

Along with enzymes and amino acids, RNA's assist in the building of proteins. There are two stages of protein synthesis:

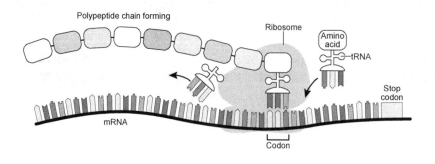

Transcription - basically, this phase allows for the assembly of mRNA   and occurs in the nucleus where the DNA is found. The DNA splits open   and the mRNA reads the code and "transcribes" the sequence onto a   single strand of mRNA. For example, if the code on the DNA is T A C C T C G T A C G A , the mRNA will make a complementary strand reading A U G G A G C A U G C U (Remember that uracil replaces thymine in RNA). Each group of three bases is called a codon. The codon will eventually code for a specific amino acid to be carried to the ribosome. "Start" codons begin the building of the protein and "stop" codons end transcription. When the stop codon is reached, the mRNA separates from the DNA and leaves the nucleus for the cytoplasm.

Translation - basically, this is the assembly of the amino acids to build the protein and occurs in the cytoplasm. The nucleotide sequence is translated to choose the correct amino acid sequence. As the rRNA translates the code at the ribosome, tRNA's, which contain an anticodon, seek out the correct amino acid and bring it back to the ribosome. For example, using the codon sequence from the example above:

the mRNA reads A U G / G A G / C A U / G C U
the anticodons are UA C / C U C / G U A / C G A (which you would be given and are not expected to memorize), and the amino acid
    sequence would be:

Methionine (start) - Glu - His - Ala. Be sure to note if the table you are given is written according to the codon sequence or the anticodon sequence. It will be specified.

This whole process is accomplished through the assistance of activating enzymes. Each of the twenty amino acids has their own enzyme. The enzyme binds the amino acid to the tRNA. When the amino acids get close to each other on the ribosome, they bond together using peptide bonds. The start and stop codons are called nonsense codons. There is one start codon (AUG) and three stop codons. (UAA, UGA, and UAG). Addition mutations will cause the whole code to shift, thereby producing the wrong protein or, at times, no protein at all.

Inheritable changes in DNA are called mutations. Mutations may be errors in replication or a spontaneous rearrangement of one or more segments by factors like radioactivity, drugs, or chemicals. The amount of the change is not as critical as where the change is. Mutations may occur on somatic or sex cells. Usually the ones on sex cells are more dangerous since they contain the basis of all information for the developing offspring. Mutations are not always bad. They are the basis of evolution, and if they make a more favorable variation that enhances the organism's survival, then they are beneficial. Unfortunately, mutations may also lead to abnormalities, birth defects, and death.

There are several types of mutations. Let's suppose a normal sequence was as follows:

Normal: A B C D E F

Duplication - one gene is repeated.   A B C C D E F

Inversion - a segment of the sequence is flipped around.   A E D C B F

Deletion - a gene is left out.   A B C E F

Insertion or Translocation - a segment from another place on the DNA is inserted in the wrong place.   A B C R S D E F

Breakage - a piece is lost.   A B C (DEF is lost)

Nondisjunction - during meiosis, chromosomes fail to separate properly. One sex cell may get both genes and another may get none. Depending on the chromosomes involved, this may or may not be serious. Offspring end up with either an extra chromosome or are missing one. An example of nondisjunction is Down Syndrome, where three #21 chromosomes are present.

Skill 8.2   Demonstrate knowledge of the roles of genes and chromosomes in the transfer of biological traits between generations

SOME DEFINITIONS TO KNOW

Dominant - the stronger of the two traits. If a dominant gene is present, it will be expressed. It is designated by a capital letter.

Recessive - the weaker of the two traits. In order for the recessive gene to be expressed, there must be two recessive genes present. It is designated by a lower case letter.

Homozygous - (purebred) having two of the same genes present; an organism may be homozygous dominant with two dominant genes or homozygous recessive with two recessive genes.

Heterozygous - (hybrid) having one dominant gene and one recessive gene. The dominant gene will be expressed according to the Law of Dominance.

Genotype - the genes the organism has. Genes are represented with letters. AA, Bb, and tt are examples of genotypes.

Phenotype - how the trait is expressed in an organism. Blue eyes, brown hair, and red flowers are examples of phenotypes.

Incomplete dominance - neither gene masks the other; a new phenotype is formed. For example, red flowers and white flowers may have equal strength. A heterozygote (Rr) would have pink flowers. If a third phenotype occurs, incomplete dominance is responsible.

Codominance - genes may form new phenotypes. The ABO blood grouping is an example of co-dominance. A and B are of equal strength and O is recessive. Therefore, type A blood may have the genotypes of AA or AO, type B blood may have the genotypes of BB or BO, type AB blood has the genotype A and B, and type O blood has two recessive O genes.

Linkage - genes that are found on the same chromosome usually appear together unless crossing over has occurred in meiosis (example - blue eyes and blonde hair).

Lethal alleles - these are usually recessive due to the early death of the offspring. If a 2:1 ratio of alleles is found in offspring, a lethal gene combination is usually the reason. Some examples of lethal alleles include sickle cell anemia, Tay-Sachs, and cystic fibrosis. Usually the coding for an important protein is affected.

Inborn errors of metabolism - these occur when the protein affected is an enzyme. Examples include PKU (phenylketonuria) and albinism.

Polygenic characters - many alleles code for a phenotype. There may be as many as twenty genes that code for skin color. This is why there is such a variety of skin tones. Another example is height. A couple of medium height may have very tall offspring.

Sex linked traits - the Y chromosome, found only in males (XY), carries very little genetic information, whereas the X chromosome found in females (XX) carries very important information. Since men have no second X chromosome to dominate over a recessive gene, the recessive trait is expressed more often in men. Women need the recessive gene on both X chromosomes to show the trait. Examples of sex linked traits include hemophilia and color-blindness.

Sex influenced traits - traits that are influenced by the sex hormones. Male pattern baldness is an example of a sex influenced trait. Testosterone influences the expression of the gene. Mostly men loose their hair due to this condition.

Skill 8.3   Differentiate sexual and asexual reproduction in organisms

The purpose of cell division is to provide growth and repair in body (somatic) cells and to replenish or create sex cells for reproduction. There are two forms of cell division. Mitosis is the division of somatic cells and meiosis is the division of sex cells (eggs and sperm). The table below summarizes the major differences between the two processes.

<u>MITOSIS</u>

1. Division of somatic cell
2. Two cells result from each division
3. Chromosome number is identical to parent cells.
4. For cell growth and repair

<u>MEIOSIS</u>

1. Division of sex cells
2. Four cells or polar bodies result from each division
3. Chromosome number is half the number of parent cells
4. Recombinations provide genetic diversity

Mitosis

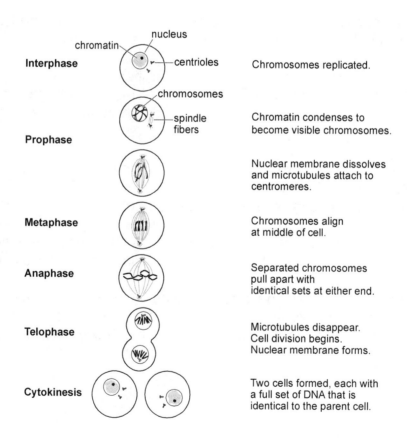

Interphase	Chromosomes replicated.
Prophase	Chromatin condenses to become visible chromosomes.
	Nuclear membrane dissolves and microtubules attach to centromeres.
Metaphase	Chromosomes align at middle of cell.
Anaphase	Separated chromosomes pull apart with identical sets at either end.
Telophase	Microtubules disappear. Cell division begins. Nuclear membrane forms.
Cytokinesis	Two cells formed, each with a full set of DNA that is identical to the parent cell.

Meiosis

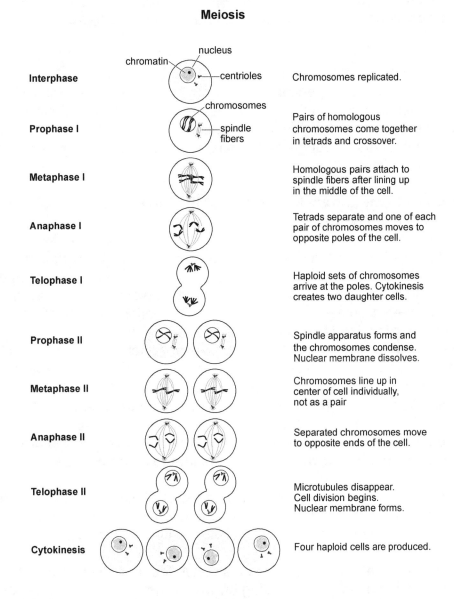

Interphase	Chromosomes replicated.
Prophase I	Pairs of homologous chromosomes come together in tetrads and crossover.
Metaphase I	Homologous pairs attach to spindle fibers after lining up in the middle of the cell.
Anaphase I	Tetrads separate and one of each pair of chromosomes moves to opposite poles of the cell.
Telophase I	Haploid sets of chromosomes arrive at the poles. Cytokinesis creates two daughter cells.
Prophase II	Spindle apparatus forms and the chromosomes condense. Nuclear membrane dissolves.
Metaphase II	Chromosomes line up in center of cell individually, not as a pair
Anaphase II	Separated chromosomes move to opposite ends of the cell.
Telophase II	Microtubules disappear. Cell division begins. Nuclear membrane forms.
Cytokinesis	Four haploid cells are produced.

Bacteria reproduce by binary fission. This asexual process is simply dividing the bacterium in half. All new organisms are exact clones of the parent.

The obvious advantage of asexual reproduction is that it does not require a partner. This is a huge advantage for organisms, such as the hydra, which do not move. Not having to move around to reproduce also allows organisms to conserve energy. Asexual reproduction also tends to be faster. There are disadvantages, as in the case of regeneration, in plants if the plant is not in good condition or in the case of spore-producing plants, if the surrounding conditions are not suitable for the spores to grow. As asexual reproduction produces only exact copies of the parent organism, it does not allow for genetic variation, which means that mutations, or weaker qualities, will always be passed on. This can also be detrimental to a species well adapted to a particular environment when the conditions of that environment change suddenly. On the whole, asexual reproduction is more reliable because it requires fewer steps and less can go wrong.

Sexual reproduction shares genetic information between gametes, thereby producing variety in the species. This can result in a better species with an improved chance of survival. There is the disadvantage that sexual reproduction requires a partner, which in turn often requires courtship, finding a mate, and mating. Another disadvantage is that sexually reproductive organisms require special mechanisms.

Skill 8.4   Demonstrate knowledge of the basic principles of inheritance and Mendel's laws

Gregor Mendel is recognized as the father of genetics. His work in the late 1800's is the basis of our knowledge of genetics. Although unaware of the presence of DNA or genes, Mendel realized there were factors (now known as genes) that were transferred from parents to their offspring. Mendel worked with pea plants and fertilized the plants himself, keeping track of subsequent generations, which led to the Mendelian laws of genetics. Mendel found that two "factors" governed each trait, one from each parent. Traits or characteristics came in several forms, known as alleles. For example, the trait of flower color had white alleles and purple alleles. Mendel formed three laws:

Law of dominance - in a pair of alleles, one trait may cover up the allele of the other trait. Example: brown eyes are dominant to blue eyes.

Law of segregation - only one of the two possible alleles from each parent is passed on to the offspring from each parent. (During meiosis, the haploid number insures that half the sex cells get one allele, half get the other).

Law of independent assortment - alleles sort independently of each other. (Many combinations are possible depending on which sperm ends up with which egg (compare this to the many combinations of hands possible when dealing a deck of cards).

Skill 8.5   Solve problems involving the probability of inheriting a specific trait (e.g., dominant/recessive, incomplete dominant, sex-linked, multiple-allele)

Punnet squares - these are used to show the possible ways that genes combine or probability of the occurrence of a certain genotype or phenotype. One parent's genes are put at the top of the box and the other parent at the side of the box. Genes combine on the square just like numbers that are added in addition tables.

Example: Monohybrid Cross - a cross using only one trait. It shows four possible gene combinations.

Example: Dihybrid Cross - a cross using two traits. More (16) gene combinations are possible.

This Punnet square shows the result of the cross of two F_1 hybrids.

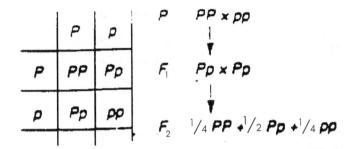

This cross results in a 1:2:1 ratio of F_2 offspring. Here, the P is the dominant allele and the p is the recessive allele. The F_1 cross produces three offspring with the dominant allele expressed (two PP and Pp) and one offspring with the recessive allele expressed (pp). Some other important terms to know:

Homozygous – having a pair of identical alleles. For example, PP and pp are homozygous pairs.

Heterozygous – having two different alleles. For example, Pp is a heterozygous pair.

Phenotype – the organism's physical appearance.

Genotype – the organism's genetic makeup. For example, PP and Pp have the same phenotype (purple in color), but are different genotypes.

The law of independent assortment states that alleles sort independently of each other. The law of segregation applies for monohybrid crosses (only one character, in this case flower color, is investigated). In a dihybrid cross, two characters are being explored. Two of the seven characters Mendel studied were seed shape and color. Yellow is the dominant seed color (Y) and green is the recessive color (y). The dominant seed shape is round (R) and the recessive shape is wrinkled (r). A cross between a plant with yellow round seeds ($YYRR$) and a plant with green wrinkled seeds ($yyrr$) produces an F_1 generation with the genotype $YyRr$. The production of F_2 offspring results in a 9:3:3:1 phenotypic ratio.

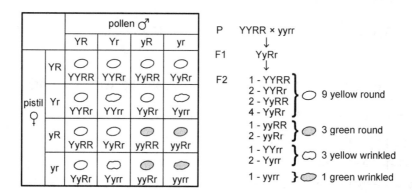

Based on Mendelian genetics, the more complex hereditary pattern of dominance was discovered. In Mendel's law of segregation, the F_1 generation have either purple or white flowers. This is an example of complete dominance. Incomplete dominance is when the F_1 generation results in an appearance somewhere between the two parents. For example, red flowers are crossed with white flowers, resulting in an F_1 generation with pink flowers. The red and white traits are still carried by the F_1 generation, resulting in an F_2 generation with a phenotypic ration of 1:2:1. In codominance, the genes may form new phenotypes. The ABO blood grouping is an example of codominance.

Sex linked traits - the Y chromosome, found only in males (XY), carries very little genetic information, whereas the X chromosome, found in females (XX), carries very important information. Since men have no second X chromosome to dominate over a recessive gene, the recessive trait is expressed more often in men. Women need the recessive gene on both X chromosomes to show the trait. Examples of sex linked traits include hemophilia and color-blindness.

Sex influenced traits - traits are influenced by the sex hormones. Male pattern baldness is an example of a sex influenced trait. Testosterone influences the expression of the gene. Mostly men loose their hair due to this condition.

Nondisjunction - during meiosis, chromosomes fail to separate properly. One sex cell may get both chromosomes and another may get none. Depending on the chromosomes involved, this may or may not be serious. Offspring end up with either an extra chromosome or are missing one. An example of nondisjunction is Down Syndrome, where three #21 chromosomes are present.

Skill 8.6   Identify applications of genetic engineering technology (e.g., agriculture, medicine, forensics)

In its simplest form, genetic engineering requires enzymes to cut DNA, a vector, and a host organism for the recombinant DNA. A restriction enzyme is a bacterial enzyme that cuts foreign DNA in specific locations. The restriction fragment that results can be inserted into a bacterial plasmid (vector). Other vectors that may be used include viruses and bacteriophage. The splicing of restriction fragments into a plasmid results in a recombinant plasmid. This recombinant plasmid can now be placed inside a host cell, usually a bacterial cell, and replicated.

The use of recombinant DNA provides a means to transplant genes among species. This opens the door for cloning specific genes of interest. Hybridization can be used to find a gene of interest. A probe is a molecule complementary in sequence to the gene of interest. The probe, once it has bonded to the gene, can be detected by labeling it with a radioactive isotope or a fluorescent tag.

Gel electrophoresis is another method for analyzing DNA. Electrophoresis separates DNA or proteins by size or electrical charge. The DNA runs towards the positive charge as it separates the DNA fragments by size. The gel is treated with a DNA-binding dye that fluoresces under ultraviolet light. A picture of the gel can be taken and used for analysis.

One of the most widely used genetic engineering techniques is polymerase chain reaction (PCR). PCR is a technique in which a piece of DNA can be amplified into billions of copies within a few hours. This process requires a primer to specify the segment to be copied and an enzyme (usually taq polymerase) to amplify the DNA. PCR has allowed scientists to perform several procedures on the smallest amounts of DNA.

Forensic scientists regularly use DNA technology to solve crimes. DNA testing can determine a person's guilt or innocence. A suspect's DNA fingerprint is compared to the DNA found at the crime scene. If the fingerprints match, guilt can then be established.

Genetic engineering has made enormous contributions to medicine. Genetic engineering has opened the door to DNA technology. The use of DNA probes and polymerase chain reaction (PCR) has enabled scientists to identify and detect elusive pathogens. Diagnosis of genetic disease is now possible before the onset of symptoms.

Genetic engineering has allowed for the treatment of some genetic disorders. Gene therapy is the introduction of a normal allele to the somatic cells to replace the defective allele. The medical field has had success in treating patients with a single enzyme deficiency disease. Gene therapy has allowed doctors and scientists to introduce a normal allele that would provide the missing enzyme.

Insulin and mammalian growth hormones have been produced in bacteria by gene-splicing techniques. Insulin treatment helps control diabetes for millions of people who suffer from the disease. The insulin produced in genetically engineered bacteria is chemically identical to that made in the pancreas. Human grown hormone (HGH) has been genetically engineered for the treatment of dwarfism caused by insufficient amounts of HGH. HGH is being further researched for the possible treatment of broken bones and severe burns.

Biotechnology has advanced the techniques used to create vaccines. Genetic engineering allows for the modification of a pathogen in order to attenuate it for vaccine use. In fact, vaccines created by a pathogen attenuated by gene-splicing may be safer than using the traditional mutants.

Many microorganisms are used to detoxify toxic chemicals and to recycle waste. Sewage treatment plants use microbes to degrade organic compounds. Some compounds, like chlorinated hydrocarbons, cannot be easily degraded. Scientists are working on genetically modifying microbes to be able to degrade the harmful compounds that today's microbes cannot.

Genetic engineering has also benefited agriculture. For example, many dairy cows are given bovine growth hormone to increase milk production. Commercially grown plants are often genetically modified for optimal growth.

Strains of wheat, cotton, and soybeans have been developed to resist the herbicides used to control weeds. This allows for the successful growth of the plants while destroying the weeds. Crop plants are also being engineered to resist infections and pests. Scientists can genetically modify crops to contain a viral gene that does not affect the plant and will "vaccinate" the plant from a virus attack. Crop plants are now being modified to resist insect attacks. This allows farmers to reduce the amount of pesticide used on plants.

COMPETENCY 9.0   UNDERSTAND THE DEPENDENCE OF
                  ORGANISMS ON ONE ANOTHER AND
                  UNDERSTAND THE FLOW OF ENERGY AND
                  MATTER IN ECOSYSTEMS

**Skill 9.1   Identify the roles of producers, consumers, and
              decomposers in ecosystems**

Trophic levels are based on the feeding relationships that determine energy flow and
chemical cycling.

Autotrophs are the primary producers of the ecosystem. Producers mainly consist of
plants. Primary consumers are the next trophic level. The primary consumers are the
herbivores that eat plants or algae. Secondary consumers are the carnivores that eat
the primary consumers. Tertiary consumers eat the secondary consumers. These
trophic levels may go higher depending upon the ecosystem. Decomposers are
consumers that feed off of animal waste and dead organisms. This pathway of food
transfer is known as the food chain.

**Skill 9.2   Demonstrate knowledge of the flow of energy and matter
              through a food web, food chain, or ecosystem**

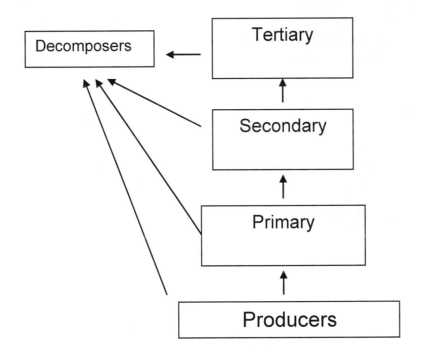

Most food chains are more elaborate, becoming food webs.

Biogeochemical Cycles

Essential elements are recycled through an ecosystem. At times, the element needs to be "fixed" in a useable form. Cycles are dependent on plants, algae, and bacteria to fix nutrients for use by animals.

Water cycle – Two percent of all the available water is fixed and unavailable in ice or in the bodies of organisms. Available water includes surface water (lakes, oceans, and rivers) and ground water (aquifers and wells). Ninety-six percent (96%) of all available water is from ground water. Water is recycled through the processes of evaporation and precipitation. The water present now is the water that has been here since our atmosphere formed.

Carbon cycle - Ten percent of all available carbon in the air (from carbon dioxide gas) is fixed by photosynthesis. Plants fix carbon in the form of glucose, animals eat the plants and are able to obtain their source of carbon. When animals release carbon dioxide through respiration, the plants gain a source of carbon to fix again.

Nitrogen cycle - Eighty percent of the atmosphere is in the form of nitrogen gas. Nitrogen must be fixed and taken out of the gaseous form to be incorporated into an organism. Only a few genera of bacteria have the correct enzymes to break the triple bond between nitrogen atoms. These bacteria live within the roots of legumes (peas, beans, alfalfa) and add bacteria to the soil so it may be taken up by the plant. Nitrogen is necessary to make amino acids and the nitrogenous bases of DNA.

Phosphorus cycle - Phosphorus exists as a mineral and is not found in the atmosphere. Fungi and plant roots have a structure called mycorrhizae that are able to fix insoluble phosphates into useable phosphorus. Urine and decayed matter returns phosphorus to the soil where it can be fixed in the plant. Phosphorus is needed for the backbone of DNA and for ATP manufacture.

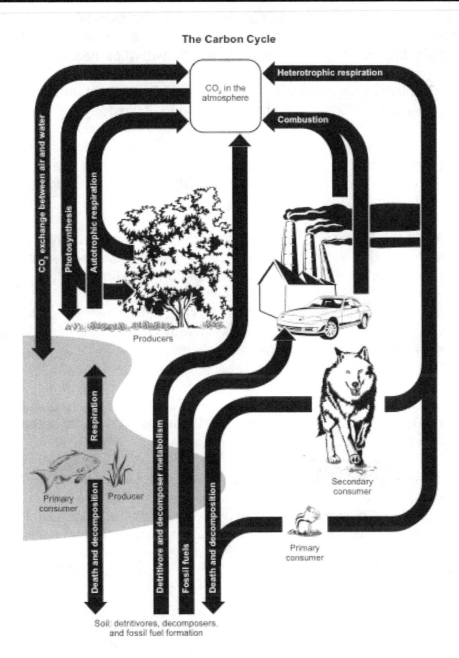

The Carbon Cycle

Skill 9.3   Evaluate how changes in environmental conditions can affect the survival of individuals or entire species

Biotic factors - living things in an ecosystem; plants, animals, bacteria, fungi, etc. If one population in a community increases, it affects the ability of another population to succeed by limiting the available amount of food, water, shelter, and space.

Abiotic factors - non-living aspects of an ecosystem; soil quality, rainfall, temperature. Changes in climate and soil can cause effects at the beginning of the food chain, thus limiting or accelerating the growth of population.

Ecological Problems - nonrenewable resources are fragile and must be conserved for use in the future. Man's impact and knowledge of conservation will control our future.

Biological magnification - chemicals and pesticides accumulate along the food chain. Tertiary consumers have more accumulated toxins than animals at the bottom of the food chain.

Simplification of the food web - Three major crops feed the world (rice, corn, and wheat). The planting of these foods limits other habitats and forces those inhabitants into other areas, causing overpopulation or extinction.

Fuel sources - strip mining and the overuse of oil reserves have depleted these resources. At the current rate of consumption, only conservation or alternative fuel sources will guarantee our future as a species.

Pollution - although technology gives us many advances, pollution is a side effect of production. Waste disposal and the burning of fossil fuels have polluted our land, water, and air. Global warming and acid rain are two results of the burning of hydrocarbons and sulfur.

Global warming - rainforest depletion and the use of fossil fuels and aerosols have caused an increase in carbon dioxide production. This leads to a decrease in the amount of oxygen which is directly proportional to the amount of ozone. As the ozone layer depletes, more heat enters our atmosphere and is trapped. This causes an overall warming effect which may eventually melt polar ice caps, causing a rise in water levels and changes in climate which will affect weather systems.

Endangered species - construction to house our overpopulated world has caused a destruction of habitat for other animals leading to their extinction.

Overpopulation - the human race is still growing at an exponential rate. Carrying capacity has not been met due to our ability to use technology to produce more food and housing. Space and water can not be manufactured and eventually our overuse affects every living thing on this planet.

Skill 9.4   Recognize the types and characteristics of relationships between organisms (e.g., competition, parasitism, mutualism)

Definitions of feeding relationships:

Parasitism - two species that occupy a similar place; the parasite benefits from the relationship, the host is harmed.

Commensalism - two species that occupy a similar place; neither species is harmed or benefits from the relationship.

Mutualism (symbiosis)- two species that occupy a similar place; both species benefit from the relationship.

Competition - two species that occupy the same habitat or eat the same food are said to be in competition with each other.

Predation - animals that eat other animals are called predators. The animals they feed on are called the prey. Population growth depends upon competition for food, water, shelter, and space. The amount of predators determines the amount of prey, which in turn affects the number of predators.

Carrying Capacity - this is the total amount of life a habitat can support. Once the habitat runs out of food, water, shelter, or space, the carrying capacity decreases and then stabilizes.

Skill 9.5   Demonstrate knowledge of harmful and beneficial microorganisms

Although bacteria and fungi may cause disease, they are also beneficial for use as medicines and food. Penicillin is derived from a fungus that is capable of destroying the cell wall of bacteria. Most antibiotics work in this way. Viral diseases have been fought through the use of vaccination, where a small amount of the virus is introduced so that the immune system is able to recognize it upon later infection. Antibodies are more quickly manufactured when the host has had prior exposure. Viruses are difficult to treat because antibiotics are ineffective against them. That is why doctors do not usually prescribe antibiotics for those who have a cold or the flu—common viral infections.

Skill 9.6   Identify characteristics of the Earth's major terrestrial biomes (e.g., tropical rain forest, desert, tundra) and aquatic communities (e.g., freshwater, estuarine, marine)

Ecology is the study of organisms, where they live and their interactions with the environment. A population is a group of the same species in a specific area. A community is a group of populations residing in the same area. Communities that are ecologically similar in regards to temperature, rainfall, and the species that live there are called biomes. Specific biomes include:

Marine - covers 75% of the earth. This biome is organized by the depth of the water. The intertidal zone is from the tide line to the edge of the water. The littoral zone is from the water's edge to the open sea. It includes coral reef habitats and is the most densely populated area of the marine biome. The open sea zone is divided into the epipelagic zone and the pelagic zone. The epipelagic zone receives more sunlight and has a larger number of species. The ocean floor is called the benthic zone and is populated with bottom feeders.

Tropical Rain Forest - temperature is constant (25 degrees C), rainfall exceeds 200 cm per year. Located around the area of the equator, the rain forest has abundant and diverse species of plants and animals.

Savanna - temperatures range from 0-25 degrees C depending on the location. Rainfall is from 90 to 150 cm per year. Plants include shrubs and grasses. The savanna is a transitional biome between the rain forest and the desert.

Desert - temperatures range from 10-38 degrees C. Rainfall is under 25 cm per year. Plant species include xerophytes and succulents. Lizards, snakes, and small mammals are common here.

Temperate Deciduous Forest - temperature ranges from -24 to 38 degrees C. Rainfall is between 65 and 150 cm per year. Deciduous trees are common, as well as deer, bear, and squirrels.

Taiga - temperatures range from -24 to 22 degrees C. Rainfall is between 35 and 40 cm per year. Taiga is located very north and very south of the equator, getting close to the poles. Plant life includes conifers and plants that can withstand harsh winters. Animals include weasels, mink, and moose.

Tundra - temperatures range from -28 to 15 degrees C. Rainfall is limited, ranging from 10 to 15 cm per year. The tundra is located even further north and south of the taiga. Common plants include lichens and mosses. Animals include polar bears and musk ox.

Polar or Permafrost - temperature ranges from -40 to 0 degrees C. It rarely gets above freezing. Rainfall is below 10 cm per year. Most water is bound up as ice. Life is limited.

Succession - Succession is an orderly process of replacing a community that has been damaged or has begun where no life previously existed. Primary succession occurs after a community has expired due to a natural disaster or, where life never existed before as in a flooded area. Secondary succession takes place in communities that were once flourishing but disturbed by some source, either man or nature, but not totally stripped. A climax community is a community that is established and flourishing.

COMPETENCY 10.0   UNDERSTAND THE THEORY OF EVOLUTION AND THE ROLE OF NATURAL SELECTION

Skill 10.1   Recognize the roles of variation and natural selection in the process of evolution

Darwin defined the theory of Natural Selection in the mid-1800's. Through the study of finches on the Galapagos Islands, Darwin theorized that nature selects the traits that are advantageous to a given species. Those organisms in a given species, which do not possess the desirable trait, die and do not pass on their genes. Those organisms in a species that are more fit survive to reproduce, thus increasing specific gene traits in the population. Darwin listed four principles to define natural selection:

1. The individuals in a certain species vary from generation to generation.
2. Some of the variations are determined by the genetic makeup of the species.
3. More individuals are produced than will survive.
4. Some genes allow for better survival of an animal.

Causes of evolution - Certain factors increase the chances of variability in a population, thus leading to evolution. Items that increase variability include mutations, sexual reproduction, immigration, large population size, and variation in geographic local. Items that decrease variation would be natural selection, emigration, small population size, and random mating.

Sexual selection - Genes that come together determine the makeup of the gene pool. Animals that use mating behaviors may be successful or unsuccessful. An animal that lacks attractive plumage or has a weak mating call will not attract the female, thereby eventually limiting its gene in the gene pool. Mechanical isolation, where sex organs do not fit the female, has an obvious disadvantage.

Skill 10.2   Recognize evidence for the evolution of species (e.g., Darwin's finches, fossils, genetics)

The idea of evolution is actually an ancient one, but scientists typically credit the theory of evolution to Charles Darwin and Alfred Russel Wallace. These scientists jointly presented the theory of evolution by natural selection in 1858. One of the more famous historical incidents leading up the formulation of this theory was Darwin's travel aboard the HMS Beagle. During the Beagle's 5-year journey across the Atlantic and along the coast of South America, Darwin made many observations regarding the plant and animal life. He later collected and published these findings, which were the basis for the theory he later developed, in "The Voyage of the Beagle."

Since the development of the theory of evolution, some of the best supporting evidence has come from molecular genetic studies. However, during the time of Darwin there were several "lower tech" pieces of evidence. For instance, the fossil record and comparative anatomy demonstrated possible relationships between both living and extinct organisms. One of the most famous examples of this involves "Darwin's finches." While onboard the Beagle, Darwin observed 13 species of finches in the Galapagos Islands. These finches were similar in size but had dramatically different sized and shaped beaks and extremely varied behavior. While Darwin did not at first realize that all these birds were related species of finches, their relations became apparent when he returned specimens to England and consulted with other naturalists. He later discovered that these were all related species that had adapted to take advantage of different food sources and slightly different ecological niches.

Skill 10.3   Identify and compare features and behaviors of organisms that allow them to survive or reproduce more effectively than organisms that do not have those features or behaviors (e.g., camouflage, use of hibernation, protection)

Anatomical structures and physiological processes that evolve over geological time to increase the overall reproductive success of an organism in its environment are known as biological adaptations. Such evolutionary changes occur through natural selection, the process by which individual organisms with favorable traits survive to reproduce more frequently than those with unfavorable traits. The heritable component of such favorable traits is passed down to offspring during reproduction, increasing the frequency of the favorable trait in a population over many generations.

Adaptations increase long-term reproductive success by making an organism better suited for survival under particular environmental conditions and pressures. These biological changes can increase an organism's ability to obtain air, water, food and nutrients, to cope with environmental variables, and to defend themselves. The term adaptation may apply to changes in biological processes that, for example, enable on organism to produce venom or to regulate body temperature, and also to structural adaptations, such as an organism's shape and skin color. Adaptations can occur in behavioral traits and survival mechanisms as well.

One well-known structural change that demonstrates the concept of adaptation is the development of the primate and human opposable thumb, the first digit of the hand that can be moved around to touch other digits and to grasp objects. The history of the opposable thumb is one of complexly linked structural and behavioral adaptations in response to environmental stressors.

Skill 10.4   Demonstrate knowledge of factors that affect the evolution of species (e.g., geographic isolation, genetic mutations)

Causes of evolution - Certain factors increase the chances of variability in a population, thus leading to evolution. Items that increase variability include mutations, sexual reproduction, immigration, and large population size. Items that decrease variation would be natural selection, emigration, small population size, and random mating.

The most commonly used species concept is the Biological Species Concept (BSC). This states that a species is a reproductive community of populations that occupy a specific niche in nature. It focuses on reproductive isolation of populations as the primary criterion for recognition of species status. The biological species concept does not apply to organisms that are completely asexual in their reproduction, fossil organisms, or distinctive populations that hybridize.

Reproductive isolation is caused by any factor that impedes two species from producing viable, fertile offspring. Reproductive barriers can be categorized as prezygotic (pre-mating) or postzygotic (post-mating).

The prezygotic barriers are as follows:

1.   Habitat isolation – species occupy different habitats in the same territory.
2.   Temporal isolation – populations reaching sexual maturity/flowering at different times of the year.
3.   Ethological isolation – behavioral differences that reduce or prevent interbreeding between individuals of different species (including pheromones and other attractants).
4.   Mechanical isolation – structural differences that make gamete transfer difficult or impossible.
5.   Gametic isolation – male and female gametes do not attract each other; no fertilization.

The postzygotic barriers are as follows:

1.   Hybrid inviability – hybrids die before sexual maturity.
2.   Hybrid sterility – disrupts gamete formation; no normal sex cells.
3.   Hybrid breakdown – reduces viability or fertility in progeny of the F_2 backcross.

Geographical isolation can also lead to the origin of species. Allopatric speciation is speciation without geographic overlap. It is the accumulation of genetic differences through division of a species' range, either through a physical barrier separating the population or through expansion by dispersal such that gene flow is halted. In sympatric speciation, new species arise within the range of parent populations. Populations are sympatric if their geographical range overlaps. This usually involves the rapid accumulation of genetic differences (usually chromosomal rearrangements) that prevent interbreeding with adjacent populations.

Sexual selection - Genes that come together determine the makeup of the gene pool. Animals that use mating behaviors may be successful or unsuccessful. An animal that lacks attractive plumage or has a weak mating call will not attract the female, thereby eventually limiting that gene from the gene pool. Mechanical isolation, where sex organs do not fit the female, has an obvious disadvantage.

COMPETENCY 11.0   UNDERSTAND THE NATURE OF MATTER AND ITS CLASSIFICATION

Skill 11.1   Demonstrate knowledge of the difference between pure substances (e.g., elements, compounds) and mixtures (e.g., solutions, alloys)

An element is a substance that can not be broken down into other substances. Today, scientists have identified 109 elements: 89 are found in nature and 20 are synthetic.

An atom is the smallest particle of the element that has the properties of that element. All of the atoms of a particular element are the same. The atoms of each element are different from the atoms of the other elements.

Elements are assigned an identifying symbol of one or two letters. The symbol for oxygen is O and stands for one atom of oxygen. However, because oxygen atoms in nature are joined together is pairs, the symbol O_2 represents oxygen. This pair of oxygen atoms is a molecule. A molecule is the smallest particle of a substance that can exist independently and has all of the properties of that substance. A molecule of most elements is made up of one atom. However, oxygen, hydrogen, nitrogen, and chlorine molecules are made of two atoms each.

A compound is made of two or more elements that have been chemically combined. The result is that the elements lose their individual identities when they are joined. The compound that they become has different properties than the individual elements it is made of.

We use a formula to show the elements of a chemical compound. A chemical formula is a shorthand way of showing what is in a compound by using symbols and subscripts. The letter symbols let us know what elements are involved and the number subscript tells how many atoms of each element are involved. No subscript is used if there is only one atom involved. For example, carbon dioxide is made up of one atom of carbon (C) and two atoms of oxygen (O_2), so the formula would be represented as CO_2.

Substances can combine without a chemical change. A mixture is any combination of two or more substances in which the substances keep their own properties. A fruit salad is a mixture. So is an ice cream sundae, although you might not recognize each part if it is stirred together. Colognes and perfumes are other examples. You may not readily recognize the individual elements; however, they can be separated.

Compounds and mixtures are similar in that they are made up of two or more substances. However, they have the following opposing characteristics:

Compounds:
1. Made up of one kind of particle
2. Formed during a chemical change
3. Broken down only by chemical changes
4. Properties are different from its parts
5. Has a specific amount of each ingredient.

Mixtures:
1. Made up of two or more particles
2. Not formed by a chemical change
3. Can be separated by physical changes
4. Properties are the same as its parts.
5. Does not have a definite amount of each ingredient.

Common compounds are acids, bases, salts, and oxides, and these are classified according to their characteristics.

An acid contains one element of hydrogen (H). Although it is never wise to taste a substance to identify it, acids have a sour taste. Vinegar and lemon juice are both acids, and acids occur in many foods in a weak state. Strong acids can burn skin and destroy materials. Common acids include:

Sulfuric acid (H_2SO_4)	-	Used in medicines, alcohol, dyes, and car batteries.
Nitric acid (HNO_3)	-	Used in fertilizers, explosives, cleaning materials.
Carbonic acid (H_2CO_3)	-	Used in soft drinks.
Acetic acid ($HC_2H_3O_2$)	-	Used in making plastics, rubber, photographic film, and as a solvent.

Bases have a bitter taste and the stronger ones feel slippery. Like acids, strong bases can be dangerous and should be handled carefully. All bases contain the elements oxygen and hydrogen (OH). Many household cleaning products contain bases. Common bases include:

Sodium hydroxide	NaOH	-	Used in making soap, paper, vegetable oils, and refining petroleum.

Ammonium hydroxide	NH₄OH	-	Making deodorants, bleaching compounds, cleaning compounds.
Potassium hydroxide	KOH	-	Making soaps, drugs, dyes, alkaline batteries, and purifying industrial gases.
Calcium hydroxide	Ca(OH)₂	-	Making cement and plaster

An indicator is a substance that changes color when it comes in contact with an acid or a base. Litmus paper is an indicator. Blue litmus paper turns red in an acid. Red litmus paper turns blue in a base.

A substance that is neither acid nor base is neutral. Neutral substances do not change the color of litmus paper.

PH SCALE

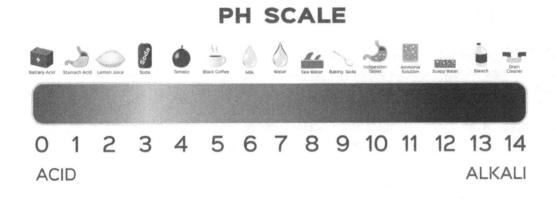

Salt is formed when an acid and a base combine chemically. Water is also formed. The process is called neutralization. Table salt (NaCl) is an example of this process. Salts are also used in toothpaste, Epsom salts, and cream of tartar. Calcium chloride (CaCl₂) is used on frozen streets and walkways to melt the ice.

Oxides are compounds that are formed when oxygen combines with another element. Rust is an oxide formed when oxygen combines with iron.

Skill 11.2   Identify the component parts of a substance (e.g., atoms, ions, molecules)

The atomic theory of matter suggests that:

1. All matter consists of atoms
2. All atoms of an element are identical
3. Different elements have different atoms
4. Atoms maintain their properties in a chemical reaction

An atom is a nucleus surrounded by a cloud with moving electrons.

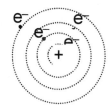

The nucleus is the center of the atom. The positive particles inside the nucleus are called protons. The mass of a proton is about 2,000 times that of the mass of an electron. The number of protons in the nucleus of an atom is called the atomic number. All atoms of the same element have the same atomic number.

Neutrons are another type of particle in the nucleus. Neutrons and protons have about the same mass, but neutrons have no charge. Neutrons were discovered because scientists observed that not all atoms in neon gas have the same mass.

Isotopes of an element have the same number of protons in the nucleus, but have different masses. Neutrons explain the difference in mass.

The mass of matter is measured against a standard mass such as the gram. Scientists measure the mass of an atom by comparing it to that of a standard atom. The result is relative mass. The relative mass of an atom is its mass expressed in terms of the mass of the standard atom. The isotope of the element carbon is the standard atom. It has six (6) neutrons and is called carbon-12. It is assigned a mass of 12 atomic mass units (amu). Therefore, the atomic mass unit (amu) is the standard unit for measuring the mass of an atom. It is equal to the mass of a carbon atom.

The mass number of an atom is the sum of its protons and neutrons. In any element, there is a mixture of isotopes, some having slightly more or slightly fewer protons and neutrons. The atomic mass of an element is an average of the mass numbers of its atoms.

The following table summarizes the terms used to describe atomic nuclei.

Term	Example	Meaning	Characteristic
Atomic Number	# protons (p)	same for all atoms of a given element	Carbon (C) atomic number = 6 (6p)
Mass number	# protons + # neutrons (p + n)	changes for different isotopes of an element	C-12 (6p + 6n) C-13 (6p + 7n)
Atomic mass	average mass of the atoms of the element	usually not a whole number	atomic mass of carbon equals 12.011

Each atom has an equal number of electrons (negative) and protons (positive). Therefore, atoms are neutral. Electrons orbiting the nucleus occupy energy levels that are arranged in order and the electrons tend to occupy the lowest energy level available. A stable electron arrangement is an atom that has all of its electrons in the lowest possible energy levels.

Each energy level holds a maximum number of electrons. However, an atom with more than one level does not hold more than 8 electrons in its outermost shell.

Level	Name	Max. # of Electrons
First	K shell	2
Second	L shell	8
Third	M shell	18
Fourth	N shell	32

This can help explain why chemical reactions occur. Atoms react with each other when their outer levels are unfilled. When atoms either exchange or share electrons with each other, these energy levels become filled and the atom becomes more stable.

As an electron gains energy, it moves from one energy level to a higher energy level. The electron can not leave one level until it has enough energy to reach the next level. Excited electrons are electrons that have absorbed energy and have moved farther from the nucleus.

Electrons can also lose energy. When they do, they fall to a lower level. However, they can only fall to the lowest level that has room for them. This explains why atoms do not collapse.

Skill 11.3   Distinguish between physical and chemical properties of matter (e.g., density, melting point, combustibility)

Substances can have two variables of conductivity. A conductor is a material that transfers a substance easily. That substance may be thermal or electrical in nature. Metals are known for being good thermal and electrical conductors. Touch your hand to a hot piece of metal and you know it is a good conductor- the heat transfers to your hand and you may be burnt. Materials through which electric charges can easily flow are called electrical conductors. Metals that are good electric conductors include silicon and boron. On the other hand, an insulator is a material through which electric charges do not move easily, if at all. The nonmetal elements of the periodic table are examples of electrical insulators.

Solubility is defined as the amount of substance (referred to as solute) that will dissolve into another substance, called the solvent. The amount that will dissolve can vary according to the conditions, most notably temperature. The process is called solvation.

Melting point refers to the temperature at which a solid becomes a liquid. Boiling point refers to the temperature at which a liquid becomes a gas. Melting takes place when there is sufficient energy available to break the intermolecular forces that hold molecules together in a solid. Boiling occurs when there is enough energy available to break the intermolecular forces holding molecules together as a liquid.

Hardness describes how difficult it is to scratch or indent a substance. The hardest natural substance is a diamond.

Skill 11.4   Identify the characteristics of ionic and covalent chemical bonds and their influence on the chemical and physical properties of a substance

The outermost electrons in the atoms are called valence electrons. Since they are the electrons involved in the bonding process, they determine the properties of the element.

A chemical bond is a force of attraction that holds atoms together. When atoms are bonded chemically, they cease to have their individual properties. For instance, hydrogen and oxygen combine into water and no longer look like hydrogen and oxygen. They look like water.

A covalent bond is formed when two atoms share electrons. Recall that atoms whose outer shells are not filled with electrons are unstable. When they are unstable, they readily combine with other unstable atoms. By combining and sharing electrons, they act as a single unit. Covalent bonding happens among nonmetals. Covalent bonds are always polar when between two non-identical

MIDDLE GRADES SCIENCE   88

atoms. Covalent compounds are compounds whose atoms are joined by covalent bonds. Table sugar, methane, and ammonia are examples of covalent compounds.

An ionic bond is a bond formed by the transfer of electrons. It happens when metals and nonmetals bond. Before chlorine and sodium combine, the sodium has one valence electron and chlorine has seven. Neither valence shell is filled, but the chlorine's valence shell is almost full. During the reaction, the sodium gives one valence electron to the chlorine atom. Both atoms then have filled shells and are stable. Something else has happened during the bonding. Before the bonding, both atoms were neutral. When one electron was transferred, it upset the balance of protons and electrons in each atom. The chlorine atom took on one extra electron and the sodium atom released one atom. The atoms have now become ions. Ions are atoms with an unequal number of protons and electrons. To determine whether the ion is positive or negative, compare the number of protons (+charge) to the electrons (-charge). If there are more electrons the ion will be negative. If there are more protons, the ion will be positive.

Compounds that result from the transfer of metal atoms to nonmetal atoms are called ionic compounds. Sodium chloride (table salt), sodium hydroxide (drain cleaner), and potassium chloride (salt substitute) are examples of ionic compounds.

Spontaneous diffusion occurs when random motion leads particles to increase entropy by equalizing concentrations. Particles tend to move into places of lower concentration. For example, sodium will move into a cell if the concentration is greater outside than inside of the cell. Spontaneous diffusion keeps cells balanced.

Skill 11.5   Demonstrate knowledge of the organization of the periodic table and its relationship to the properties of matter

The periodic table of elements is an arrangement of the elements in rows and columns so that it is easy to locate elements with similar properties. The elements of the modern periodic table are arranged in numerical order by atomic number.

The periods are the rows down the left side of the table. They are called first period, second period, etc. The columns of the periodic table are called groups, or families. Elements in a family have similar properties.

There are three types of elements that are grouped by color: metals, nonmetals, and metalloids.

Element Key

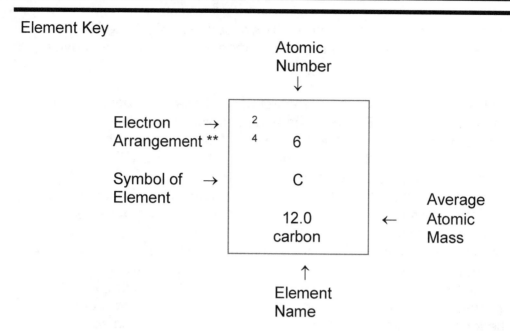

** Number of electrons on each level. Top number represents the innermost level.

Periodic Table of the Elements

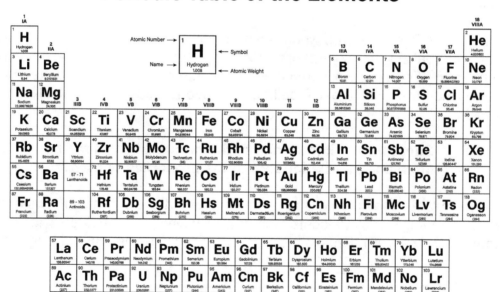

Humdan/Shutterstock.com

The periodic table arranges metals into families with similar properties. The periodic table has its columns marked IA - VIIIA. These are the traditional group numbers. Arabic numbers 1 - 18 are also used, as suggested by the Union of Physicists and Chemists.

Metals

With the exception of hydrogen, all elements in Group 1 are alkali metals. These metals are shiny, soft, less dense, and the most chemically active.

Group 2 metals are the alkaline earth metals. They are harder, denser, have higher melting points, and are chemically active.

The transition elements can be found by finding the periods (rows) from 4 to 7 under the groups (columns) 3-12. They are metals that do not show a range of properties as you move across the chart. They are hard and have high melting points. Compounds of these elements are colorful such as silver, gold, and mercury.

Elements can be combined to make metallic objects. An alloy is a mixture of two or more elements having properties of metals. The elements do not have to be all metals. For instance, steel is made up of the metal iron and the non-metal carbon.

Nonmetals

Nonmetals are not as easy to recognize as metals because they do not always share physical properties. In general the properties of nonmetals are the opposite of metals. They are not shiny, they are brittle, and they are not good conductors of heat and electricity.

Nonmetals are solids, gases, and one is a liquid (bromine).

Nonmetals have four to eight electrons in their outermost energy level and tend to attract electrons to their outer energy levels. As a result, the outer levels are usually filled with eight electrons. This difference in the number of electrons is what causes the differences between metals and nonmetals. The outstanding chemical property of nonmetals is that they react with metals.

The halogens can be found in Group 17. Halogens combine readily with metals to form salts. Table salt, fluoride toothpaste, and bleach all have an element from the halogen family.

The Noble Gases got their name from the fact that they did not react chemically with other elements, much like the nobility did not mix with the masses. These gases (found in Group 18) will only combine with other elements under very specific conditions. They are inert (inactive).

In recent years, scientists have found this to be only generally true, since chemists have been able to prepare compounds of krypton and xenon.

Metalloids

Metalloids have properties in between metals and nonmetals. They can be found in Groups 13-16, but do not occupy the entire group. They are arranged in stair steps across the groups.

Physical Properties:
1. All are solids having the appearance of metals.
2. All are white or gray, but not shiny.
3. They will conduct electricity, but not as well as a metal.

Chemical Properties:
1. Have some characteristics of metals and nonmetals.
2. Properties do not follow patterns like metals and nonmetals. Each must be studied individually.

Boron is the first element in Group 13. It is a poor conductor of electricity at low temperatures. However, increase its temperature and it becomes a good conductor. By comparison, metals, which are good conductors, lose their ability as they are heated. It is because of this property that boron is so useful. Boron is a semiconductor. Semiconductors are used in electrical devices that have to function at temperatures too high for metals.

Silicon is the second element in Group 14. It is also a semiconductor and is found in great abundance in the Earth's crust. Sand is made of a silicon compound, silicon dioxide. Silicon is also used in the manufacture of glass and cement.

Skill 11.6   Identify chemical symbols and interpret formulas

One or more substances are formed during a chemical reaction. Also, energy is released during some chemical reactions. Sometimes the energy release is slow and sometimes it is rapid. In a fireworks display, energy is released very rapidly. However, the chemical reaction that produces tarnish on a silver spoon happens very slowly.

Chemical equilibrium is defined as when the quantities of reactants and products are at a 'steady state' and are no longer shifting, but the reaction may still proceed forward and backward. The rate of forward reaction must equal the rate of backward reaction.

In one kind of chemical reaction, two elements combine to form a new substance. We can represent the reaction and the results in a chemical equation.

Carbon and oxygen form carbon dioxide. The equation can be written:

$$C \quad + \quad O_2 \quad \rightarrow \quad CO_2$$

1 atom of   +   1 molecule $\rightarrow$ 1 molecule of
carbon   oxygen $\rightarrow$ carbon dioxide

No matter is ever gained or lost during a chemical reaction; therefore the chemical equation must be *balanced*. This means that there must be the same number of molecules on both sides of the equation. Remember that the subscript numbers indicate the number of atoms in the elements. If there is no subscript, assume there is only one atom.

In a second kind of chemical reaction, the molecules of a substance split, forming two or more new substances. An electric current can split water molecules into hydrogen and oxygen gas.

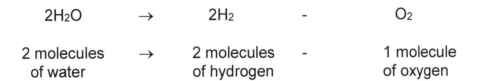

$$2H_2O \quad \rightarrow \quad 2H_2 \quad - \quad O_2$$

2 molecules $\rightarrow$ 2 molecules   -   1 molecule
of water   of hydrogen   of oxygen

The number of molecules is shown by the number in front of an element or compound. If no number appears, assume that it is 1 molecule.

A third kind of chemical reaction is when elements change places with each other. An example of one element taking the place of another is when iron changes places with copper in the compound copper sulfate:

$CuSo_4$	+	Fe	$\rightarrow$	$FeSO_4$	+	Cu
copper	+	iron		iron		copper
sulfate		(steel wool)		sulfate		

Sometimes two sets of elements change places. In this example, an acid and a base are combined:

HCl	+	NaOH	$\rightarrow$	NaCl	+	H_2O
hydrochloric		sodium		sodium		water
acid		hydroxide		chloride		
				(table salt)		

Matter can change, but it can not be created nor destroyed. The sample equations show two things:

1. In a chemical reaction, matter is changed into one or more different kinds of matter.
2. The amount of matter present before and after the chemical reaction is the same.

Many chemical reactions give off energy. Like matter, energy can change form but it can neither be created nor destroyed during a chemical reaction. This is the law of conservation of energy.

COMPETENCY 12.0   UNDERSTAND CHANGES IN MATTER.

Skill 12.1   Identify physical, chemical, and nuclear changes in matter and examples of those changes in everyday life

Physical properties and chemical properties of matter describe the appearance or behavior of a substance. A physical property can be observed without changing the identity of a substance. For instance, you can describe the color, mass, shape, and volume of a book. Chemical properties describe the ability of a substance to be changed into new substances. Baking powder goes through a chemical change as it changes into carbon dioxide gas during the baking process.

Matter constantly changes. A physical change is a change that does not produce a new substance. The freezing and melting of water is an example of physical change. A chemical change (or chemical reaction) is any change of a substance into one or more other substances. Burning materials turn into smoke, a seltzer tablet fizzes into gas bubbles.

The phase of matter (solid, liquid, or gas) is identified by its shape and volume. A solid has a definite shape and volume. A liquid has a definite volume, but no shape. A gas has no shape or volume because it will spread out to occupy the entire space of whatever container it is in.

Energy is the ability to cause change in matter. Applying heat to a frozen liquid changes it from solid back to liquid. Continue heating it and it will boil and give off steam, a gas.

Evaporation is the change in phase from liquid to gas. Condensation is the change in phase from gas to liquid.

Chemical reactions involve the breaking and forming of bonds between atoms. Bonds involve only the outer electrons and do not affect the nucleus. When a reaction involves a nucleus, elements are changed into different elements. This is called a nuclear reaction.

The binding energy is released when the nuclei of atoms are split apart in a nuclear reaction. This binding energy is called nuclear energy.

There are two types of nuclear reactions. These are fission and fusion.

Nuclear fission occurs when the nuclei are split apart. Smaller nuclei are formed and energy is released. The fission of many atoms in a short time period releases a large amount of energy. "Heavy water" is used in a nuclear reactor to slow down neutrons, controlling and moderating the nuclear reactions. Controlling the release so that energy is released slowly gives us nuclear submarines and nuclear power plants.

Nuclear fusion is the opposite. It occurs when small nuclei combine to form a larger nucleus. It begins with the hydrogen atom, which has the smallest nuclei. During one type of fusion, four hydrogen nuclei are fused at very high pressures and temperatures. They form one helium atom. The sun and stars are examples of fusion. They are made mostly of hydrogen that is constantly fusing. As the hydrogen forms helium, it releases an energy that we see as light. When all of the hydrogen is used, the star will no longer shine. Scientists estimate that the sun has enough hydrogen to keep it glowing for another four billion years.

During a nuclear reaction, elements change into other elements called radioactive elements. Uranium is a radioactive element. The element uranium breaks down and changes into the element lead. Most natural radioactive elements breakdown slowly, so energy is released over a long period of time.

Radioactive particles are used in the treatment of cancer because they can kill cancer cells. However, if they are powerful enough, they can also cause death. People working around such substances must protect themselves with the correct clothing, equipment, and safety procedures.

Skill 12.2   Apply knowledge of the law of conservation of matter to the analysis of physical changes and chemical changes (e.g., cutting, dissolving, forming a precipitate)

There are four kinds of chemical reactions:

In a composition reaction, two or more substances combine to form a compound.

$A + B \rightarrow AB$
i.e. silver and sulfur yield silver dioxide

In a decomposition reaction, a compound breaks down into two or more simpler substances.

$AB \rightarrow A + B$
i.e. water breaks down into hydrogen and oxygen

In a single replacement reaction, a free element replaces an element that is part of a compound.

$A + BX \rightarrow AX + B$
i.e. iron plus copper sulfate yields iron sulfate plus copper

In a double replacement reaction, parts of two compounds replace each other. In this case, the compounds seem to switch partners.

$AX + BY \rightarrow AY + BX$
i.e. sodium chloride plus mercury nitrate yields sodium nitrate plus mercury chloride

A chemical reaction is an interaction in which atoms exchange or share electrons, forming new chemicals. The substance or substances initially involved in this process are called reactants. Such reactions are characterized by a chemical change, and yield one or more products that are different from the reactants.

There are several distinct indications that a chemical reaction has occurred, depending on the type of reaction that takes place and the reactants involved.

1.   Formation of a precipitate is one indicator of a chemical reaction. Precipitation is the term used to describe the formation of a solid out of solution during a chemical reaction. In most cases, the precipitate falls out of solution, and then sinks or floats in solution depending on its density. The formation of a precipitate can occur when solutions containing ionic compounds are mixed and an insoluble product is formed. Precipitates may also be seen in single displacement reactions when one metal ion in solution is replaced by another metal ion. A common experiment used to demonstrate precipitation is the mixing of silver nitrate and sodium chloride. This reaction is:

$$AgNO_3 + NaCl \rightarrow AgCl + NaNO_3$$

In this case, the precipitate is $AgCl$, which is insoluble in water.

2.   A change in the color of a solution may also indicate that a chemical reaction has taken place. When two solutions are mixed, a color change indicates that a chemical reaction has occurred if the change does not simply result from the dilution of one reactant in another. The Briggs-Rauscher reaction, also known as 'the oscillating clock,' is one of the most common demonstrations of a color change reaction In this experiment, three colorless solutions are mixed together, and the resulting mixture oscillates between clear, amber, and deep blue, and over time becomes stable in color as a blue-black mixture.

   This reaction is:

$$IO_3^- + 2 H_2O_2 + CH_2(CO_2H)_2 + H^+ \rightarrow$$
$$ICH(CO_2H)_2 + 2 O_2 + 3 H_2O$$

The amber color results from the formation of I_2, which is then consumed to produce the deep blue color as it binds to the starch present in solution.

3. The formation of a gas is the third sign that a reaction may have occurred, and is seen when bubbles form after two solutions have been mixed, or a solid is added to a solution. For example, in the reaction:

$$Zn + 2HCl \rightarrow ZnCl_2 + H_2$$

hydrogen gas is released after zinc is added to hydrochloric acid.

4. An increase or decrease in temperature also indicates that a chemical reaction (exothermic or endothermic reaction, respectively) has taken place. For example, when solutions of barium hydroxide and ammonium nitrate are mixed, the following endothermic reaction occurs, producing temperatures as low as – 20 degrees Celsius.

$$Ba(OH)_2 + 8H2O_{(s)} + 2NH_4NO_{3(s)} \rightarrow Ba(NO_3)_{2(s)} + 2NH_{3\ (aq)} + 10H_2O_{(li)}$$

Skill 12.3 Recognize the characteristics of physical states of matter (e.g., temperature, density, molecular motion)

Everything in our world is made up of matter, whether it is a rock, a building, an animal, or a person. Matter is defined by its characteristics: it takes up space and it has mass.

Mass is a measure of the amount of matter in an object. Two objects of equal mass will balance each other on a simple balance scale no matter where the scale is located. For instance, two rocks with the same amount of mass that are in balance on Earth will also be in balance on the Moon. They will feel heavier on Earth than on the Moon because of the gravitational pull of the Earth. So, although the two rocks have the same mass, they will have different weight.

Weight is the measure of the Earth's pull of gravity on an object. It can also be defined as the pull of gravity between other bodies. The units of weight measure that we commonly use are the pound in English measure and the kilogram in metric measure.

In addition to mass, matter also has the property of volume. Volume is the amount of cubic space that an object occupies. Volume and mass together give a more exact description of the object. Two objects may have the same volume, but different mass, the same mass but different volumes, etc. For instance, consider two cubes that are each one cubic centimeter, one made from plastic, one from lead. They have the same volume, but the lead cube has more mass. The measure that we use to describe the cubes takes into consideration both the mass and the volume. Density is the mass of a substance contained per unit of volume. If the density of an object is less than the density of a liquid, the object will float in the liquid. If the object is denser than the liquid, then the object will sink.

Density is stated in grams per cubic centimeter (g / cm^3) where the gram is the standard unit of mass. To find an object's density, you must measure its mass and its volume. Then divide the mass by the volume ($D = m / V$).

To find an object's density, first use a balance to find its mass. Then calculate its volume. If the object is a regular shape, you can find the volume by multiplying the length, width, and height together. However, if it is an irregular shape, you can find the volume by seeing how much water it displaces. Measure the water in the container before and after the object is submerged. The difference will be the volume of the object.

Specific gravity is the ratio of the density of a substance to the density of water. For instance, the specific density of one liter of turpentine is calculated by comparing its mass (0.81 kg) to the mass of one liter of water (1 kg):

$$\frac{\text{mass of 1 L alcohol}}{\text{mass of 1 L water}} = \frac{0.81 \text{ kg}}{1.00 \text{ kg}} = 0.81$$

Skill 12.4   Identify the properties of solutions (e.g., concentration, ph, conductivity)

When two or more pure materials mix in a homogeneous way (with their molecules intermixing on a molecular level), the mixture is called a solution. When a pure liquid and a gas or solid form a liquid solution, the pure liquid is called the solvent and the non-liquids are called solutes. When all components in the solution were originally liquids, then the one present in the greatest amount is called the solvent and the others are called solutes. A solution at equilibrium with undissolved solute is a saturated solution. The amount of solute required to form a saturated solution in a given amount of solvent is called the solubility of that solute. If less solute is present, the solution is called unsaturated. It is also possible to have more solute than the equilibrium amount, resulting in a solution that is termed supersaturated.

An acid contains one element of hydrogen (H). Although it is never wise to taste a substance to identify it, acids have a sour taste. Vinegar and lemon juice are both acids, and acids occur in many foods in a weak state. Strong acids can burn skin and destroy materials. Common acids include:

| Sulfuric acid (H_2SO_4) | - | Used in medicines, alcohol, dyes, and car batteries. |
| Nitric acid (HNO_3) | - | Used in fertilizers, explosives, cleaning materials. |

Bases have a bitter taste and the stronger ones feel slippery. Like acids, strong bases can be dangerous and should be handled carefully. All bases contain the elements oxygen and hydrogen (OH). Many household cleaning products contain bases. Common bases include:

| Sodium hydroxide | NaOH | - | Used in making soap, paper, vegetable oils, and refining petroleum. |
| Ammonium hydroxide | NH_4OH | - | Making deodorants, bleaching compounds, cleaning compounds. |

A neutral substance has a pH of 7. An acidic substance has a pH below 7. A basic substance has a pH above 7. pH can easily be detected through the use of an indicator. An indicator is a substance that changes color when it comes in contact with an acid or a base. Litmus paper is an indicator. Blue litmus paper turns red in an acid. Red litmus paper turns blue in a base.

A substance that is neither acid nor base is neutral. Neutral substances do not change the color of litmus paper.

Salt is formed when an acid and a base combine chemically. Water is also formed. The process is called neutralization. Table salt (NaCl) is an example of this process. Salts are also used in toothpaste, Epsom salts, and cream of tartar. Calcium chloride ($CaCl_2$) is used on frozen streets and walkways to melt the ice.

Skill 12.5   Analyze factors that affect rates of physical changes and chemical reactions (e.g., temperature, catalysts)

The rate of most simple reactions increases with temperature because a greater fraction of molecules have the kinetic energy required to overcome the reaction's activation energy. The chart below shows the effect of temperature on the distribution of kinetic energies in a sample of molecules. These curves are called Maxwell-Boltzmann distributions. The shaded areas represent the fraction of molecules containing sufficient kinetic energy for a reaction to occur. This area is larger at a higher temperature; so more molecules are above the activation energy and more molecules react per second.

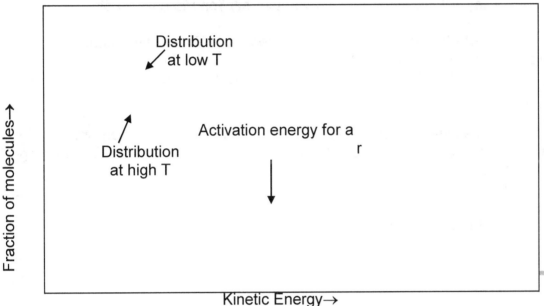

Kinetic molecular theory may be applied to reaction rates in addition to physical constants like pressure. Reaction rates increase with reactant concentration because more reactant molecules are present and more are likely to collide with one another in a certain volume at higher concentrations. The nature of these relationships determines the rate law for the reaction. For ideal gases, the concentration of a reactant is its molar density, and this varies with pressure and temperature.

Kinetic molecular theory also predicts that reaction rate constants (values for k) increase with temperature because of two reasons:

1. More reactant molecules will collide with each other per second.
2. These collisions will each occur at a higher energy that is more likely to overcome the activation energy of the reaction.

A catalyst is a material that increases the rate of a chemical reaction without changing itself permanently in the process. Catalysts provide an alternate reaction mechanism for the reaction to proceed in the forward and in the reverse direction. Therefore, catalysts have no impact on the chemical equilibrium of a reaction. They will not make a less favorable reaction more favorable.

Catalysts reduce the activation energy of a reaction. This is the amount of energy needed for the reaction to begin. Molecules with such low energies that they would have taken a long time to react will react more rapidly if a catalyst is present.

The impact of a catalyst may also be represented on an energy diagram. A catalyst increases the rate of both the forward and reverse reactions by lowering the activation energy for the reaction. Catalysts provide a different activated complex for the reaction at a lower energy state.

Biological catalysts are called enzymes.

COMPETENCY 13.0   UNDERSTAND PRINCIPLES AND CONCEPTS RELATED TO ENERGY

Skill 13.1   Compare the characteristics of different forms of energy (e.g., heat, light, kinetic, potential)

Abstract concept it might be, but energy is one of the most fundamental concepts in our world. We use it to move people and things from place to place, to heat and light our homes, to entertain us, to produce food and goods, and to communicate with each other. It is not some sort of magical invisible fluid, poured, weighed, or bottled. It is not a substance but rather the ability possessed by things.

Technically, energy is the ability to do work or supply heat. Work is the transfer of energy to move an object a certain distance. It is motion against an opposing force. Lifting a chair into the air is work; the opposing force is gravity. Pushing a chair across the floor is work; the opposing force is friction.

Heat, on the other hand, is not a form of energy but a method of transferring energy. This energy, according to the First Law of Thermodynamics, is conserved. That means energy is neither created nor destroyed in ordinary physical and chemical processes (non-nuclear). Energy is merely changed from one form to another. Energy in all of its forms must be conserved. In any system, $\Delta E = q + w$ (E = energy, q = heat, and w = work).

The temperature exhibited by an object is proportional to the average kinetic energy of the particles in the substance. Increase the temperature of a substance and its particles move faster so their average kinetic energies increase as well. But temperature is NOT an energy, it is not conserved.
The energy an object has, due to its position or arrangement of its parts, is called potential energy. Potential energy due to position is equal to the mass of the object times the gravitational pull on the object times the height of the object, or

$$PE = mgh$$

where PE = potential energy; m = mass of object; g = gravity; and h = height.

Heat is energy that is transferred between objects caused by differences in their temperatures. Heat passes spontaneously from an object of higher temperature to one of lower temperature. This transfer continues until both objects reach the same temperature. Both kinetic energy and potential energy can be transformed into heat energy. When you step on the brakes in your car, the kinetic energy of the car is changed to heat energy by friction between the brakes and the wheels. Other transformations can occur from kinetic to potential as well. Since most of the energy in our world is in a form that is not easily used, man and mother nature have developed some clever ways of changing one form of energy into another form that may be more useful.

MIDDLE GRADES SCIENCE   103

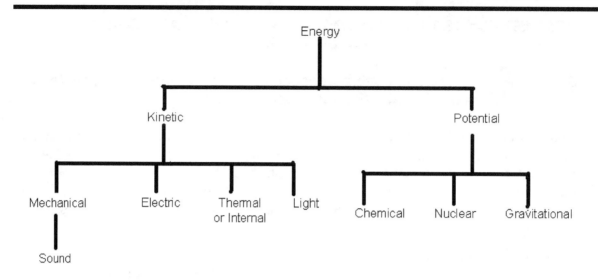

Gravitational Potential Energy

When something is lifted or suspended in air, work is done on the object against the pull of gravity. This work is converted to a form of potential energy called gravitational potential energy.

Nuclear Potential Energy

Nuclear energy trapped inside of an atom is referred to as nuclear energy. When the atom is split, tremendous energy is released in the form of heat and light.

Chemical Potential Energy

The energy generated from chemical reactions in which the chemical bonds of a substance are broken and rearranged to form new substances is called chemical potential energy.

Electrical Kinetic energy

The flow of electrons along a circuit is called electrical energy. The movement of electrons creates an electric current which generates electricity.

Mechanical Kinetic Energy

Mechanical energy is the energy of motion doing work, like a pendulum moving back and forth in a grandfather clock.

Thermal Kinetic Energy

Thermal Energy is defined as the energy that a substance has due to the chaotic motion of its molecules. Molecules are in constant motion, and always possess some amount of kinetic energy. It is also called Internal Energy and is not the same as heat.

Light or Radiant Kinetic Energy

Radiant energy comes from a light source, such as the Sun. Energy released from the Sun is in the form of photons. These tiny particles, invisible to the human eye, move in a way similar to a wave.

Energy transformations make it possible for us to use energy, to do work. The following are some examples of how energy is transformed to do work.

1. Different types of stoves are used to transform the chemical energy of fuel (gas, coal, wood, etc.) into heat.

2. Solar collectors can be used to transform solar energy into electrical energy.

3. Windmills make use of the kinetic energy of the air molecules, transforming it into mechanical or electrical energy.

4. Hydroelectric plants transform the kinetic energy of falling water into electrical energy.

5. A flashlight converts chemical energy stored in batteries to light energy and heat. Most of the energy is converted to heat, only a small amount is actually changed into light energy.

Skill 13.2 Applying knowledge of the law of conservation of energy in the analysis of physical and chemical systems

The relationship between heat, forms of energy, and work (mechanical, electrical, etc.) are the Laws of Thermodynamics. These laws deal strictly with systems in thermal equilibrium and not those within the process of rapid change or in a state of transition. Systems that are nearly always in a state of equilibrium are called reversible systems.

The first law of thermodynamics is a restatement of conservation of energy. The change in heat energy supplied to a system (Q) is equal to the sum of the change in the internal energy (U) and the change in the work done by the system against internal forces. $\Delta Q = \Delta U + \Delta W$

The second law of thermodynamics is stated in two parts:

1. No machine is 100% efficient. It is impossible to construct a machine that only absorbs heat from a heat source and performs an equal amount of work because some heat will always be lost to the environment.

2. Heat can not spontaneously pass from a colder to a hotter object. An ice cube sitting on a hot sidewalk will melt into a little puddle, but it will never spontaneously cool and form the same ice cube. Certain events have a preferred direction called the arrow of time.

Entropy is the measure of how much energy or heat is available for work. Work occurs only when heat is transferred from hot to cooler objects. Once this is done, no more work can be extracted. The energy is still being conserved, but is not available for work as long as the objects are the same temperature. Theory has it that, eventually, all things in the universe will reach the same temperature. If this happens, energy will no longer be usable.

Skill 13.3   Recognize the relationship between potential energy and kinetic energy

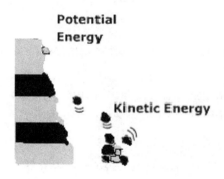

Potential Energy

Kinetic Energy

Energy exists in two basic forms, potential and kinetic. Kinetic energy is the energy of a moving object. Potential energy is the energy stored in matter due to its position relative to other objects.

In any object, solid, liquid or gas, the atoms and molecules that make up the object are constantly moving (vibrational, translational, and rotational motion) and are colliding with each other. They are not stationary.

Due to this motion, the object's particles have varying amounts of kinetic energy. A fast moving atom can push a slower moving atom during a collision, so it has energy. All moving objects have energy and that energy depends on the object's mass and velocity. Kinetic energy is calculated: $KE = \frac{1}{2} mv^2$.

Skill 13.4   Demonstrate knowledge of energy transformations and the processes by which energy Is transferred (i.e., conduction, radiation, convection)

Heat energy that is transferred into or out of a system is heat transfer. The temperature change is positive for a gain in heat energy and negative when heat is removed from the object or system.

The formula for heat transfer is $Q = mc\Delta T$ where Q is the amount of heat energy transferred, m is the amount of substance (in kilograms), c is the specific heat of the substance, and ΔT is the change in temperature of the substance. It is important to assume that the objects in thermal contact are isolated and insulated from their surroundings.

If a substance in a closed container loses heat, then another substance in the container must gain heat.

A calorimeter uses the transfer of heat from one substance to another to determine the specific heat of the substance.

When an object undergoes a change of phase, it goes from one physical state (solid, liquid, or gas) to another. For instance, water can go from liquid to solid (freezing) or from liquid to gas (boiling). The heat that is required to change from one state to the other is called latent heat.

The heat of fusion is the amount of heat that it takes to change from a solid to a liquid or the amount of heat released during the change from liquid to solid.

The heat of vaporization is the amount of heat that it takes to change from a liquid to a gaseous state.

Heat is transferred in three ways: conduction, convection, and radiation.

Conduction occurs when heat travels through the heated solid.

The transfer rate is the ratio of the amount of heat per amount of time it takes to transfer heat from area of an object to another. For example, if you place an iron pan on a flame, the handle will eventually become hot. How fast the handle gets too hot to manage is a function of the amount of heat and how long it is applied. Because the change in time is in the denominator of the function, the shorter the amount of time it takes to heat the handle, the greater the transfer rate.

Convection is heat transported by the movement of a heated substance. Warmed air rising from a heat source such as a fire or electric heater is a common example of convection. Convection ovens make use of circulating air to more efficiently cook food.

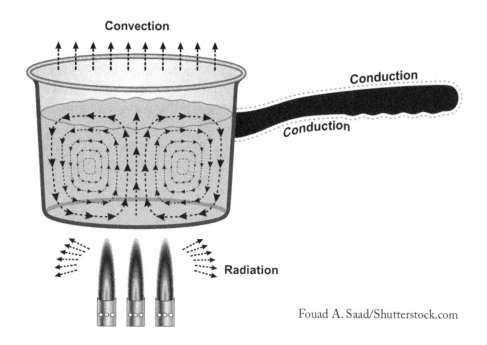

Fouad A. Saad/Shutterstock.com

Radiation is heat transfer as the result of electromagnetic waves. The Sun warms the Earth by emitting radiant energy.

An example of all three methods of heat transfer occurs in the thermos bottle or Dewar flask. The bottle is constructed of double walls of Pyrex glass that have a space in between. Air is evacuated from the space between the walls and the inner wall is silvered. The lack of air between the walls lessens heat loss by convection and conduction. The heat inside is reflected by the silver lining, cutting down heat transfer by radiation. Hot liquids remain hotter and cold liquids remain colder for longer periods of time.

Skill 13.5 Interpret diagrams that illustrate changes in the physical states of matter (e.g., phase diagrams)

Heat and temperature are different physical quantities. Heat is a measure of energy. Temperature is the measure of how hot (or cold) a body is with respect to a standard object.

Two concepts are important in the discussion of temperature changes. Objects are in thermal contact if they can affect each other's temperatures. Set a hot cup of coffee on a desk top. The two objects are in thermal contact with each other and will begin affecting each other's temperatures. The coffee will become cooler and the desktop warmer. Eventually, they will have the same temperature. When this happens, they are in thermal equilibrium.

We can not rely on our sense of touch to determine temperature because the heat from a hand may be conducted more efficiently by certain objects, making them feel colder. Thermometers are used to measure temperature. A small amount of mercury in a capillary tube will expand when heated. The thermometer and the object whose temperature it is measuring are put in contact long enough for them to reach thermal equilibrium. Then the temperature can be read from the thermometer scale.

Skill 13.6   Apply knowledge of the kinetic molecular model to the analysis of the properties and behaviors of matter as solids, liquids, gases, and plasmas

Molecules have kinetic energy (they move around), and they also have intermolecular attractive forces (they stick to each other). The relationship between these two determines whether a collection of molecules will be a gas, liquid, or solid.

A gas has an indefinite shape and an indefinite volume. The kinetic model for a gas is a collection of widely separated molecules, each moving in a random and free fashion, with negligible attractive or repulsive forces between them. Gases will expand to occupy a larger container so there is more space between the molecules. Gases can also be compressed to fit into a small container so the molecules are less separated. Diffusion occurs when one material spreads into or through another. Gases diffuse rapidly and move from one place to another.

A liquid assumes the shape of the portion of any container that it occupies and has a specific volume. The kinetic model for a liquid is a collection of molecules attracted to each other with sufficient strength to keep them close to each other but with insufficient strength to prevent them from moving around randomly. Liquids have a higher density and are much less compressible than gases because the molecules in a liquid are closer together. Diffusion occurs more slowly in liquids than in gases because the molecules in a liquid stick to each other and are not completely free to move.

A solid has a definite volume and definite shape. The kinetic model for a solid is a collection of molecules attracted to each other with sufficient strength to essentially lock them in place. Each molecule may vibrate, but it has an average position relative to its neighbors. If these positions form an ordered pattern, the solid is called crystalline. Otherwise, it is called amorphous. Solids have a high density and are almost incompressible because the molecules are close together. Diffusion occurs extremely slowly because the molecules almost never alter their position.

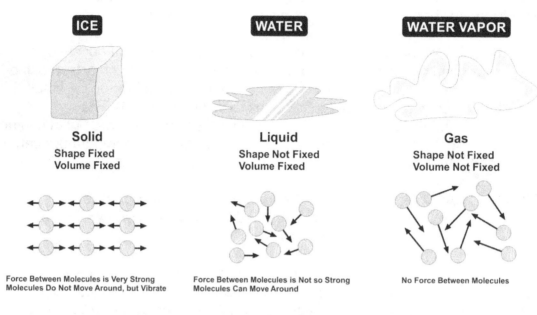

Udaix/Shutterstock.com

In a solid, the energy of intermolecular attractive forces is much stronger than the kinetic energy of the molecules, so kinetic energy and kinetic molecular theory are not very important. As temperature increases in a solid, the vibrations of individual molecules grow more intense and the molecules spread slightly further apart, decreasing the density of the solid. In a liquid, the energy of intermolecular attractive forces is about as strong as the kinetic energy of the molecules and both play a role in the properties of liquids. In a gas, the energy of intermolecular forces is much weaker than the kinetic energy of the molecules. Kinetic molecular theory is usually applied for gases and is best applied by imagining ourselves shrinking down to become a molecule and picturing what happens when we bump into other molecules and into container walls.

COMPETENCY 14.0   **UNDERSTAND THE RELATIONSHIPS AMONG FORCE, MASS, AND MOTION OF OBJECTS**

Skill 14.1   **Distinguish between the mass and weight of an object**

Mass and weight are not the same quantities. An object's mass gives it a reluctance to change its current state of motion. It is also the measure of an object's resistance to acceleration. The force that the Earth's gravity exerts on an object with a specific mass is called the object's weight on Earth. Weight is a force that is measured in Newtons. Weight (W) = mass times acceleration due to gravity. (W = mg). To illustrate the difference between mass and weight, picture two rocks of equal mass on a balance scale. If the scale is balanced in one place, it will be balanced everywhere, regardless of the gravitational field. However, the weight of the stones would vary on a spring scale, depending upon the gravitational field. In other words, the stones would be balanced on both Earth and the Moon. However, the weight of the stones would be greater on Earth than on the Moon.

Skill 14.2   **Identify characteristics of forces that act on objects (e.g., frictional, gravitational)**

Push and pulls –Pushing a volleyball or pulling a bowstring applies muscular force when the muscles expand and contract. When the bow is released it is called elastic force (when an object returns to its original shape).

Rubbing – Friction opposes the motion of one surface past another. Friction is common when slowing down a car or sled.

Pull of gravity – is a force of attraction between two objects. Gravity questions can be raised not only on Earth but also between planets and even black hole discussions.

Forces on objects at rest – The formula F= ma means that force equals mass times acceleration. An object will not move unless the force is strong enough to move the mass. Also there can be opposing forces holding the object in place. For instance, a boat may want to be forced by the currents to drift away but an equal and opposite force is a rope holding it to a dock.

Forces on a moving object - Overcoming inertia is the tendency of any object to oppose a change in motion. An object at rest tends to stay at rest. An object that is moving tends to keep moving.

Inertia and circular motion – Centripetal force is provided by the high banking of the curved road and by friction between the wheels and the road. This inward force keeps an object moving and is called centripetal force.

Skill 14.3   Determine the relationship between the velocity and acceleration of an object

The science of describing the motion of bodies is known as kinematics. The motion of bodies is described using words, diagrams, numbers, graphs, and equations.

The following words are used to describe motion: vectors, scalars, distance, displacement, speed, velocity, and acceleration.

The two categories of mathematical quantities that are used to describe the motion of objects are scalars and vectors. Scalars are quantities that are fully described by magnitude alone. Examples of scalars are 5m and 20 degrees Celsius. Vectors are quantities that are fully described by magnitude and direction. Examples of vectors are 30m/sec, and 5 miles north.

Distance is a scalar quantity that refers to how much ground an object has covered while moving. Displacement is a vector quantity that refers to the object's change in position.

Example:

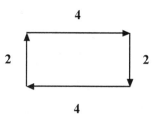

Jamie walked 2 miles north, 4 miles east, 2 miles south, and then 4 miles west. In terms of distance, she walked 12 miles. However, there is no displacement because the directions cancelled each other out, and she returned to her starting position.

Speed is a scalar quantity that refers to how fast an object is moving (ex. the car was traveling 60 mi./hr). Velocity is a vector quantity that refers to the rate at which an object changes its position. In other words, velocity is speed with direction (ex. the car was traveling 60 mi./hr east).

$$\text{Average speed} = \frac{\text{Distance traveled}}{\text{Time of travel}}$$

$$v = \frac{d}{t}$$

$$\text{Average velocity} = \frac{\square}{\text{time}} = \frac{\text{displacement}}{\text{time}}$$

Instantaneous Speed - speed at any given instant in time.

Average Speed - average of all instantaneous speeds, found simply by a distance/time ratio.

Acceleration is a vector quantity defined as the rate at which an object changes its velocity.

$$a = \frac{\square}{time} = \frac{v_f - v_i}{t}$$ where v_f represents the final velocity and v_i represents the initial velocity

Since acceleration is a vector quantity, it always has a direction associated with it. The direction of the acceleration vector depends on

- whether the object is speeding up or slowing down
- whether the object is moving in the positive or negative direction.

Skill 14.4   Solve quantitative problems involving force, mass, and motion of objects

Laws of Motion

Newton's first law of motion is also called the law of inertia. It states that an object at rest will remain at rest and an object in motion will remain in motion at a constant velocity unless acted upon by an external force.

Newton's second law of motion states that if a net force acts on an object, it will cause the acceleration of the object. The relationship between force and motion is Force equals mass times acceleration (F = ma).

Newton's third law states that for every action there is an equal and opposite reaction. Therefore, if an object exerts a force on another object, that second object exerts an equal and opposite force on the first.

Using these laws of motion and algebra, we can solve for force, mass, or acceleration, provided that we have two of the three variables. The force of gravity on Earth is always equal to the weight of the object as found by the equation:

F_{grav} = m * g

where g = 9.8 m/s^2 (on Earth)
and m = mass (in kg)

Momentum is the amount of moving mass. Its SI unit is kg m/s because it is calculated as the mass multiplied by the velocity of an object. Momentum is the mathematical restatement of Newton's laws- it is the tendency of an object to continue to move in its direction of travel, unless acted on by a net external force. Momentum is 'conserved' (the total momentum of a closed system cannot be changed).

Skill 14.5   Demonstrate knowledge of Newton's three laws of motion and their applications to everyday situations

Dynamics is the study of the relationship between motion and the forces affecting motion. Force causes motion.

Newton's laws of motion

Newton's first law of motion is also called the law of inertia. It states that an object at rest will remain at rest and an object in motion will remain in motion at a constant velocity unless acted upon by an external force.

Newton's second law of motion states that if a net force acts on an object, it will cause the acceleration of the object. The relationship between force and motion is Force equals mass times acceleration ($F = ma$).

Newton's third law states that for every action there is an equal and opposite reaction. Therefore, if an object exerts a force on another object, that second object exerts an equal and opposite force on the first.

Surfaces that touch each other have a certain resistance to motion. This resistance is friction.

1.   The materials that make up the surfaces will determine the magnitude of the frictional force.
2.   The frictional force is independent of the area of contact between the two surfaces.
3.   The direction of the frictional force is opposite to the direction of motion.
4.   The frictional force is proportional to the normal force between the two surfaces in contact.

Static friction describes the force of friction of two surfaces that are in contact but do not have any motion relative to each other, such as a block sitting on an inclined plane. Kinetic friction describes the force of friction of two surfaces in contact with each other when there is relative motion between the surfaces.

When an object moves in a circular path, a force must be directed toward the center of the circle in order to keep the motion going. This constraining force is called centripetal force. Gravity is the centripetal force that keeps a satellite circling the Earth.

MIDDLE GRADES SCIENCE   114

Skill 14.6   Apply knowledge of the concepts of work and power to the analysis of everyday activities

Work is done on an object when an applied force moves through a distance.

Energy and Work

Whenever work is done upon an object by an external force, there will be a change in the total mechanical energy of the object. If only internal forces are doing work, there is no change in total mechanical energy, the total mechanical energy is "conserved." The quantitative relationship between work and mechanical energy is expressed by the following equation:

$$TME_i + W_{ext} = TME_f$$

The equation states that the initial amount of total mechanical energy (TME_i) plus the work done by external forces (W_{ext}) is equal to the final amount of total mechanical energy (TME_f).

Power

Power is the rate at which work is done. It is the work/time ratio. The following equation is the formula used to compute power:

$$Power = \frac{Work}{Time}$$

The standard metric unit of power is the Watt. A unit of power is equivalent to a unit of work divided by a unit of time. Therefore, a Watt is equivalent to a Joule/second.

Mechanical Advantage

There are two types of mechanical advantage, ideal and actual. Ideal mechanical advantage is the mechanical advantage of an ideal machine. Because such a machine does not really exist, we use physics principles to "theoretically" solve such equations. The ideal mechanical advantage (IMA) is found using the following formula:

$$IMA = D_E / D_R$$

The effort distance over the resistance distance gives us the IMA.

Actual mechanical advantage it the mechanical advantage of a real machine and takes into consideration factors such as energy lost to friction. Actual mechanical advantage (AMA) is calculated using the following formula:

AMA = R / E_{actual}

By dividing the resistance force by the actual effort force we can determine the actual mechanical advantage of a machine.

Efficiency is the relationship between energy input and energy output. Efficiency is expressed as a percentage. The more efficient a system is, the less energy that is lost within that system. The percentage efficiency of any machine can be calculated as long as you know how much energy has to be put into the machine and how much useful energy comes out. The following equation is used:

% efficiency = useful energy produced x 100 / total energy used

Skill 14.7 Demonstrate knowledge of types and characteristics of simple machines and their effect on work

There are four types of simple machines:
1. Inclined plane
2. Lever
3. Wheel and axle
4. Pulley

<u>Work and energy</u>

Work is done on an object when an applied force moves through a distance.

Power is the work done divided by the amount of time that it took to do it. (Power = Work / time)

COMPETENCY 15.0   UNDERSTAND THE PROPERTIES OF WAVES, SOUND, AND LIGHT

Skill 15.1   Recognize the characteristics of mechanical waves (e.g., wavelength, amplitude)

Waves are divided into two main categories, electromagnetic and mechanical.

Electromagnetic waves

Light, microwaves, x-rays, and TV and radio transmissions are all kinds of electromagnetic waves. They are all a wavy disturbance that repeats itself over a distance called the wavelength. Electromagnetic waves come in varying sizes and properties, by which they are organized along the electromagnetic spectrum. The electromagnetic spectrum is measured in frequency (f) in hertz and wavelength (λ) in meters. The frequency times the wavelength of every electromagnetic wave equals the speed of light (3.0×10^9 meters/second).

Mechanical waves

A wave is simply a disturbance that travels through a medium (material). As it moves through the medium, it transports energy from one location to another. Sound and light are examples of mechanical waves. Waves can be described by a specific set of vocabulary, including pitch, frequency, wavelength and amplitude.

The pitch of a sound depends on the frequency that the ear receives. The frequency of a wave is the equivalent of how often the particles in the medium vibrate when the wave passes through that medium. Frequency is measured in vibrations per second. High-pitched sound waves have high frequencies. High notes are produced by an object that is vibrating at a greater number of times per second than one that produces a low note.

The intensity of a sound is the amount of energy that crosses a unit of area in a given unit of time. The loudness of the sound is subjective and depends upon the effect on the human ear. Two tones of the same intensity but different pitches may appear to have different loudness. The intensity of sound is measured in decibels. Normal conversation is about 60 decibels. A power saw is about 110 decibels.

The amplitude of a sound wave determines its loudness. Loud sound waves have large amplitudes. The larger the sound wave, the more energy is needed to create the wave.

Wavelength is the distance measured between two repeating portions of a wave pattern. This can be measured between the crests (high points) or troughs (low points), but is not measured between crest and trough.

Skill 15.2   Demonstrate knowledge of the properties of sound in everyday phenomena (e.g., echoes, Doppler effect)

When a piano tuner tunes a piano, he only uses one tuning fork, even though there are many strings on the piano. He adjusts to first string to be the same as that of the tuning fork. Then he listens to the beats that occur when both the tuned and untuned strings are struck. He adjusts the untuned string until he can hear the correct number of beats per second. This process of striking the untuned and tuned strings together and timing the beats is repeated until all of the piano strings are tuned.

Pleasant sounds have a regular wave pattern that is repeated over and over. Sounds that have an irregular pattern are unpleasant and are called noise.

Change in experienced frequency due to relative motion of the source of the sound is called the Doppler Effect. When a siren approaches, the pitch is high. When it passes, the pitch drops. As a moving sound source approaches a listener, the sound waves are closer together, causing an increase in frequency of the sound that is heard. As the source passes the listener, the waves spread out and the frequency experienced by the listener is lower.

An echo is a wave that has been reflected by a medium, and returns to your ear. The delay between its reflection and your perception of its return is equal to the distance divided by the speed of sound.

Skill 15.3   Recognize how the behavior of waves is affected by the medium (e.g., air, water, solids) through which the waves are passing

Sound waves need a medium in which to spread; light waves do not. The speed of any wave depends upon the elastic and inertial properties of the medium through which it travels. The density of a medium is an example of an inertial property. Sound usually travels faster in denser material. A sound wave will travel nearly three times as fast through helium than through air. On the other hand, the speed of light is slower in denser materials. The speed of light is slower in glass than in air. (The standard for the speed of light, c, is actually the speed of light in a vacuum, such as empty space.)

Elastic properties are properties related to the tendency of a medium to maintain its shape when acted upon by force or stress. Sound waves travel faster in solids than they do in liquids, and faster in liquids than they do in gases. The inertial factor would seem to indicate otherwise. However, the elastic factor has a greater influence on the speed of the wave.

When a wave strikes an object, some of the wave energy is reflected off the object, some of the energy goes into and is absorbed by the object, and some of the energy goes through the object. For example, sound waves can penetrate walls. However, sound waves from the air cannot penetrate water, and sound waves from water cannot penetrate the air. Light passes through some materials, such as glass, but not through many other materials.

Skill 15.4   Recognize characteristics of the electromagnetic spectrum

The electromagnetic spectrum is measured in frequency (f) in hertz and wavelength (λ) in meters. The frequency times the wavelength of every electromagnetic wave equals the speed of light (3.0×10^9 meters/second).

Roughly, the range of wavelengths of the electromagnetic spectrum is:

	λ		f	
Radio waves	$10^5 - 10^{-1}$ meters		$10^3 - 10^9$ hertz	
Microwaves	$10^{-1} - 10^{-3}$ meters		$10^9 - 10^{11}$ hertz	
Infrared radiation	$10^{-3} - 10^{-6}$ meters		$10^{11.2} - 10^{14.3}$ hertz	
Visible light	$10^{-6.2} - 10^{-6.9}$ meters		$10^{14.3} - 10^{15}$ hertz	
Ultraviolet radiation	$10^{-7} - 10^{-9}$ meters		$10^{15} - 10^{17.2}$ hertz	
X-Rays	$10^{-9} - 10^{-11}$ meters		$10^{17.2} - 10^{19}$ hertz	
Gamma Rays	$10^{-11} - 10^{-15}$ meters		$10^{19} - 10^{23.25}$ hertz	

Skill 15.5   Identify the effect of mirrors, lenses, and prisms on the behavior of light

Shadows illustrate one of the basic properties of light. Light travels in a straight line. If you put your hand between a light source and a wall, you will interrupt the light and produce a shadow.

When light hits a surface, it is reflected. The angle of the incoming light - the angle of incidence - is the same as the angle of the reflected light - the angle of reflection. It is this reflected light that allows you to see objects. You see the objects when the reflected light reaches your eyes.

Different surfaces reflect light differently. Rough surfaces scatter light in many different directions. A smooth surface reflects the light in one direction. If it is smooth and shiny (like a mirror), the reflection allows you to see your image in the surface.

When light enters a different medium, it bends. This bending, or change of speed, is called refraction.

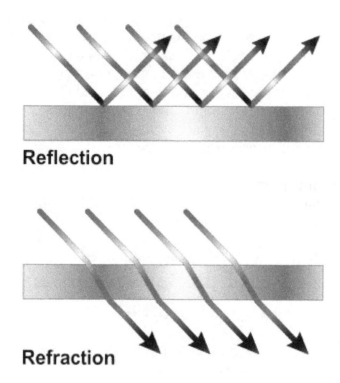

Reflection

Refraction

Fouad A. Saad/Shutterstock.com

Light can be diffracted, or bent, around the edges of an object. Diffraction occurs when light goes through a narrow slit. As light passes through it, the light bends slightly around the edges of the slit. You can demonstrate this by pressing your thumb and forefinger together, making a very thin slit between them. Hold them about 8 cm from your eye and look at a distant source of light. The pattern you observe is caused by the diffraction of light.

Light and other electromagnetic radiation can be polarized because the waves are transverse. The distinguishing characteristic of transverse waves is that they are perpendicular to the direction of the motion of the wave. Polarized light has vibrations confined to a single plane that is perpendicular to the direction of motion. Light is able to be polarized by passing it through special filters that block all vibrations except those in a single plane. By blocking out all but one place of vibration, polarized sunglasses cut down on glare.

Light can travel through thin fibers of glass or plastic without escaping the sides. Light on the inside of these fibers is reflected so that it stays inside the fiber until it reaches the other end. Such fiber optics are being used to carry telephone messages. Sound waves are converted to electric signals which are coded into a series of light pulses which move through the optical fiber until they reach the other end. At that time, they are converted back into sound.

The image that you see in a bathroom mirror is a virtual image because it only seems to be where it is. However, a curved mirror can produce a real image. A real image is produced when light passes through the point where the image appears. A real image can be projected onto a screen.

Cameras use a convex lens to produce an image on the film. A convex lens is thicker in the middle than at the edges. The image size depends upon the focal length (distance from the focus to the lens). The longer the focal length, the larger the image. A converging lens produces a real image whenever the object is far enough from the lens so that the rays of light from the object can hit the lens and be focused into a real image on the other side of the lens.

Eyeglasses can help correct sight deficiencies by changing where the image is focused on the retina of the eye. If a person is nearsighted, the lens of his eye focuses images in front of the retina. In this case, the corrective lens placed in the eyeglasses will be concave so that the image will reach the retina. In the case of farsightedness, the lens of the eye focuses the image behind the retina. The correction will call for a convex lens to be fitted into the glass frames so that the image is brought forward into sharper focus.

Skill 15.6   Demonstrate knowledge of the relationship between the properties of waves and how they are perceived by humans (e.g., color, pitch)

The pitch of a sound depends on the frequency that the ear receives. High-pitched sound waves have high frequencies. High notes are produced by an object that is vibrating at a greater number of times per second than one that produces a low note.

The intensity of a sound is the amount of energy that crosses a unit of area in a given unit of time. The loudness of the sound is subjective and depends upon the effect on the human ear. Two tones of the same intensity but different pitches may appear to have different loudness. The intensity level of sound is measured in decibels. Normal conversation is about 60 decibels. A power saw is about 110 decibels.

The amplitude of a sound wave determines its loudness. Loud sound waves have large amplitudes. The larger the sound wave, the more energy is needed to create the wave.

An oscilloscope is useful in studying waves because it gives a picture of the wave that shows the crest and trough of the waves. Interference is the interaction of two or more waves that meet. If the waves interfere constructively, the crest of each one meets the crests of the others. They combine into a crest with greater amplitude. As a result, you hear a louder sound. If the waves interfere destructively, then the crest of one meets the trough of another. They produce a wave with lower amplitude that produces a softer sound.

If you have two tuning forks that produce different pitches, then one will produce sounds of a slightly higher frequency. When you strike the two forks simultaneously, you may hear beats. Beats are a series of loud and soft sounds. This is because when the waves meet, the crests combine at some points and produce loud sounds. At other points, they nearly cancel each other out and produce soft sounds.

A great example absorption is apparent when discussing light. Transparent materials allow one or more of the frequencies of visible light to be transmitted through them; whatever color(s) is/are not transmitted by such objects are typically absorbed by them. The appearance of a transparent object is dependent upon what color(s) of light is/are incident upon the object and what color(s) of light is/are transmitted through the object.

COMPETENCY 16.0 UNDERSTAND ELECTRICITY AND MAGNETISM

Skill 16.1   Recognize the characteristics of static electricity

Electrostatics is the study of stationary electric charges. A plastic rod that is rubbed with fur or a glass rod that is rubbed with silk will become electrically charged and will attract small pieces of paper. The charge on the plastic rod rubbed with fur is negative and the charge on glass rod rubbed with silk is positive.

Electrically charged objects share these characteristics:

1. Like charges repel one another.
2. Opposite charges attract each other.
3. Charge is conserved. A neutral object has no net change. If the plastic rod and fur are initially neutral, when the rod becomes charged by the fur a negative charge is transferred from the fur to the rod. The net negative charge on the rod is equal to the net positive charge on the fur.

Materials through which electric charges can easily flow are called conductors. On the other hand, an insulator is a material through which electric charges do not move easily, if at all. A simple device used to indicate the existence of a positive or negative charge is called an electroscope. An electroscope is composed of a conducting knob and attached to that are very lightweight conducting leaves - usually made of gold foil or aluminum foil. When a charged object touches the knob, the leaves push away from each other because like charges repel. It is not possible to tell whether the charge is positive or negative.

Charging by induction

Touch the knob with a finger while a charged rod is nearby. The electrons will be repulsed and flow out of the electroscope through the hand. If the hand is removed while the charged rod remains close, the electroscope will retain the charge.

When an object is rubbed with a charged rod, the object will take on the same charge as the rod. However, charging by induction gives the object the opposite charge as that of the charged rod.

Grounding charge

Charge can be removed from an object by connecting it to the Earth through a conductor. The removal of static electricity by conduction is called grounding.

Skill 16.2   Demonstrate knowledge of the components of an electric circuit and their functions

An electric circuit is a path along which electrons flow. A simple circuit can be created with a dry cell, wire, and a bell, or light bulb. When all are connected, the electrons flow from the negative terminal, through the wire to the device and back to the positive terminal of the dry cell. If there are no breaks in the circuit, the device will work. The circuit is closed. Any break in the flow will create an open circuit and cause the device to shut off.

The device (bell, bulb) is an example of a load. A load is a device that uses energy. Suppose that you also add a buzzer so that the bell rings when you press the buzzer button. The buzzer is acting as a switch. A switch is a device that opens or closes a circuit. Pressing the buzzer makes the connection complete and the bell rings. When the buzzer is not engaged, the circuit is open and the bell is silent.

When an electron goes through a load, it does work and therefore loses some of its energy. The measure of how much energy is lost is called the potential difference. The potential difference between two points is the work needed to move a charge from one point to another.

Potential difference is measured in a unit called the volt. Voltage is potential difference. The higher the voltage, the more energy the electrons have. This energy is measured by a device called a voltmeter. To use a voltmeter, place it in a circuit parallel with the load you are measuring.

Current is the number of electrons per second that flow past a point in a circuit. Current is measured with a device called an ammeter. To use an ammeter, put it in series with the load you are measuring.

As electrons flow through a wire, they lose potential energy. Some energy is changed into heat energy because of resistance. Resistance is the ability of the material to oppose the flow of electrons through it. All substances have some resistance, even if they are a good conductor, such as copper. This resistance is measured in units called ohms. A thin wire will have more resistance than a thick one because it will have less room for electrons to travel. In a thicker wire, there will be more possible paths for the electrons to flow. Resistance also depends upon the length of the wire. The longer the wire, the more resistance it will have. Potential difference, resistance, and current form a relationship know as Ohm's Law. Current (I) is equal to potential difference (V) divided by resistance (R).

$$I = V / R$$

If you have a wire with resistance of 5 ohms and a potential difference of 75 volts, you can calculate the current by

I = 75 volts / 5 ohms
I = 15 amperes

A current of 10 or more amperes will cause a wire to get hot; 22 amperes is about the maximum for a house circuit. Currents above 25 amperes can reach temperatures high enough to start a fire.

Electricity can be used to change the chemical composition of a material. For instance, when electricity is passed through water, it breaks the water down into hydrogen gas and oxygen gas.

Circuit breakers in a home monitor the electric current. If there is an overload, the circuit breaker will create an open circuit, stopping the flow of electricity.

Computers can be made small enough to fit inside a plastic credit card by creating what is known as a solid state device. In this device, electrons flow through solid material such as silicon.

Resistors are used to regulate volume on a television or radio or through a dimmer switch for lights.

A bird can sit on an electrical wire without being electrocuted because the bird and the wire have about the same potential. However, if that same bird would touch two wires at the same time he would not have to worry about flying south next year.

When caught in an electrical storm, a car is a relatively safe place from lightening because of the resistance of the rubber tires. A metal building would not be safe unless there was a lightening rod that would attract the lightening and conduct it to the ground.

Skill 16.3   Compare series and parallel circuits

A series circuit is one where the electrons have only one path along which they can move. When one load in a series circuit goes out, the circuit is open. An example of this is a set of Christmas tree lights that is missing a bulb. None of the bulbs will work.

A parallel circuit is one where the electrons have more than one path to move along. Each possible direction of flow is known as a path. If a load goes out in a parallel circuit, the other load will still work because the electrons can still find a way to continue moving along the path.

Skill 16.4   Identifying the properties of magnets and the characteristics of magnetic fields.

Magnets have a north pole and a south pole. Like poles repel and different poles attract. A magnetic field is the space around a magnet where its force will affect objects. The closer you are to a magnet, the stronger the force. As you move away, the force becomes weaker.

Some materials act as magnets and some do not. This is because magnetism is a result of electrons in motion. The most important motion in this case is the spinning of the individual electrons. Electrons spin in pairs in opposite directions in most atoms. Each spinning electron has the magnetic field that it creates canceled out by the electron that is spinning in the opposite direction.

In an atom of iron, there are four unpaired electrons. The magnetic fields of these are not canceled out. Their fields add up to make a tiny magnet. Their fields exert forces on each other, setting up small areas in the iron called magnetic domains where atomic magnetic fields line up in the same direction.

You can make a magnet out of an iron nail by stroking the nail in the same direction repeatedly with a magnet. This causes poles in the atomic magnets of the nail to be attracted to the magnet. The tiny magnetic fields in the nail line up in the direction of the magnet. The magnet causes the domains pointing in its direction to grow in the nail. Eventually, one large domain results and the nail becomes a magnet.

A bar magnet has a north pole and a south pole. If you break the magnet in half, each piece will have a north and a south pole.

The Earth has a magnetic field. In a compass, a tiny, lightweight magnet is suspended and will line its south pole up with the North Pole magnet of the Earth.

Skill 16.5   Demonstrate knowledge of the relationship between moving electric charges and magnetic fields and applications of electromagnetism in everyday life (e.g., motors, generators)

A magnet can be made out of a coil of wire by connecting the ends of the coil to a battery. When the current goes through the wire, the wire acts in the same way that a magnet does, it is called an electromagnet.

The poles of the electromagnet will depend upon which way the electric current runs. An electromagnet can be made more powerful in three ways:

1. Make more coils.
2. Put an iron core (nail) inside the coils.
3. Use more battery power.

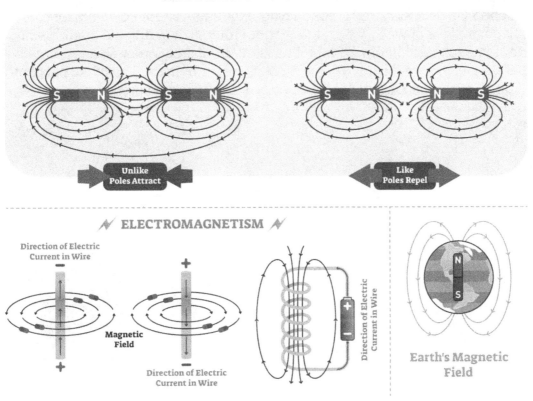

VectorMine/Shutterstock.com

Telegraphs use electromagnets to work. When a telegraph key is pushed, current flows through a circuit, turning on an electromagnet which attracts an iron bar. The iron bar hits a sounding board which responds with a click. Release the key and the electromagnet turns off. Messages can be sent around the world in this way.

Scrap metal can be removed from waste materials by the use of a large electromagnet that is suspended from a crane. When the electromagnet is turned on, the metal in the pile of waste will be attracted to it. All other materials will stay on the ground.

Air conditioners, vacuum cleaners, and washing machines use electric motors. In a motor, electricity is used to create magnetic fields that oppose each other and cause the rotor to move. The wiring loops attached to the rotating shaft have a magnetic field opposing the magnetic field caused by the wiring in the housing of the motor that cannot move. The repelling action of the opposing magnetic fields turns the rotor.

A generator is a device that turns rotary mechanical energy into electrical energy. The process is based on the relationship between magnetism and electricity. As a wire or any other conductor moves across a magnetic field, an electric current occurs in the wire. The large generators used by the electric companies have a stationary conductor. A magnet attached to the end of a rotating shaft is positioned inside a stationary, conducting ring that is wrapped with a long, continuous piece of wire. When the magnet rotates, it induces a small electric current in each section of wire that it passes. Each section of wire is a small, separate electric conductor. All the small currents of these individual sections add up to one large current, which is what is used for electric power.

DOMAIN IV.   CHARACTERISTICS OF SCIENCE

COMPETENCY 17.0   UNDERSTAND THE CHARACTERISTICS OF
                       SCIENTIFIC KNOWLEDGE AND THE PROCESS
                       OF SCIENTIFIC INQUIRY

Skill 17.1   Demonstrating knowledge of the nature, purpose, and characteristics of science and the limitations of science in terms of the kinds of questions that can be answered

Science may be defined as a body of knowledge that is systematically derived from study, observations, and experimentation. Its goal is to identify and establish principles and theories which may be applied to solve problems. Pseudoscience, on the other hand, is a belief that is not warranted. There is no scientific methodology or application. Some of the more classic examples of pseudoscience include witchcraft, alien encounters, or any topics that are explained by hearsay.

Only certain types of questions can truly be answered by science because the scientific method relies on observable phenomenon. That is, only hypotheses that can be tested are valid. Often this means that we can control the variables in a system to an extent that allows us to truly determine their effects. If we don't have full control over the variables, for instance in environmental biology, we can study several different naturally occurring systems in which the desired variable is different. Scientific research serves two purposes:

1.   To investigate and acquire knowledge which is theoretical and
2.   To do research which is of practical value.

Science is in a unique position to be able to serve humanity. Scientific research comes from inquiry. An inquiring mind craves answers. The two most important questions – why and how, are the starting points. A person who is inquisitive asks questions and wants to find solutions.

Scientific research uses the scientific method to methodically answer questions. Those who research must follow the scientific method, which consists of a series of steps designed to solve a problem or find an answer to the problem.
The aim of the scientific method is to eliminate bias/prejudice from the scientist/researcher. As human beings, we are influenced by our bias/prejudice and this method helps to eliminate it. If all the steps of the scientific method are followed as outlined, bias is eliminated.

Scientific research is clearly different from learning in other specialties. Science demands evidence. Science requires experimenting to prove one's ideas or propositions. Science does not answer all our questions. Science doesn't say anything about the cultural, moral, and religious beliefs of the individuals. It is up to us to use the information science provides and make our own decisions according to our beliefs and norms.

Skill 17.2   Recognize the dynamic nature of scientific knowledge through the continual testing, revision, and occasional rejection of existing theories

The first step in a scientific inquiry is posing a question to be answered. Next, a hypothesis is formed to provide a plausible explanation. An experiment is then proposed and performed to test this hypothesis. A comparison between the predicted and observed results is the next step. Conclusions are then formed and it is determined whether the hypothesis is correct or incorrect. If incorrect, the next step is to form a new hypothesis and the process is repeated.

Science is limited by the available technology. An example of this would be the relationship of the discovery of the cell and the invention of the microscope. As our technology improves, more hypotheses will become theories and possibly laws. Science is also limited by the data that is able to be collected. Data may be interpreted differently on different occasions. Scientific limitations cause explanations to be changeable as new technologies emerge.

Skill 17.3   Determine an appropriate scientific hypothesis or investigative design for addressing a given problem

The scientific method is the basic process behind science. It involves several steps as outlined below.

Posing a question
Although many discoveries happen by chance, the standard thought process of a scientist begins with forming a question to research. The more limited the question, the easier it is to set up an experiment to answer it.

Form a hypothesis
Once the question is formulated, take an educated guess about the answer to the problem or question.

Conduct the test
To make a test fair, data from an experiment must have a variable or any condition that can be changed such as temperature or mass. A well designed test will try to manipulate as few variables as possible to clearly determine which variable is responsible for the result. This requires a second example called a control. A control is an extra setup in which all the conditions are the same except for the variable being tested.

MIDDLE GRADES SCIENCE   130

Observe and record the data
Reporting of the data should state specifics of how the measurements were calculated. A graduated cylinder needs to be read with proper procedures. As beginning students, technique must be part of the instructional process so as to give validity to the data.

Drawing a conclusion
After you record data it should be compared with the data from other groups. A conclusion is the judgment derived from the data results.

Graphing data
Graphing takes numbers and visually demonstrates patterns that might otherwise be more difficult to conclude.

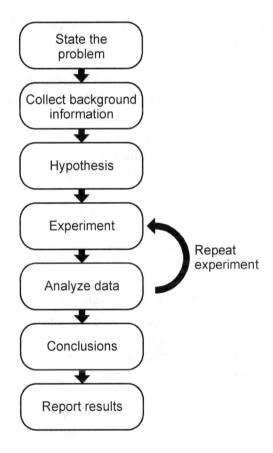

Skill 17.4 **Identify the characteristics and uses of various types of scientific investigations (e.g., observation, controlled experiment)**

Most research in the scientific field is conducted using the scientific method to discover the answer to a problem. The scientific method is the process of thinking through possible solutions and testing each possibility to find the best solution. The scientific method generally involves the following steps: forming a hypothesis, choosing a method and design, conducting experimentation (collecting data), analyzing data, drawing a conclusion, and reporting the findings. Depending on the hypothesis and data to be collected and analyzed, different types of scientific investigation may be used.

Descriptive studies are often the first form of investigation used in new areas of scientific inquiry. The most important element in descriptive reporting is a specific, clear, and measurable definition of the disease, condition, or factor in question. Descriptive studies always address the five W's: who, what, when, where, and why. Descriptive studies include case reports, case-series reports, cross-sections, surveillance studies with individuals, and correlational studies with populations. Descriptive studies are used primarily for trend analysis, health-care planning, and hypothesis generation.

A controlled experiment is a form of scientific investigation in which one variable, the independent or control variable, is manipulated to reveal the effect on another variable, the dependent (experimental) variable, while other variables in the system remain fixed. The control group is virtually identical to the dependent variable except for the one aspect whose effect is being tested. Testing the effects of bleach water on a growing plant, the plant receiving bleach water would be the dependent group, while the plant receiving plain water would be the control group. It is good practice to have several replicate samples for the experiment being performed, which allows for results to be averaged or obvious discrepancies to be discarded.

Comparative data analysis is a statistical form of investigation that allows the researcher to gain new or unexpected insight into data. Comparative data analysis, whether within the research of an individual project or a meta-analysis, allows the researcher to maximize the understanding of the particular data set, uncover underlying structural similarities between research, extract important variables, test underlying assumptions, and detect outliers and anomalies. Most comparative data analysis techniques are graphical in nature with a few quantitative techniques. The use of graphics to compare data allows the researcher to explore the data open-mindedly.

Skill 17.5   Demonstrate knowledge of the principles and procedures for designing and carrying out scientific investigations (e.g., changing one variable at a time)

An experiment is proposed and performed with the sole objective of testing a hypothesis. The purpose should always be defined and will state the problem. The purpose should include the hypothesis (educated guess) of what is expected from the outcome of the experiment. The entire experiment should relate to this problem. It is important to describe exactly what was done to prove or disprove a hypothesis. A control is necessary to prove that the results occurred from the changed conditions and would not happen normally. Only one variable should be manipulated at one time. Observations and results of the experiment should be recorded including all results from data. Drawings, graphs, and illustrations should be included to support information. Observations are objective, whereas analysis and interpretation is subjective. A conclusion should explain why the results of the experiment either proved or disproved the hypothesis.

When evaluating an experiment, it is important to first look at the question it was supposed to answer. How logically did the experiment flow from there? How many variables existed? It is best to only test one variable at a time. You discover a scientist conducting an experiment with the following characteristics: He has two rows each set up with four stations. The first row has a piece of tile as the base at each station. The second row has a piece of linoleum as the base at each station. The scientist has eight eggs and is prepared to drop one over each station. What is he testing? He is trying to answer whether or not the egg is more likely to break when dropped over one material as opposed to the other. His hypothesis might have been: The egg will be less likely to break when dropped on linoleum. This is a simple experiment. If the experiment was more complicated, or for example, conducted on a microscopic level, one might want to examine the appropriateness of the instruments utilized and their calibration.

Skill 17.6   Recognize the importance of and strategies for avoiding bias in scientific investigations

Scientific research can be biased in the choice of what data to consider, in the reporting or recording of the data, and/or in how the data are interpreted. The scientist's emphasis may be influenced by his/her nationality, sex, ethnic origin, age, or political convictions. For example, when studying a group of animals, male scientists may focus on the social behavior of the males and typically male characteristics.

Although bias related to the investigator, the sample, the method, or the instrument may not be completely avoidable in every case, it is important to know the possible sources of bias and how bias could affect the evidence. Moreover, scientists need to be attentive to possible bias in their own work as well as that of other scientists.

Objectivity may not always be attained. However, one precaution that may be taken to guard against undetected bias is to have many different investigators or groups of investigators working on a project. By different, it is meant that the groups are made up of various nationalities, ethnic origins, ages, and political convictions, and are composed of both males and females. It is also important to note one's aspirations, and to make sure to be truthful to the data, even when grants, promotions, and notoriety are at risk.

COMPETENCY 18.0   UNDERSTAND SCIENTIFIC TOOLS, INSTRUMENTS, MATERIALS, AND SAFETY PRACTICES

Skill 18.1   Recognize procedures for the safe and proper use of scientific tools, instruments, chemicals, and other materials in investigations

Bunsen burners - Hot plates should be used whenever possible to avoid the risk of burns or fire. If Bunsen burners are used, the following precautions should be followed:

1. Know the location of fire extinguishers and safety blankets and educate students in their use. Long hair and long sleeves should be secured and out of the way.

2. Turn the gas all the way on and make a spark with the striker.

3. Adjust the air valve at the bottom of the Bunsen burner until the flame shows an inner cone.

4. Adjust the flow of gas to the desired flame height by using the adjustment valve.

5. Do not touch the barrel of the burner (it is hot).

6. The preferred method to light burners is to use strikers rather than matches.

Graduated Cylinder - These are used for precise measurements. They should always be placed on a flat surface. The surface of the liquid will form a meniscus (a lens-shaped curve). The measurement is read at the <u>bottom</u> of this curve.

Balance - Electronic balances are easier to use, but are more expensive. An electronic balance should always be tarred (returned to zero) before measuring and placed on a flat surface. Substances should be placed on a piece of paper to avoid messes and damage to the instrument. Triple beam balances must be used on a level surface. There are screws located at the bottom of the balance to make any adjustments. Start with the largest counterweight first, sliding it to the last notch that does not tip the balance. Do the same with the next largest, etc. until the pointer remains at zero. The mass is the total of all the readings on the beams. Again, use paper under the substance to protect the equipment.

Buret – A buret (or burette) is used to dispense precisely measured volumes of liquid. A stopcock is used to control the volume of liquid being dispensed at a time.

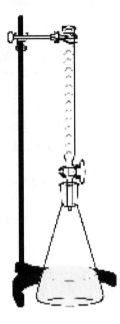

Light microscopes are commonly used in laboratory experiments. Several procedures should be followed to properly care for this equipment:

- Clean all lenses with lens paper only.
- Carry microscopes with two hands; one on the arm and one on the base.
- Always begin focusing on low power, then switch to high power.
- Store microscopes with the low power objective down.
- Always use a coverslip when viewing wet mount slides.
- Bring the objective down to its lowest position then focus, moving up to avoid breaking the slide or scratching the lens.

Wet mount slides should be made by placing a drop of water on the specimen and then putting a glass coverslip on top of the drop of water. Dropping the coverslip at a forty-five degree angle will help you to avoid the presence of air bubbles on the slide. Total magnification is determined by multiplying the ocular (usually 10X) and the objective (usually 10X on low, 40X on high).

All laboratory solutions should be prepared as directed in the lab manual. Care should be taken to avoid contamination. All glassware should be rinsed thoroughly with distilled water before using, and cleaned well after each use. Safety goggles should be worn while working with glassware in case of an accident. All solutions should be made with distilled water (tap water contains dissolved particles which may affect the results of an experiment). Chemical storage should be located in a secure, dry area. Chemicals should be stored in accordance with reactability. Acids are to be locked in a separate area. Used solutions should be disposed of according to local disposal procedures. Any questions regarding safe disposal or chemical safety may be directed to the local fire department.

Skill 18.2   Select and use appropriate tools and international system (SI) units for measuring objects or substances

Science uses the metric system which is accepted worldwide. This consistency allows for ease of comparison among experiments done by scientists around the world. Learn the following basic units and prefixes:

> meter - measure of length
> liter - measure of volume
> gram - measure of mass

deca-(meter, liter, gram) = 10X the base unit   deci = 1/10 the base unit
hecto-(meter, liter, gram)= 100X the base unit   centi = 1/100 the base unit
kilo-(meter, liter, gram) = 1000X the base unit   milli = 1/1000 the base unit

Skill 18.3   Identify potential safety hazards associated with scientific equipment, materials, procedures, and settings

Safety in the science classroom and laboratory is of paramount importance to the science educator. The following is a general summary of the types of safety equipment that should be made available within a given school system as well as general locations where the protective equipment or devices should be maintained and used. Please note that this is only a partial list and that your school system should be reviewed for unique and site-specific hazards at each facility.

The key to maintaining a safe learning environment is through proactive training and regular in-service updates for all staff and students who utilize the science laboratory. Proactive training should include how to identify potential hazards, evaluate potential hazards, and how to prevent or respond to hazards.

The following types of training should be considered:

a) Right to Know (OSHA training on the importance and benefits of properly recognizing and safely working with hazardous materials) along with some basic chemical hygiene and how to read and understand a material safety data sheet,
b) instruction in how to use a fire extinguisher,
c) instruction in how to use a chemical fume hood,
d) general guidance in when and how to use personal protective equipment (e.g. safety glasses or gloves), and
e) instruction in how to monitor activities for potential impacts on indoor air quality.

It is also important for the instructor to utilize Material Data Safety Sheets. Maintain a copy of the material safety data sheet for every item in your chemical inventory. This information will assist you in determining how to store and handle your materials by outlining the health and safety hazards posed by the substance. In most cases the manufacturer will provide recommendations with regard to protective equipment, ventilation, and storage practices. This information should be your first guide when considering the use of a new material.

Frequent monitoring and in-service training on all equipment, materials, and procedures will help to ensure a safe and orderly laboratory environment. It will also provide everyone who uses the laboratory the safety fundamentals necessary to discern a safety hazard and to respond appropriately.

Skill 18.4   Demonstrate knowledge of procedures for the ethical use and care of living organisms in scientific research

Dissections - Animals which are not obtained from recognized sources should not be used. Decaying animals or those of unknown origin may harbor pathogens and/or parasites. Specimens should be rinsed before handling. Latex gloves are desirable. If gloves are not available, students with sores or scratches should be excused from the activity. Formaldehyde is a carcinogenic and should be avoided or disposed of according to district regulations. Students objecting to dissections for moral reasons should be given an alternative assignment.

Live specimens - No dissections may be performed on living mammalian vertebrates or birds. Lower order life and invertebrates may be used. Biological experiments may be done with all animals except mammalian vertebrates or birds. No physiological harm may result to the animal. All animals housed and cared for in the school must be handled in a safe and humane manner. Animals are not to remain on school premises during extended vacations unless adequate care is provided. Many state laws stipulate that any instructor who intentionally refuses to comply with the laws may be suspended or dismissed.

Microbiology - Pathogenic organisms must never be used for experimentation. Students should adhere to the following rules at all times when working with microorganisms to avoid accidental contamination:

1. Treat all microorganisms as if they were pathogenic.
2. Maintain sterile conditions at all times

If you are taking a national level exam you should check the Department of Education for your state's safety procedures. You will want to know what your state expects of you, not only for the test but also for performance in the classroom and for the welfare of your students.

Skill 18.5   Recognize appropriate protocols for maintaining safety and for responding to emergencies during classroom laboratory activities

All science labs should contain the following items of safety equipment. The following are requirements by law.

- Fire blanket which is visible and accessible
- Ground Fault Circuit Interrupters (GCFI) within two feet of water supplies
- Signs designating room exits
- Emergency shower providing a continuous flow of water
- Emergency eye wash station which can be activated by the foot or forearm
- Eye protection for every student and a means of sanitizing equipment
- Emergency exhaust fans providing ventilation to the outside of the building
- Master cut-off switches for gas, electricity, and compressed air. Switches must have permanently attached handles. Cut-off switches must be clearly labeled.
- An ABC fire extinguisher
- Storage cabinets for flammable materials

Also recommended, but not required by law:
- Chemical spill control kit
- Fume hood with a motor which is spark proof
- Protective laboratory aprons made of flame retardant material
- Signs which will alert potential hazardous conditions
- Containers for broken glassware, flammables, corrosives and waste.
- Containers should be labeled.

It is the responsibility of teachers to provide a safe environment for their students. Proper supervision greatly reduces the risk of injury and a teacher should never leave a class for any reason without providing alternate supervision. After an accident, two factors are considered; foreseeability and negligence. Foreseeability is the anticipation that an event may occur under certain circumstances. Negligence is the failure to exercise ordinary or reasonable care. Safety procedures should be a part of the science curriculum and a well managed classroom is important to avoid potential lawsuits

The "Right to Know Law" covers science teachers who work with potentially hazardous chemicals. Briefly, the law states that employees must be informed of potentially toxic chemicals. An inventory must be made available if requested. The inventory must contain information about the hazards and properties of the chemicals. Training must be provided in the safe handling and interpretation of the Material Safety Data Sheet.

The following chemicals are potential carcinogens and not allowed in school facilities:

Acrylonitriel, Arsenic compounds, Asbestos, Bensidine, Benzene, Cadmium compounds, Chloroform, Chromium compounds, Ethylene oxide, Ortho-toluidine, Nickel powder, and Mercury.

COMPETENCY 19.0   UNDERSTAND SKILLS AND PROCEDURES FOR
                   ANALYZING DATA AND COMMUNICATING
                   SCIENCE.

Skill 19.1   Recognize the concepts of precision, accuracy, and error
              and identify potential sources of error in gathering and
              recording data

Accuracy and precision

Accuracy is the degree of conformity of a measured, calculated quantity to its
actual (true) value. Precision is also called reproducibility or repeatability and is
the degree to which further measurements or calculations will show the same or
similar results.

Accuracy is the degree of veracity while precision is the degree of reproducibility.
The best analogy to explain accuracy and precision is the target comparison.

Repeated measurements are compared to arrows that are fired at a target.
Accuracy describes the closeness of arrows to the bull's eye at the target center.
Arrows that strike closer to the bull's eye are considered more accurate.

Systematic and random error

All experimental uncertainty is due to either random errors or systematic errors.

Random errors are statistical fluctuations in the measured data due to the
precision limitations of the measurement device. Random errors usually result
from the experimenter's inability to take the same measurement in exactly the
same way to produce the same result.

Systematic errors, by contrast, are reproducible inaccuracies that are
consistently in the same direction. Systematic errors are often due to a problem,
which persists throughout the entire experiment.

Systematic and random errors refer to problems associated with making
measurements. Mistakes made in the calculations or in reading the instrument
are not considered in error analysis.

Skill 19.2   Apply appropriate mathematical concepts and computational skills to analyze data

Moles = mass X 1 mole/molecular weight

For example, to determine the moles of 20 grams of water, you would take the mass of the water (20 g) and multiply it by 1 mole of water divided by the molecular weight of a molecule of water (18 g).

Percent solution and proportions are basically the same thing. To find percent volume, divide the grams of the substance by the amount of the solvent. For example, 20 grams of salt divided by 100 ml of water would result in a 20% solution of saltwater. To determine percent mass, divide the ml of substance being mixed by the amount of solvent. Percent mass is not used as often as percent volume.

Rate is determined by dividing the change in distance (or the independent variable) by the change in time. If a plant grew four inches in two days, the rate of growth would be two inches per day.

Skill 19.3   Identify methods (e.g., tables, graphs) and criteria for organizing data to aid in the analysis of data (e.g., detecting patterns)

Graphing is an important skill to visually display collected data for analysis. The two types of graphs most commonly used are the line graph and the bar graph (histogram). Line graphs are set up to show two variables represented by one point on the graph. The X axis is the horizontal axis and represents the dependent variable. Dependent variables are those that would be present independently of the experiment. A common example of a dependent variable is time. Time proceeds regardless of anything else. The Y axis is the vertical axis and represents the independent variable. Independent variables are manipulated by the experiment, such as the amount of light, or the height of a plant. Graphs should be calibrated at equal intervals. If one space represents one day, the next space may not represent ten days. A "best fit" line is drawn to join the points and may not include all the data points. Axes must always be labeled. A good title will describe both the dependent and the independent variable. Bar graphs are set up similarly in regards to axes, but points are not plotted. Instead, the dependent variable is set up as a bar where the X axis intersects with the Y axis. Each bar is a separate item of data and is not joined by a continuous line.

Classifying means grouping items according to their similarities. It is important for students to realize relationships and similarity as well as differences to reach a reasonable conclusion in a lab experience.

Skill 19.4 Recognize that there may be more than one way to interpret a given set of findings

Interpreting data and analyzing observations are important. If data is not organized in a logical manner, wrong conclusions can be drawn. Also, other scientists may not be able to follow your work or repeat your results. When interpreting the data, one should ask himself: How do the patterns observed relate to other things? What conclusions can be drawn from the patterns? Science is also limited by the data that is able to be collected. Data may be interpreted differently on different occasions. Scientific limitations cause explanations to change as new technologies emerge. When new information is available, it may shed light on past assumptions or theories, causing scientists to look again and possibly reinterpret the previous findings. Observations are objective, and interpretations are subjective. There is always room for the possibility of misinterpretation, although scientists try to limit it.

Skill 19.5 Demonstrate knowledge of the use of data to support or challenge scientific arguments and claims

Conclusions must be communicated by clearly describing the information using accurate data, visual presentation, and other appropriate media such as a power point presentation. Examples of visual presentations are graphs (bar/line/pie), tables/charts, diagrams, and artwork. Modern technology must be used whenever necessary. The method of communication must be suitable to the audience. Written communication is as important as oral communication. The scientist's strongest ally is a solid set of reproducible data.

Skill 19.6 Identify appropriate methods for communicating the outcomes of scientific investigations (e.g., publications reviewed by peers)

Because people often attempt to use scientific evidence in support of political or personal agendas, the ability to evaluate the credibility of scientific claims is a necessary skill in today's society. In evaluating scientific claims made in the media, public debates, and advertising, one should follow several guidelines.

First, scientific, peer-reviewed journals are the most accepted source for information on scientific experiments and studies. One should carefully scrutinize any claim that does not reference peer-reviewed literature.

Second, the media and those with an agenda to advance (advertisers, debaters, etc.) often overemphasize the certainty and importance of experimental results. One should question any scientific claim that sounds fantastical or overly certain.

Finally, knowledge of experimental design and the scientific method is important in evaluating the credibility of studies. For example, one should look for the inclusion of control groups and the presence of data to support the given conclusions.

Skill 19.7   Demonstrate familiarity with effective resources strategies for reading to gain information about science-related topics and developing subject-area vocabulary

Science Reference Resources:

Encyclopedia Britannica, Wikipedia, PubMed, Encarta, All Science Texts

List of Science Journals http://www.loc.gov/rr/scitech/cjoulist.html

Strategies:

To optimize the amount of information and vocabulary retained by the reading student, teachers must encourage strategic reading methods. Strategic reading is the process whereby students actively construct meaning and interact with text as they read by setting purposes for reading, establishing methods of accomplishing such purposes, monitoring comprehension as they read, and evaluating the completed task.

There are several steps a strategic reader must follow before, during and after reading. Before reading, the student must build up background knowledge on the reading and the topic, set a purpose for the reading, and determine methods to accomplish this purpose. While reading, students must devote their entire attention to the task, continually confirm their understanding, use semantic and syntactic cues to construct meanings of unfamiliar words, use outside sources to define unknown words, and ask questions. After reading, strategic readers must decide if their goals for reading have been reached, evaluate their understanding of reading material, summarize major ideas, construct lists of new vocabulary, seek any additional needed information from outside sources and paraphrase what they have learned.

Teachers of strategic reading should follow several clearly defined steps. First, the teacher must introduce the strategic reading method by discussing the reasons why it is taught and explaining the steps involved. Then, the teacher must provide the opportunity for collaborative group work and individual work with the strategy. After this session, the teacher should discuss with the students what was done with the strategy and why. Finally, the steps of the strategy should be reviewed again, and the strategy should be referenced and revisited whenever possible.

Prior to reading, strategies should stress the recall of prior knowledge, prediction of what reading will teach and the selection of reading materials to suit their purpose. To teach before-reading strategies, teachers can employ "think-a-louds," a type of verbal brainstorming, and "previewing," where teachers express prior personal experiences relevant to the text and encourage students to do so while reading background information.

MIDDLE GRADES SCIENCE   143

Self-questioning is a during-reading strategy in which students generate questions about important elements of the text and new vocabulary which are used to retain information and also for group discussion when reading has been completed.

After-reading strategies help to increase comprehension and retained information. These strategies include summarizing what has been read, interpreting and evaluating ideas, applying these ideas to situations outside of the reading, creating lists of new terms and ideas, and using study strategies for note taking and locating important content.

Skill 19.8 Demonstrate knowledge of conventions and strategies for scientific writing (e.g., lab reports)

Knowledge is integrated in the form of a lab report. A report has many sections. It should include a specific title and tell exactly what is being studied. The abstract is a summary of the report written at the beginning of the paper. The purpose should always be defined and will state the problem. The purpose should include the hypothesis (educated guess) of what is expected from the outcome of the experiment. The entire experiment should relate to this problem. The procedure used to obtain data is important to the outcome. Experiments consist of controls and variables. A control is the experiment run under normal conditions. The variable includes a factor that is changed. In science, the variable may be light, temperature, pH, time, etc. The differences in tested variables may be used to make a prediction or form a hypothesis. Only one variable should be tested at a time. One would not alter both the temperature and pH of the experiment.

An independent variable is one that is changed or manipulated by the researcher. This could be the amount of light given to a plant or the temperature at which bacteria is grown. The dependent variable is that which is influenced by the independent variable.

Observations and results of the experiment should be recorded, including all results from data. Drawings, graphs, and illustrations should be included to support information. Observations are objective, whereas analysis and interpretation are subjective. A conclusion should explain why the results of the experiment either proved or disproved the hypothesis.

A scientific theory is an explanation of a set of related observations based on a proven hypothesis. A scientific law usually lasts longer than a scientific theory and has more experimental data to support it.

COMPETENCY 20.0   UNDERSTAND THE UNIFYING CONCEPTS OF SCIENCE AND TECHNOLOGY

Skill 20.1   Demonstrate knowledge of the unifying concepts (e.g., system, model, change, scale) of science and technology

Math, science, and technology have common themes in how they are applied and understood. All three use models, diagrams, and graphs to simplify a concept for analysis and interpretation. Patterns observed in these systems lead to predictions based on observations. The following are the concepts and processes generally recognized as common to all scientific disciplines:

- Systems, order, and organization

- Evidence, models, and explanation

- Constancy, change, and measurement

- Evolution and equilibrium

- Form and function

Systems, order, and organization

Because the natural world is so complex, the study of science involves the organization of items into smaller groups based on interaction or interdependence. These groups are called systems. Examples of organization are the periodic table of elements and the five-kingdom classification scheme for living organisms. Examples of systems are the solar system, cardiovascular system, Newton's laws of force and motion, and the laws of conservation.

Order refers to the behavior and measurability of organisms and events in nature. The arrangement of planets in the solar system and the life cycle of bacterial cells are examples of order.

Evidence, models, and explanations

Scientists use evidence and models to form explanations of natural events. Models are miniaturized representations of a larger event or system. Evidence is anything that furnishes proof.

Constancy, change, and measurement

Constancy and change describe the observable properties of natural organisms and events. Scientists use different systems of measurement to observe change and constancy. For example, the freezing and melting points of given substances and the speed of sound are constant under constant conditions. Growth, decay, and erosion are all examples of natural change.

Evolution and equilibrium

Evolution is the process of change over a long period of time. While biological evolution is the most common example, one can also classify technological advancement, changes in the universe, and changes in the environment as evolution.

Equilibrium is the state of balance between opposing forces of change. Homeostasis and ecological balance are examples of equilibrium.

Form and function

Form and function are properties of organisms and systems that are closely related. The function of an object usually dictates its form and the form of an object usually facilitates its function. For example, the form of the heart (e.g. muscle, valves) allows it to perform its function of circulating blood through the body.

Skill 20.2   Recognize the characteristics of systems and how the components of a system interact

In human systems, feedback loops serve to regulate bodily functions in relation to environmental conditions. Positive feedback loops enhance the body's response to external stimuli and promote processes that involve rapid deviation from the initial state. For example, positive feedback loops function in stress response and the regulation of growth and development. Negative feedback loops help maintain stability in spite of environmental changes and function in homeostasis. For example, negative feedback loops function in the regulation of blood glucose levels and the maintenance of body temperature.

Feedback loops regulate the secretion of classical vertebrate hormones in humans. The pituitary gland and hypothalamus respond to varying levels of hormones by increasing or decreasing production and secretion. High levels of a hormone cause down-regulation of the production and secretion pathways, while low levels of a hormone cause up-regulation of the production and secretion pathways.

"Fight or flight" refers to the human body's response to stress or danger. Briefly, as a response to an environmental stressor, the hypothalamus releases a hormone that acts on the pituitary gland, triggering the release of another hormone, adrenocorticotropin (ACTH), into the bloodstream. ACTH then signals the adrenal glands to release the hormones cortisol, epinephrine, and norepinephrine. These three hormones act to ready the body to respond to a threat by increasing blood pressure and heart rate, speeding reaction time, diverting blood to the muscles, and releasing glucose for use by the muscles and brain. The stress-response hormones also down-regulate growth, development, and other non-essential functions. Finally, cortisol completes the "fight or flight" feedback loop by acting on the hypothalamus to stop hormonal production after the threat has passed.

Skill 20.3   Identify types and characteristics of models used in science and technology, including the advantages and limitations of models

The model is a basic element of the scientific method. Many things in science are studied with models. A model is any simplification or substitute for what we are actually studying, understanding, or predicting. A model is a substitute, but it is similar to what it represents. We encounter models at every step of our daily living. The Periodic Table of the elements is a model chemists use for predicting the properties of the elements. Physicists use Newton's laws to predict how objects will interact, such as planets and spaceships. In geology, the continental drift model predicts the past positions of continents. Samples, ideas, and methods are all examples of models. At every step of scientific study models are extensively used. The primary activity of the hundreds of thousands of scientists is to produce new models, resulting in tens of thousands of scientific papers published per year.

Types of models:

- Scale models: some models are basically downsized or enlarged copies of their target systems like the models of protein, DNA, etc.
- Idealized models: An idealization is a deliberate simplification of something complicated with the objective of making it easier to understand. Some examples are frictionless planes, point masses, isolated systems, etc.
- Analogical models: standard examples of analogical models are the billiard model of a gas, the computer model of the mind, or the liquid drop model of the nucleus.
- Phenomenological models: These are usually defined as models that are independent of theories.
- Data models: These are corrected, rectified, regimented, and in many instances, idealized versions of the data we gain from immediate observation (raw data).
- Theory models: Any structure is a model if it represents an idea (theory). An example of this is a flow chart, which summarizes a set of ideas.

Uses of models:

- Models are crucial for understanding the structure and function of processes in science.
- Models help us to visualize the organs/systems they represent, much like putting a face to name.
- Models are very useful to predict and foresee future events like hurricanes.

Limitations:

- Though models are every useful to us, they can never replace the real thing.
- Models are not exactly like the real item they represent.
- Caution must be exercised before presenting the models to the class, as they may not be accurate.
- It is the responsibility of the educator to analyze the model critically for the proportions, content value, and other important data.
- One must be careful about the representation style. This style differs from person to person.

Sample Test

Directions: Read each item and select the correct response. The answer key follows.

1. **What is the main difference between the 'condensation hypothesis' and the 'tidal hypothesis' for the origin of the solar system?**
   (Skill 1.1)(Rigorous)

   A. The tidal hypothesis can be tested, but the condensation hypothesis cannot.

   B. The tidal hypothesis proposes a near collision of two stars pulling on each other, but the condensation hypothesis proposes condensation of rotating clouds of dust and gas.

   C. The tidal hypothesis explains how tides began on planets such as Earth, but the condensation hypothesis explains how water vapor became liquid on Earth.

   D. The tidal hypothesis is based on Aristotelian physics, but the condensation hypothesis is based on Newtonian mechanics.

2. **Which of the following is the best definition for 'meteorite'?**
   (Skill 1.2)(Rigorous)

   A. A meteorite is a mineral composed of mica and feldspar.

   B. A meteorite is material from outer space, that has struck the earth's surface.

   C. A meteorite is an element that has properties of both metals and nonmetals.

   D. A meteorite is a very small unit of length measurement.

3. **Which of the following units is *not* a measure of distance?**
   (Skill 1.6)(Average Rigor)

   A. AU (astronomical unit).

   B. Light year.

   C. Parsec.

   D. Lunar year.

4. **Which of the following is *not* true about phase change in matter?(Skill 2.1)(Rigorous)**

   A. Solid water and liquid ice can coexist at water's freezing point.

   B. At 7 degrees Celsius, water is always in liquid phase.

   C. Matter changes phase when enough energy is gained or lost.

   D. Different phases of matter are characterized by differences in molecular motion.

5. **What is the most accurate description of the Water Cycle? (Skill 2.2)(Rigorous)**

   A. Rain comes from clouds, filling the ocean. The water then evaporates and becomes clouds again.

   B. Water circulates from rivers into groundwater and back, while water vapor circulates in the atmosphere.

   C. Water is conserved except for chemical or nuclear reactions, and any drop of water could circulate through clouds, rain, ground-water, and surface-water.

   D. Weather systems cause chemical reactions to break water into its atoms.

6. **What is the source for most of the United States' drinking water?(Skill 2.2)(Rigorous)**

   A. Desalinated ocean water.

   B. Surface water (lakes, streams, mountain runoff).

   C. Rainfall into municipal reservoirs.

   D. Groundwater.

7. **The theory of 'sea floor spreading' explains _____. (Skill 2.4)(Average Rigor)**

   A. the shapes of the continents.

   B. how continents collide.

   C. how continents move apart.

   D. how continents sink to become part of the ocean floor.

8. **The salinity of ocean water is closest to _____ . (Skill 2.4)(Rigorous)**

   A. 0.035 %

   B. 0.35 %

   C. 3.5 %

   D. 35 %

9. **Which of the following instruments measures wind speed?(Skill 3.2)(Rigorous)**

   A. A barometer.

   B. An anemometer.

   C. A wind sock.

   D. A weather vane.

10. **Which of the following animals are most likely to live in a tropical rain forest? (Skill 3.3)(Easy Rigor)**

    A. Reindeer.

    B. Monkeys.

    C. Puffins.

    D. Bears.

11. **Which is not one of the three layers of the earth's interior?(Skill 4.1)(Average Rigor)**

    A. Core

    B. Mantel

    C. Crust

    D. Molten Layer

12. **Lithification refers to the process by which unconsolidated sediments are transformed into _____.(Skill 4.2)(Average Rigor)**

    A. metamorphic rocks.

    B. sedimentary rocks.

    C. igneous rocks.

    D. lithium oxide.

13. **Which of the following types of rock are made from magma? (Skill 4.2)(Average Rigor)**

    A. Fossils

    B. Sedimentary

    C. Metamorphic

    D. Igneous

14 **Which of these is a true statement about loamy soil? (Skill 4.3)(Rigorous)**

    A. Loamy soil is gritty and porous.

    B. Loamy soil is smooth and a good barrier to water.

    C. Loamy soil is hostile to microorganisms.

    D. Loamy soil is velvety and clumpy.

15. **Igneous rocks can be classified according to which of the following? (Skill 4.4)(Rigorous)**

    A. Texture.

    B. Composition.

    C. Formation process.

    D. All of the above.

16. **Which of the following is *not* a type of volcano? (Skill 4.4)(Average Rigor)**

    A. Shield Volcanoes.

    B. Composite Volcanoes.

    C. Stratus Volcanoes.

    D. Cinder Cone Volcanoes.

17. **_____are cracks in the plates of the earth's crust, along which the plates move. (Skill 4.4)(Average Rigor)**

    A. Faults.

    B. Ridges.

    C. Earthquakes.

    D. Volcanoes.

18. **Fossils are usually found in _____ rock. (Skill 4.6)(Easy Rigor)**

    A. igneous.

    B. sedimentary.

    C. metamorphic.

    D. cumulus.

19. **Which of the following is the most accurate definition of a non-renewable resource?(Skill 5.1)(Rigorous)**

    A. A nonrenewable resource is never replaced once used.

    B. A nonrenewable resource is replaced on a timescale that is very long relative to human life-spans.

    C. A nonrenewable resource is a resource that can only be manufactured by humans.

    D. A nonrenewable resource is a species that has already become extinct.

20. Which parts of an atom are located inside the nucleus? (Skill 5.3)(Rigorous)

    A. electrons and neutrons.

    B. protons and neutrons.

    C. protons only.

    D. neutrons only.

21. Which of the following is *not* a common type of acid in 'acid rain' or acidified surface water? (Skill 5.3)(Average Rigor)

    A. Nitric acid.

    B. Sulfuric acid.

    C. Carbonic acid.

    D. Hydrofluoric acid.

22. Laboratory researchers have classified fungi as distinct from plants because the cell walls of fungi_____ . (Skill 6.1)(Average Rigor)

    A. contain chitin.

    B. contain yeast.

    C. are more solid.

    D. are less solid.

23. Which kingdom is comprised of organisms made of one cell with no nuclear membrane? (Skill 6.1)(Average Rigor)

    A. Monera.

    B. Protista.

    C. Fungi.

    D. Algae.

24. Which of the following is *not* a member of Kingdom Fungi? (Skill 6.1)(Easy Rigor)

    A. Mold.

    B. Blue-green algae.

    C. Mildew.

    D. Mushrooms.

25. Which of the following organisms use spores to reproduce? (Skill 6.1)(Average Rigor)

    A. Fish.

    B. Flowering plants.

    C. Conifers.

    D. Ferns.

26. **Which is not a Kingdom? (Skill 6.1)(Rigorous)**

    A. Mammalia

    B. Eubacteria

    C. Protista

    D. Fungi

27. **Animals with a notochord or backbone are in the phylum (Skill 6.2)(Easy Rigor)**

    A. arthropoda.

    B. chordata.

    C. mollusca.

    D. mammalia.

28. **Which is the correct sequence of insect development? (Skill 6.2)(Average Rigor)**

    A. Egg, pupa, larva, adult.

    B. Egg, larva, pupa, adult.

    C. Egg, adult, larva, pupa.

    D. Pupa, egg, larva, adult.

29. **Microorganisms use all but the following to move: (Skill 7.1)(Rigorous)**

    A. Pseudopods

    B. Flagella

    C. Cilia

    D. Pili

30. **What cell organelle contains the cell's stored food? (Skill 7.1)(Average Rigor)**

    A. Vacuoles.

    B. Golgi Apparatus.

    C. Ribosomes.

    D. Lysosomes.

31. **Eukaryotic cells are found in all but the following:(Skill 7.1)(Average Rigor)**

    A. Bacteria

    B. Protists

    C. Fungi

    D. Animals

32. **The purpose of the Golgi Apparatus is: (Skill 7.1)(Average Rigor)**

A.   To break down proteins

B.   To sort, modify and package molecules

C.   To break down fats

D.   To make carbohydrates.

33. **Since ancient times, people have been entranced with bird flight. What is the key to bird flight? (Skill 7.3)(Rigorous)**

   A.   Bird wings are a particular shape and composition.

   B.   Birds flap their wings quickly enough to propel themselves.

   C.   Birds take advantage of tailwinds.

   D.   Birds take advantage of crosswinds.

34. **Which of the following is *not* a necessary characteristic of living things?(Skill 7.4)(Rigorous)**

   A.   Movement.

   B.   Reduction of local entropy.

   C.   Ability to cause change in local energy form.

   D.   Reproduction.

35. **Identify the correct sequence of organization of living things from lower to higher order: (Skill 7.6)(Average Rigor)**

   A.   Cell, Organelle, Organ, Tissue, System, Organism.

   B.   Cell, Tissue, Organ, Organelle, System, Organism.

   C.   Organelle, Cell, Tissue, Organ, System, Organism.

   D.   Organelle, Tissue, Cell, Organ, System, Organism.

36. **Amino acids are carried to the ribosome in protein synthesis by _____ . (Skill 8.1)(Average Rigor)**

   A.   transfer RNA (tRNA).

   B.   messenger RNA (mRNA).

   C.   ribosomal RNA (rRNA).

   D.   transformation RNA (trRNA).

37. **Which of the following is not a nucleotide?(Skill 8.1)(Average Rigor)**

   A.   adenine.

   B.   alanine.

   C.   cytosine.

   D.   guanine.

38. **What is not a type of RNA?**
(Skill 8.1)(Average Rigor)

A. Ribosomal

B. Transfer

C. Transcriptional

D. Messenger

39. **A child has type O blood. Her father has type A blood, and her mother has type B blood. What are the genotypes of the father and mother, respectively? (Skill 8.2)(Average Rigor)**

A. AO and BO.

B. AA and AB.

C. OO and BO.

D. AO and BB.

40. **A white flower is crossed with a red flower. Which of the following is a sign of incomplete dominance? (Skill 8.2)(Average Rigor)**

A. Pink flowers.

B. Red flowers.

C. White flowers.

D. No flowers.

41. **The first stage of mitosis is called _____ . (Skill 8.3)(Rigorous)**

A. telophase.

B. anaphase.

C. prophase.

D. mitophase.

42. **A series of experiments on pea plants formed by _____ showed that two invisible markers existed for each trait, and one marker dominated the other. (Skill 8.4)(Easy Rigor)**

A. Pasteur.

B. Watson and Crick.

C. Mendel.

D. Mendeleev.

43. **Which process(es) result(s) in a haploid chromosome number? (Skill 8.4)(Average Rigor)**

A. Mitosis.

B. Meiosis.

C. Both mitosis and meiosis.

D. Neither mitosis nor meiosis.

44. **The duplication of genetic material into another cell is called: (Skill 8.6)(Rigorous)**

    A. Replicating

    B. Cell duplication

    C. Cloning

    D. Genetic restructuring

45. **Gel electrophoresis: (Skill 8.6)(Rigorous)**

    A. isolates fragments of DNA for scientific purposes

    B. Cannot be used in proteins

    C. Requires the polymerase chain reaction

    D. Only separates DNA by size

46. **What is not true of decomposers? (Skill 9.1)(Rigorous)**

    A. Decomposers recycle the carbon accumulated in durable organic material

    B. Ammonification is the decomposition of organic nitrogen back to ammonia.

    C. Decomposers add phosphorous back to the soil

    D. Decomposers belong to the Genus Escherichia.

47. **What eats secondary consumers? (Skill 9.1)(Easy Rigor)**

    A. Producers

    B. Tertiary consumers

    C. Primary consumers

    D. Decomposers

48. **Which of the following is found in the least abundance in organic molecules? (Skill 9.2)(Rigorous)**

    A. Phosphorus.

    B. Potassium.

    C. Carbon.

    D. Oxygen.

49. **What is not true of the carbon cycle? (Skill 9.2)(Average Rigor)**

    A. Ten percent of all available carbon is in the air.

    B. Carbon dioxide is fixed by glycosylation.

    C. Plants fix carbon in the form of glucose.

    D. Animals release carbon through respiration.

50. **A wrasse (fish) cleans the teeth of other fish by eating away plaque. This is an example of _____ between the fish.**
(Skill 9.4)(Rigorous)

A. parasitism.

B. symbiosis (mutualism).

C. competition.

D. predation.

51. **Viruses are responsible for many human diseases including all of the following** *except* **_____ ?(Skill 9.5)(Average Rigor)**

A. influenza.

B. A.I.D.S.

C. the common cold.

D. strep throat.

52. **Which of the following does not result in the detriment of one species and the advancement of another? (Skill 9.4)(Rigorous)**

A. Parasitism

B. Mutualism

C. Predation

D. Herbivory

53. **Darwin supported the evolutionary theory of: (Skill 10.1)(Rigorous)**

A. Punctualism

B. Gradualism

C. Equilibrium

D. Convergency

54. **Which of the following is a correct explanation for scientific 'evolution'?(Skill 10.1)(Rigorous)**

A. Giraffes need to reach higher for leaves to eat, so their necks stretch. The giraffe babies are then born with longer necks. Eventually, there are more long-necked giraffes in the population.

B. Giraffes with longer necks are able to reach more leaves, so they eat more and have more babies than other giraffes. Eventually, there are more long-necked giraffes in the population.

C. Giraffes want to reach higher for leaves to eat, so they release enzymes into their bloodstream, which in turn causes fetal development of longer-necked giraffes. Eventually, there are more long-necked giraffes in the population.

D. Giraffes with long necks are more attractive to other giraffes, so they get the best mating partners and have more babies. Eventually, there are more long-necked giraffes in the population.

55. **What is true about natural selection? (Skill 10.1)(Average Rigor)**

A. It acts on an individual genotype

B. It does not happen currently

C. It is a phenomenon of animals only

D. It acts on the individual phenotype

56. **Members of the same animal species _____ . (Skill 10.2)(Average Rigor)**

A. look identical.

B. never adapt differently.

C. are able to reproduce with one another.

D. are found in the same location.

57. **A duck's webbed feet are examples of_____. (Skill 10.3)(Average Rigor)**

A. mimicry.

B. structural adaptation.

C. protective resemblance.

D. protective coloration.

58. **What is not true about reproductive isolation? (Skill 10.4)(Rigorous)**

    A. It prevents populations from exchanging genes

    B. It can occur by preventing fertilization.

    C. It can result in speciation

    D. It is not a phenomenon of islands.

59. **Vinegar is an example of a _____ .(Skill 11.1)(Easy Rigor)**

    A. strong acid.

    B. strong base.

    C. weak acid.

    D. weak base.

60. **Which of the following will not change in a chemical reaction?(Skill 11.2)(Average Rigor)**

    A. Number of moles of products.

    B. Atomic number of one of the reactants.

    C. Mass (in grams) of one of the reactants.

    D. Rate of reaction.

61. **Carbon bonds with hydrogen by _____ .(Skill 11.4)(Rigorous)**

    A. ionic bonding.

    B. non-polar covalent bonding.

    C. polar covalent bonding.

    D. strong nuclear force.

62. **What is necessary for ion diffusion to occur spontaneously? (Skill 11.4)(Average Rigor)**

    A. Carrier proteins.

    B. Energy from an outside source.

    C. A concentration gradient.

    D. Cell flagellae.

63. **Which of the following is *not* a property of metalloids? (Skill 11.5)(Rigorous)**

    A. Metalloids are solids at standard temperature and pressure.

    B. Metalloids can conduct electricity to a limited extent.

    C. Metalloids are found in groups 13 through 17.

    D. Metalloids all favor ionic bonding.

64. **The elements in the modern Periodic Table are arranged _____ .(Skill 11.5)(Average Rigor)**

   A. in numerical order by atomic number.

   B. randomly.

   C. in alphabetical order by chemical symbol.

   D. in numerical order by atomic mass.

65. **Which of the following is a correct definition for 'chemical equilibrium'? (Skill 11.6)(Rigorous)**

   A. Chemical equilibrium is when the forward and backward reaction rates are equal. The reaction may continue to proceed forward and backward.

   B. Chemical equilibrium is when the forward and backward reaction rates are equal, and equal to zero. The reaction does not continue.

   C. Chemical equilibrium is when there are equal quantities of reactants and products.

   D. Chemical equilibrium is when acids and bases neutralize each other fully.

66. **The chemical equation for water formation is: $2H_2 + O_2 \rightarrow 2H_2O$. Which of the following is an *incorrect* interpretation of this equation?(Skill 11.6)(Rigorous)**

   A. Two moles of hydrogen gas and one mole of oxygen gas combine to make two moles of water.

   B. Two grams of hydrogen gas and one gram of oxygen gas combine to make two grams of water.

   C. Two molecules of hydrogen gas and one molecule of oxygen gas combine to make two molecules of water.

   D. Four atoms of hydrogen (combined as a diatomic gas) and two atoms of oxygen (combined as a diatomic gas) combine to make two molecules of water.

67. **The measure of the pull of the earth's gravity on an object is called _____ . (Skill 12.3)(Average Rigor)**

   A. mass number.

   B. atomic number.

   C. mass.

   D. weight.

68. **What is the main obstacle to using nuclear fusion for obtaining electricity? (Skill 12.1)(Rigorous)**

   A. Nuclear fusion produces much more pollution than nuclear fission.

   B. There is no obstacle; most power plants us nuclear fusion today.

   C. Nuclear fusion requires very high temperature and activation energy.

   D. The fuel for nuclear fusion is extremely expensive.

69. **Which reaction below is a decomposition reaction? (Skill 12.2)(Rigorous)**

   A. $HCl + NaOH \rightarrow NaCl + H_2O$

   B. $C + O_2 \rightarrow CO_2$

   C. $2H_2O \rightarrow 2H_2 + O_2$

   D. $CuSO_4 + Fe \rightarrow FeSO_4 + Cu$

70. **Which of the following is a correct explanation for astronaut 'weightlessness'? (Skill 12.3)(Rigorous)**

   A. Astronauts continue to feel the pull of gravity in space, but they are so far from planets that the force is small.

   B. Astronauts continue to feel the pull of gravity in space, but spacecraft have such powerful engines that those forces dominate, reducing effective weight.

   C. Astronauts do not feel the pull of gravity in space, because space is a vacuum.

   D. Astronauts do not feel the pull of gravity in space, because black hole forces dominate the force field, reducing their masses.

71. **What is specific gravity? (Skill 12.3)(Average Rigor)**

   A. The mass of an object.

   B. The ratio of the density of a substance to the density of water.

   C. Density.

   D. The pull of the earth's gravity on an object.

72. **Enzymes speed up reactions by _____ .(Skill 12.5)(Average Rigor)**

    A. utilizing ATP.

    B. lowering pH, allowing reaction speed to increase.

    C. increasing volume of substrate.

    D. lowering energy of activation.

73. **Catalysts assist reactions by _____ .(Skill 12.5)(Rigorous)**

    A. lowering effective activation energy.

    B. maintaining precise pH levels.

    C. keeping systems at equilibrium.

    D. adjusting reaction speed.

74. **All of the following measure energy *except* for _____ (Skill 13.1)(Easy Rigor)**

    A. joules.

    B. calories.

    C. watts.

    D. ergs.

75. **Energy is measured with the same units as _____. (Skill 13.1)(Easy Rigor)**

    A. force.

    B. momentum.

    C. work.

    D. power.

76. **The Law of Conservation of Energy states that _____. (Skill 13.2)(Rigorous)**

    A. There must be the same number of products and reactants in any chemical equation.

    B. Objects always fall toward large masses such as planets.

    C. Energy is neither created nor destroyed, but may change form.

    D. Lights must be turned off when not in use, by state regulation.

77. A ball rolls down a smooth hill. You may ignore air resistance. Which of the following is a true statement?
(Skill 13.3)(Rigorous)

A. The ball has more energy at the start of its descent than just before it hits the bottom of the hill, because it is higher up at the beginning.

B. The ball has less energy at the start of its descent than just before it hits the bottom of the hill, because it is moving more quickly at the end.

C. The ball has the same energy throughout its descent, because positional energy is converted to energy of motion.

D. The ball has the same energy throughout its descent, because a single object (such as a ball) cannot gain or lose energy.

78. A long silver bar has a temperature of 50 degrees Celsius at one end and 0 degrees Celsius at the other end. The bar will reach thermal equilibrium (barring outside influence) by the process of heat _____.
(Skill 13.4)(Rigorous)

A. conduction.

B. convection.

C. radiation.

D. phase change.

79. Which of the following is a true statement about radiation exposure and air travel?
(Skill 13.4)(Rigorous)

A. Air travel exposes humans to radiation, but the level is not significant for most people.

B. Air travel exposes humans to so much radiation that it is recommended as a method of cancer treatment.

C. Air travel does not expose humans to radiation.

D. Air travel may or may not expose humans to radiation, but it has not yet been determined.

80. When you step out of the shower, the floor feels colder on your feet than the bathmat. Which of the following is the correct explanation for this phenomenon? (Skill 13.4)(Rigorous)

A. The floor is colder than the bathmat.

B. Your feet have a chemical reaction with the floor, but not the bathmat.

C. Heat is conducted more easily into the floor.

D. Water is absorbed from your feet into the bathmat.

81. The transfer of heat by electromagnetic waves is called _____ .(Skill 13.4)(Average Rigor)

A. conduction.

B. convection.

C. phase change.

D. radiation.

82. When heat is added to most solids, they expand. Why is this the case?(Skill 13.4)(Average Rigor)

A. The molecules get bigger.

B. The faster molecular motion leads to greater distance between the molecules.

C. The molecules develop greater repelling electric forces.

D. The molecules form a more rigid structure.

83. If the volume of a confined gas is increased, what happens to the pressure of the gas? You may assume that the gas behaves ideally, and that temperature and number of gas molecules remain constant. (Skill 13.6)(Average Rigor)

A. The pressure increases.

B. The pressure decreases.

C. The pressure stays the same.

D. There is not enough information givento answer this question.

84. **Which of the following is most accurate? (Skill 14.1)(Average Rigor)**

    A. Mass is always constant; Weight may vary by location.

    B. Mass and Weight are both always constant.

    C. Weight is always constant; Mass may vary by location.

    D. Mass and Weight may both vary by location.

85. **A Newton is fundamentally a measure of _____ . (Skill 14.1)(Easy Rigor)**

    A. force.

    B. momentum.

    C. energy.

    D. gravity.

86. **The force of gravity on earth causes all bodies in free fall to _____ . (Skill 14.2)(Easy Rigor)**

    A. fall at the same speed.

    B. accelerate at the same rate.

    C. reach the same terminal velocity.

    D. move in the same direction.

87. **All of the following are considered Newton's Laws *except* for: (Skill 14.5)(Rigorous)**

    A. An object in motion will continue in motion unless acted upon by an outside force.

    B. For every action force, there is an equal and opposite reaction force.

    C. Nature abhors a vacuum.

    D. Mass can be considered the ratio of force to acceleration.

88. **Sound can be transmitted in all of the following *except* _____ . (Skill 1 5.1)(Average Rigor)**

    A. air.

    B. water.

    C. a diamond.

    D. a vacuum.

89. **The electromagnetic radiation with the longest wave length is/are _____. (Skill 15.1)(Average Rigor)**

    A. radio waves.

    B. red light.

    C. X-rays.

    D. ultraviolet light.

90. Sound waves are produced by _____ .(Skill 15.1)(Easy Rigor)

    A. pitch.

    B. noise.

    C. vibrations.

    D. sonar.

91. The Doppler Effect is associated most closely with which property of waves? (Skill 15.2)(Rigorous)

    A. amplitude.

    B. wavelength.

    C. frequency.

    D. intensity.

92. As a train approaches, the whistle sounds _____ . (Skill 15.2)(Rigorous)

    A. higher, because it has a higher apparent frequency.

    B. lower, because it has a lower apparent frequency.

    C. higher, because it has a lower apparent frequency.

    D. lower, because it has a higher apparent frequency.

93. The speed of light is different in different materials. This is responsible for _____ . (Skill 15.3)(Rigorous)

    A. interference.

    B. refraction.

    C. reflection.

    D. relativity.

94. A converging lens produces a real image _____. (Skill 15.5)(Average Rigor)

    A. always.

    B. never.

    C. when the object is within one focal length of the lens.

    D. when the object is further than one focal length from the lens.

95. Resistance is measured in units called _____ . (Skill 16.2)(Average Rigor)

    A. watts.

    B. volts.

    C. ohms.

    D. current.

96. **Rough endoplasmic reticulum contains: (Skill 7.1)(Average Rigor)**

    A. Vacuoles

    B. Mitochondria

    C. Microfilaments

    D. Ribosomes

97. **What is the scientific method? (Skill 17.1)(Rigorous)**

    A. It is the process of doing an experiment and writing a laboratory report.

    B. It is the process of using open inquiry and repeatable results to establish theories.

    C. It is the process of reinforcing scientific principles by confirming results.

    D. It is the process of recording data and observations.

98. **In an experiment, the scientist states that he believes a change in the color of a liquid is due to a change of pH. This is an example of _____ . (Skill 17.2)(Easy Rigor)**

    A. observing.

    B. inferring.

    C. measuring.

    D. classifying.

99. **When is a hypothesis formed? (Skill 17.3)(Easy Rigor)**

    A. Before the data is taken.

    B. After the data is taken.

    C. After the data is analyzed.

    D. Concurrent with graphing the data.

100. Identify the control in the following experiment: A student had four corn plants and was measuring photosynthetic rate (by measuring growth mass). Half of the plants were exposed to full (constant) sunlight, and the other half were kept in 50% (constant) sunlight.(Skill 17.3)(Rigorous)

A. The control is a set of plants grown in full (constant) sunlight.

B. The control is a set of plants grown in 50% (constant) sunlight.

C. The control is a set of plants grown in the dark.

D. The control is a set of plants grown in a mixture of natural levels of sunlight.

101. Which is the correct order of methodology?
(Skill 17.3)(Rigorous)

1. collecting data
2. planning a controlled ex periment
3. drawing a conclusion
4. hypothesizing a result
5. re-visiting a hypothesis to answer a question

A. 1,2,3,4,5

B. 4,2,1,3,5

C. 4,5,1,3,2

D. 1,3,4,5,2

102. Who determines the laws regarding the use of safety glasses in the classroom? (Skill 18.1)(Average Rigor)

A. The state.

B. The school site.

C. The Federal government.

D. The district level.

103. When measuring the volume of water in a graduated cylinder, where does one read the measurement? (Skill 18.1)(Easy Rigor)

A. At the highest point of the liquid.

B. At the bottom of the meniscus curve.

C. At the closest mark to the top of the liquid.

D. At the top of the plastic safety ring.

104. Under a 440 power microscope, an object with diameter 0.1 millimeter appears to have a diameter of _____ .
(Skill 18.1)(Rigorous)

A. 4.4 millimeters.

B. 44 millimeters.

C. 440 millimeters.

D. 4400 millimeters.

105. **Which is the most desirable tool to use to heat substances in a middle school laboratory?**
(Skill 18.1)(Easy Rigor)

A. Alcohol burner.

B. Freestanding gas burner.

C. Bunsen burner.

D. Hot plate.

106. **Chemicals should be stored**
(Skill 18.1)(Easy Rigor)

A. in the principal's office.

B. in a dark room.

C. in an off-site research facility.

D. according to their reactivity with other substances.

107. **Which item should always be used when handling glassware?**
(Skill 18.1)(Easy Rigor)

A. Tongs.

B. Safety goggles.

C. Gloves.

D. Buret stand.

108. **In a science experiment, a student needs to dispense very small measured amounts of liquid into a well-mixed solution. Which of the following is the best choice for his/her equipment to use?**
(Skill 18.1)(Easy Rigor)

A. Buret with Buret Stand, Stir-plate, Stirring Rod, Beaker.

B. Buret with Buret Stand, Stir-plate, Beaker.

C. Volumetric Flask, Dropper, Graduated Cylinder, Stirring Rod.

D. Beaker, Graduated Cylinder, Stir-plate.

109. **A laboratory balance is most appropriately used to measure the mass of which of the following?**
(Skill 18.1)(Easy Rigor)

A. Seven paper clips.

B. Three oranges.

C. Two hundred cells.

D. One student's elbow.

110. **All of the following are measured in units of length, *except* for: (Skill 18.2)(Easy Rigor)**

    A. Perimeter.

    B. Distance.

    C. Radius.

    D. Area.

111. **If one inch equals 2.54 cm how many mm in 1.5 feet (approx.)? (Skill 18.2)(Rigorous)**

    A. 18 mm.

    B. 1800 mm.

    C. 460 mm.

    D. 4,600 mm.

112. **Which of the following is the worst choice for a school laboratory activity? (Skill 18.4)(Average Rigor)**

    A. A genetics experiment tracking the fur color of mice.

    B. Dissection of a preserved fetal pig.

    C. Measurement of goldfish respiration rate at different temperatures.

    D. Pithing a frog to watch the circulatory system.

113. **Who should be notified in the case of a serious chemical spill? (Skill 18.5)(Rigorous)**

    A. The custodian.

    B. The fire department or their municipal authority.

    C. The science department chair.

    D. The School Board.

114. **In which situation would a science teacher be legally liable? (Skill 18.5)(Average Rigor)**

    A. The teacher leaves the classroom for a telephone call and a student slips and injures him/herself.

    B. A student removes his/her goggles and gets acid in his/her eye.

    C. A faulty gas line in the classroom causes a fire.

    D. A student cuts him/herself with a dissection scalpel.

115. **Which of these is the best example of 'negligence'? (Skill 18.5)(Rigorous)**

    A. A teacher fails to give oral instructions to those with reading disabilities.

    B. A teacher fails to exercise ordinary care to ensure safety in the classroom.

    C. A teacher displays inability to supervise a large group of students.

    D. A teacher reasonably anticipates that an event may occur, and plans accordingly.

116. **For her first project of the year, a student is designing a science experiment to test the effects of light and water on plant growth. You should recommend that she _____.(Skill 18.3)(Easy Rigor)**

    A. manipulate the temperature also.

    B. manipulate the water pH also.

    C. determine the relationship between light and water unrelated to plant growth.

    D. omit either water or light as a variable.

117. **Formaldehyde should not be used in school laboratories for the following reason:(Skill 18.4)(Easy Rigor)**

    A. it smells unpleasant.

    B. it is a known carcinogen.

    C. it is expensive to obtain.

    D. it is explosive.

118. **Experiments may be done with any of the following animals except _____. (Skill 18.4)(Easy Rigor)**

    A. birds.

    B. invertebrates.

    C. lower order life.

    D. frogs.

119. **In an experiment measuring the growth of bacteria at different temperatures, what is the independent variable? (Skill 19.2)(Rigorous)**

    A. Number of bacteria.

    B. Growth rate of bacteria.

    C. Temperature.

    D. Light intensity.

120. **When designing a scientific experiment, a student considers all the factors that may influence the results. The process goal is to _____.(Skill 19.2)(Average Rigor)**

    A. recognize and manipulate independent variables.

    B. recognize and record independent variables.

    C. recognize and manipulate dependent variables.

    D. recognize and record dependent variables.

121. **Which of the following data sets is properly represented by a bar graph?(Skill 19.3)(Average Rigor)**

    A. Number of people choosing to buy cars, vs. Color of car bought.

    B. Number of people choosing to buy cars, vs. Age of car customer.

    C. Number of people choosing to buy cars, vs. Distance from car lot to customer home.

    D. Number of people choosing to buy cars, vs. Time since last car purchase.

122. **A scientific law_____. (Skill 19.8)(Average Rigor)**

    A. proves scientific accuracy.

    B. may never be broken.

    C. may be revised in light of new data.

    D. is the result of one excellent experiment.

123. **In a laboratory report, what is the abstract? (Skill 19.8)(Easy Rigor)**

    A. The abstract is a summary of the report, and is the first section of the report.

    B. The abstract is a summary of the report, and is the last section of the report.

    C. The abstract is predictions for future experiments, and is the first section of the report.

    D. The abstract is predictions for future experiments, and is the last section of the report.

124. **Newton's Laws are taught in science classes because _____. (Skill 20.3)(Average Rigor)**

   A. they are the correct analysis of inertia, gravity, and forces.

   B. they are a close approximation to correct physics, for usual Earth conditions.

   C. they accurately incorporate relativity into studies of forces.

   D. Newton was a well-respected scientist in his time.

125. **The theory of 'continental drift' is supported by which of the following?(Skill 20.3)(Average Rigor)**

   A. The way the shapes of South America and Europe fit together.

   B. The way the shapes of Europe and Asia fit together.

   C. The way the shapes of South America and Africa fit together.

   D. The way the shapes of North America and Antarctica fit together.

Answer Key

1. B	45. A	89. A
2. B	46. D	90. C
3. D	47. B	91. C
4. B	48. B	92. A
5. C	49. B	93. B
6. D	50. B	94. D
7. C	51. B	95. C
8. C	52. D	96. D
9. B	53. B	97. B
10. B	54. B	98. B
11. D	55. D	99. A
12. B	56. C	100. A
13. D	57. B	101. B
14. D	58. D	102. A
15. D	59. C	103. B
16. C	60. B	104. B
17. A	61. C	105. D
18. B	62. C	106. D
19. B	63. D	107. B
20. B	64. A	108. B
21. D	65. A	109. A
22. A	66. B	110. D
23. A	67. D	111. C
24. B	68. C	112. D
25. D	69. C	113. B
26. A	70. A	114. A
27. B	71. B	115. B
28. B	72. D	116. D
29. D	73. A	117. B
30. A	74. C	118. A
31. A	75. C	119. C
32. B	76. C	120. A
33. A	77. C	121. A
34. A	78. A	122. C
35. C	79. A	123. A
36. A	80. C	124. B
37. B	81. D	125. C
38. C	82. B	
39. A	83. B	
40. A	84. A	
41. C	85. A	
42. C	86. B	
43. B	87. C	
44. C	88. D	

Rigor Table

Easy Rigor 20 %	Average Rigor 40%	Rigorous 40%
10,18, 24, 27, 42, 47, 59, 74, 75, 85, 86, 90, 98, 99, 103, 105, 106, 107, 108, 109, 110, 116, 117, 118, 123	3, 7, 11, 12, 13, 16, 17, 21, 22, 23, 25, 28, 30, 31, 32, 35, 36, 37, 38, 39, 40, 43, 49, 51, 55, 56, 57, 60, 66, 64, 67, 71, 72, 81, 82, 83, 84, 88, 89, 94, 95, 96, 102, 112, 114, 120, 121, 122, 124, 125	1, 2, 4, 5, 6, 8, 9, 14, 15, 19, 20, 26, 29, 33, 34, 41, 44, 45, 46, 48, 50, 52, 53, 54, 58, 61, 63, 65, 66, 68, 69, 70, 73, 76, 77, 78, 79, 80, 87, 91, 92, 93, 97, 100, 101, 104, 111, 113, 115, 119

Sample Questions with Rationale

1.   **What is the main difference between the 'condensation hypothesis' and the 'tidal hypothesis' for the origin of the solar system?(Skill 1.1)(Rigorous)**

A.   The tidal hypothesis can be tested, but the condensation hypothesis cannot.

B.   The tidal hypothesis proposes a near collision of two stars pulling on each other, but the condensation hypothesis proposes condensation of rotating clouds of dust and gas.

C.   The tidal hypothesis explains how tides began on planets such as Earth, but the condensation hypothesis explains how water vapor became liquid on Earth.

D.   The tidal hypothesis is based on Aristotelian physics, but the condensation hypothesis is based on Newtonian mechanics.

Answer B.   The tidal hypothesis proposes a near collision of two stars pulling on each other, but the condensation hypothesis proposes condensation of rotating clouds of dust and gas.

Most scientists believe the 'condensation hypothesis,' i.e. that the solar system began when rotating clouds of dust and gas condensed into the sun and planets. A minority opinion is the 'tidal hypothesis,' i.e. that the sun almost collided with a large star. The large star's gravitational field would have then pulled gases out of the sun; these gases are thought to have begun to orbit the sun and condense into planets. Because both of these hypotheses deal with ancient, unrepeatable events, neither can be tested, eliminating answer (A). Note that both 'tidal' and 'condensation' have additional meanings in physics, but those are not relevant here, eliminating answer (C). Both hypotheses are based on best guesses using modern physics, eliminating answer (D). Therefore, the **answer is (B)**.

2.   Which of the following is the best definition for 'meteorite'?
        (Skill 1.2)(Rigorous)

A.   A meteorite is a mineral composed of mica and feldspar.

B.   A meteorite is material from outer space, that has struck the earth's
        surface.

C.   A meteorite is an element that has properties of both metals and
        nonmetals.

D.   A meteorite is a very small unit of length measurement.

**Answer: B.   A meteorite is material from outer space, that has struck the
        earth's surface.**

Meteoroids are pieces of matter in space, composed of particles of rock and
metal. If a meteoroid travels through the earth's atmosphere, friction causes
burning and a "shooting star"—i.e. a meteor. If the meteor strikes the earth's
surface, it is known as a meterorite. Note that although the suffix –ite often
means a mineral, answer (A) is incorrect. Answer (C) refers to a 'metalloid'
rather than a 'meteorite', and answer (D) is simply a misleading pun on
'meter'. Therefore, the **answer is (B)**.

3.   Which of the following units is *not* a measure of distance?(Skill
        1.6)(Average Rigor)

A.   AU (astronomical unit).

B.   Light year.

C.   Parsec.

D.   Lunar year.

Answer: D.   Lunar year.

Although the terminology is sometimes confusing, it is important to remember
that a 'light year' (B) refers to the distance that light can travel in a year.
Astronomical Units (AU) (A) also measure distance, and one AU is the
distance between the sun and the earth. Parsecs (C) also measure distance,
and are used in astronomical measurement- they are very large, and are
usually used to measure interstellar distances. A lunar year, or any other kind
of year for a planet or moon, is the *time* measure of that body's orbit.
Therefore, the answer to this **question is (D)**.

4.   **Which of the following is *not* true about phase change in matter? (Skill 2.1)(Rigorous)**

A.   Solid water and liquid ice can coexist at water's freezing point.

B.   At 7 degrees Celsius, water is always in liquid phase.

C.   Matter changes phase when enough energy is gained or lost.

D.   Different phases of matter are characterized by differences in molecular motion.

Answer: B.   At 7 degrees Celsius, water is always in liquid phase.

According to the molecular theory of matter, molecular motion determines the 'phase' of the matter, and the energy in the matter determines the speed of molecular motion. Solids have vibrating molecules that are in fixed relative positions; liquids have faster molecular motion than their solid forms, and the molecules may move more freely but must still be in contact with one another; gases have even more energy and more molecular motion. (Other phases, such as plasma, are yet more energetic.) At the 'freezing point' or 'boiling point' of a substance, both relevant phases may be present. For instance, water at zero degrees Celsius may be composed of some liquid and some solid, or all liquid, or all solid. Pressure changes, in addition to temperature changes, can cause phase changes. For example, nitrogen can be liquefied under high pressure, even though its boiling temperature is very low. Therefore, the **correct answer must be (B)**. Water may be a liquid at that temperature, but it may also be a solid, depending on ambient pressure.

5.   **What is the most accurate description of the Water Cycle?(Skill 2.2)(Rigorous)**

A.   Rain comes from clouds, filling the ocean. The water then evaporates and becomes clouds again.

B.   Water circulates from rivers into groundwater and back, while water vapor circulates in the atmosphere.

C.   Water is conserved except for chemical or nuclear reactions, and any drop of water could circulate through clouds, rain, ground-water, and surface-water.

D.   Weather systems cause chemical reactions to break water into its atoms.

Answer: C. Water is conserved except for chemical or nuclear reactions, and any drop of water could circulate through clouds, rain, ground-water, and surface-water.

All natural chemical cycles, including the Water Cycle, depend on the principle of Conservation of Mass. (For water, unlike for elements such as Nitrogen, chemical reactions may cause sources or sinks of water molecules.) Any drop of water may circulate through the hydrologic system, ending up in a cloud, as rain, or as surface- or ground-water. Although answers (A) and (B) describe parts of the water cycle, the most comprehensive and correct **answer is (C)**.

6.   **What is the source for most of the United States' drinking water? (Skill 2.2)(Rigorous)**

A.   Desalinated ocean water.

B.   Surface water (lakes, streams, mountain runoff).

C.   Rainfall into municipal reservoirs.

D.   Groundwater.

Answer: D. Groundwater.

Groundwater currently provides drinking water for 53% of the population of the United States. (Although groundwater is often less polluted than surface water, it can be contaminated and it is very hard to clean once it is polluted. If too much groundwater is used from one area, then the ground may sink or shift, or local salt water may intrude from ocean boundaries.) The other answer choices can be used for drinking water, but they are not the most widely used. Therefore, **the answer is (D)**.

7.   **The theory of 'sea floor spreading' explains _____(Skill 2.4)(Average Rigor)**

A.   the shapes of the continents.

B.   how continents collide.

C.   how continents move apart.

D.   how continents sink to become part of the ocean floor.

Answer: C. How continents move apart.

In the theory of 'sea floor spreading', the movement of the ocean floor causes continents to spread apart from one another. This occurs because crust plates split apart, and new material is added to the plate edges. This process pulls the continents apart, or may create new separations, and is believed to have caused the formation of the Atlantic Ocean. The **answer is (C)**.

8.   **The salinity of ocean water is closest to _____ .(Skill 2.4)(Rigorous)**

A.   0.035 %

B.   0.35 %

C.   3.5 %

D.   35 %

Answer: C. 3.5 %

Salinity, or concentration of dissolved salt, can be measured in mass ratio (i.e. mass of salt divided by mass of sea water). For Earth's oceans, the salinity is approximately 3.5 %, or 35 parts per thousand. Note that answers (A) and (D) can be eliminated, because (A) is so dilute as to be hardly saline, while (D) is so concentrated that it would not support ocean life. Therefore, the **answer is (C)**.

9.   **Which of the following instruments measures wind speed?(Skill 3.2)(Rigorous)**

A.   Barometer.

B.   Anemometer.

C.   Thermometer.

D.   Weather Vane.

B.   Anemometer.

An anemometer is a device to measure wind speed, while a barometer measures pressure, a thermometer measures temperature, and a weather vane indicates wind direction. This is consistent only with **answer (B)**.

If you chose "barometer," here is an old physics joke to console you:

A physics teacher asks a student the following question:

"Suppose you want to find out the height of a building, and the only tool you have is a barometer. How could you find out the height?"

(The teacher hopes that the student will remember that pressure is inversely proportional to height, and will measure the pressure at the top of the building and then use the data to calculate the height of the building.)

"Well," says the student, "I could tie a string to the barometer and lower it from the top of the building, and then measure the amount of string required."

"You could," answers the teacher, "but try to think of a method that uses your physics knowledge from our class."

"All right," replies the student, "I could drop the barometer from the roof and measure the time it takes to fall, and then use free-fall equations to calculate the height from which it fell."

"Yes," says the teacher, "but what about using the barometer per se?"

"Oh," answers the student, "I could find the building superintendent, and offer to exchange the barometer for a set of blueprints, and look up the height!"

10. **Which of the following animals are most likely to live in a tropical rain forest?(Skill 3.3)(Easy Rigor)**

A. Reindeer.

B. Monkeys.

C. Puffins.

D. Bears.

B. Monkeys.

The tropical rain forest biome is hot and humid, and is very fertile—it is thought to contain almost half of the world's species. Reindeer (A), puffins (C), and bears (D), however, are usually found in much colder climates. There are several species of monkeys that thrive in hot, humid climates, so **answer (B) is correct.**

11. **Which is not one of the three layers of the earth's interior?(Skill 4.1)(Average Rigor)**

A. Core

B. Mantel

C. Crust

D. Molten Layer

Answer is D. The first three, the core, the mantel and the crust are the three layers of the earth's interior.

12.   **Lithification refers to the process by which unconsolidated sediments are transformed into _____(Skill 4.2)(Average Rigor)**

A.   metamorphic rocks.

B.   sedimentary rocks.

C.   igneous rocks.

D.   lithium oxide.

B.   Sedimentary rocks.

Lithification is the process of sediments coming together to form rocks, i.e. sedimentary rock formation. Metamorphic and igneous rocks are formed via other processes (heat and pressure or volcano, respectively). Lithium oxide shares a word root with 'lithification' but is otherwise unrelated to this question. Therefore, the **answer must be (B)**.

13.   **Which of the following types of rock are made from magma?(Skill 4.2)(Average Rigor)**

A.   Fossils.

B.   Sedimentary.

C.   Metamorphic.

D.   Igneous.

D.   Igneous.

Few fossils are found in metamorphic rock and virtually none found in igneous rocks. Igneous rocks are formed from magma and magma is so hot that any organisms trapped by it are destroyed. Metamorphic rocks are formed by high temperatures and great pressures. When fluid sediments are transformed into solid sedimentary rocks, the process is known as lithification. The **answer is (D).**

14. **Which of these is a true statement about loamy soil?(Skill 4.3)(Rigorous)**

A. Loamy soil is gritty and porous.

B. Loamy soil is smooth and a good barrier to water.

C. Loamy soil is hostile to microorganisms.

D. Loamy soil is velvety and clumpy.

D. **Loamy soil is velvety and clumpy**.

The three classes of soil by texture are: Sandy (gritty and porous), Clay (smooth, greasy, and most impervious to water), and Loamy (velvety, clumpy, and able to hold water and let water flow through). In addition, loamy soils are often the most fertile soils. Therefore, the **answer must be (D)**.

15. **Igneous rocks can be classified according to which of the following? (Skill 4.4)(Rigorous)**

A. Texture.

B. Composition.

C. Formation process.

D. All of the above.

D. **All of the above**.

Igneous rocks, which form from the crystallization of molten lava, are classified according to many of their characteristics, including texture, composition, and how they were formed. Therefore, **the answer is (D).**

16. **Which of the following is *not* a type of volcano?(Skill 4.4)(Average Rigor)**

A. Shield Volcanoes.

B. Composite Volcanoes.

C. Stratus Volcanoes.

D. Cinder Cone Volcanoes.

C. Stratus Volcanoes.

There are three types of volcanoes. Shield volcanoes (A) are associated with non-violent eruptions and repeated lava flow over time. Composite volcanoes (B) are built from both lava flow and layers of ash and cinders. Cinder cone volcanoes (D) are associated with violent eruptions, such that lava is thrown into the air and becomes ash or cinder before falling and accumulating. **'Stratus' (C)** is a type of cloud, not volcano, so it is the correct answer to this question.

17. **_____ are cracks in the plates of the earth's crust, along which the plates move.(Skill 4.4)(Average Rigor)**

A. Faults

B. Ridges

C. Earthquakes

D. Volcanoes

A. Faults.

Faults are cracks in the earth's crust, and when the earth moves, an earthquake results. Faults may lead to mismatched edges of ground, forming ridges, and ground shape may also be determined by volcanoes. The answer to this question must **therefore be (A).**

18. **Fossils are usually found in _____ rock.(Skill 4.6)(Easy Rigor)**

A. igneous.

B. sedimentary.

C. metamorphic.

D. cumulus.

B. Sedimentary

Fossils are formed by layers of dirt and sand settling around organisms, hardening, and taking an imprint of the organisms. When the organism decays, the hardened imprint is left behind. This is most likely to happen in rocks that form from layers of settling dirt and sand, i.e. sedimentary rock. Note that igneous rock is formed from molten rock from volcanoes (lava), while metamorphic rock can be formed from any rock under very high temperature and pressure changes. 'Cumulus' is a descriptor for clouds, not rocks. The best answer is **therefore (B)**.

19. **Which of the following is the most accurate definition of a nonrenewable resource?(Skill 5.1)(Rigorous)**

A. A nonrenewable resource is never replaced once used.

B. A nonrenewable resource is replaced on a timescale that is very long relative to human life-spans.

C. A nonrenewable resource is a resource that can only be manufactured by humans.

D. A nonrenewable resource is a species that has already become extinct.

B. A nonrenewable resource is replaced on a timescale that is very long relative to human life-spans.

Renewable resources are those that are renewed, or replaced, in time for humans to use more of them. Examples include fast-growing plants, animals, or oxygen gas. (Note that while sunlight is often considered a renewable resource, it is actually a nonrenewable but extremely abundant resource.) Nonrenewable resources are those that renew themselves only on very long timescales, usually geologic timescales. Examples include minerals, metals, or fossil fuels. Therefore, the **correct answer is (B)**.

20.   **Which parts of an atom are located inside the nucleus?(Skill 5.3)(Rigorous)**

A.   Protons and Electrons.

B.   Protons and Neutrons.

C.   Protons only.

D.   Neutrons only.

B.   **Protons and Neutrons.**

Protons and neutrons are located in the nucleus, while electrons move around outside the nucleus. This is consistent only with **answer (B)**.

21.   **Which of the following is *not* a common type of acid in 'acid rain' or acidified surface water?(Skill 5.3)(Average Rigor)**

A.   Nitric acid.

B.   Sulfuric acid.

C.   Carbonic acid.

D.   Hydrofluoric acid.

D.   **Hydrofluoric acid.**

Acid rain forms predominantly from pollutant oxides in the air (usually nitrogen-based NO_x or sulfur-based SO_x), which become hydrated into their acids (nitric or sulfuric acid). Because of increased levels of carbon dioxide pollution, carbonic acid is also common in acidified surface water environments. Hydrofluoric acid can be found, but it is much less common. In general, carbon, nitrogen, and sulfur are much more prevalent in the environment than fluorine. Therefore, the **answer is (D)**.

22.   Laboratory researchers have classified fungi as distinct from plants because the cell walls of fungi. (Skill 6.1)(Average Rigor)

A.   contain chitin.

B.   contain yeast.

C.   are more solid.

D.   are less solid.

A.   **Contain chitin.**

Kingdom Fungi consists of organisms that are eukaryotic, multicellular, absorptive consumers. They have a chitin cell wall, which is the only universally present feature in fungi that is never present in plants. Thus, the **answer is (A)**.

23.   Which kingdom is comprised of organisms made of one cell with no nuclear membrane?(Skill 6.1)(Average Rigor)

A.   Monera.

B.   Protista.

C.   Fungi.

D.   Algae.

A.   **Monera.**

To answer this question, first note that algae are not a kingdom of their own. Some algae are in monera, the kingdom that consists of unicellular prokaryotes with no true nucleus. Protista and fungi are both eukaryotic, with true nuclei, and are sometimes multi-cellular. Therefore, the **answer is (A)**.

24. **Which of the following is *not* a member of Kingdom Fungi?(Skill 6.1)(Easy Rigor)**

A. Mold.

B. Blue-green algae.

C. Mildew.

D. Mushrooms.

B. Blue-green Algae.

Mold (A), mildew (C), and mushrooms (D) are all types of fungus. Blue-green algae, however, is in Kingdom Monera. Therefore, the **answer is (B)**.

25. **Which of the following organisms use spores to reproduce?(Skill 6.1)(Average Rigor)**

A. Fish.

B. Flowering plants.

C. Conifers.

D. Ferns.

D. Ferns.

Ferns, in Division Pterophyta, reproduce with spores and flagellated sperm. Flowering plants reproduce via seeds, and conifers reproduce via seeds protected in cones (e.g. pinecone). Fish, of course, reproduce sexually. Therefore, the **answer is (D)**.

26. **Which is not a Kingdom? (Skill 6.1)(Rigorous)**

A. Mammalia

B. Eubacteria

C. Protista

D. Fungi

Answer is A. Mammalia is not one of the kingdoms of animals and plants.

27. **Animals with a notochord or a backbone are in the phylum: (Skill 6.2)(Easy Rigor)**

A. arthropoda.

B. chordata.

C. mollusca.

D. mammalia.

B.   Chordata.

The phylum arthropoda contains spiders and insects and phylum mollusca contain snails and squid. Mammalia is a class in the phylum chordata. The **answer is (B).**

28. **Which is the correct sequence of insect development?(Skill 6.2)(Average Rigor)**

A. Egg, pupa, larva, adult.

B. Egg, larva, pupa, adult.

C. Egg, adult, larva, pupa.

D. Pupa, egg, larva, adult.

B.   Egg, larva, pupa, adult.

An insect begins as an egg, hatches into a larva (e.g. caterpillar), forms a pupa (e.g. cocoon), and emerges as an adult (e.g. moth). Therefore, the **answer is (B).**

29.   **Microorganisms use all but the following to move: (Skill 7.1)(Rigorous)**

A.   Pseudopods

B.   Flagella

C.   Cilia

D.   Pili

D.   Pseudopods

Pseudopods, flagella and cilia are used by microorganisms for movement. Pili are used for attachment.

30.   **What cell organelle contains the cell's stored food?(Skill 7.1)(Average Rigor)**

A.   Vacuoles.

B.   Golgi Apparatus.

C.   Ribosomes.

D.   Lysosomes.

A. Vacuoles.

In a cell, the sub-parts are called organelles. Of these, the vacuoles hold stored food (and water and pigments). The Golgi Apparatus sorts molecules from other parts of the cell; the ribosomes are sites of protein synthesis; the lysosomes contain digestive enzymes. This is consistent only with **answer (A).**

31. **Eukaryotic cells are found in all but the following:(Skill 7.1)(Average Rigor)**

A. Bacteria

B. Protists

C. Fungi

D. Animals

Answer is A. Eukaryotic cells are found in protists, fungi, plants and animals but not in bacteria.

32. **The purpose of the Golgi Apparatus is: (Skill 7.1)(Average Rigor)**

A. To break down proteins

B. To sort, modify and package molecules

C. To break down fats

D. To make carbohydrates.

Answer is B. The Golgi Apparatus takes molecules from the endoplasmic reticulum and sorts, modifies and packages the molecules for later use by the cell.

33. **Since ancient times, people have been entranced with bird flight. What is the key to bird flight? (Skill 7.3)(Rigorous)**

A. Bird wings are a particular shape and composition.

B. Birds flap their wings quickly enough to propel themselves.

C. Birds take advantage of tailwinds.

D. Birds take advantage of crosswinds.

A. **Bird wings are a particular shape and composition.**

Bird wings are shaped for wide area, and their bones are very light. This creates a large surface-area-to-mass ratio, enabling birds to glide in air. Birds do flap their wings and float on winds, but none of these is the main reason for their flight ability. Thus, the **answer is (A)**.

34. **Which of the following is *not* a necessary characteristic of living things?(Skill 7.4)(Rigorous)**

A. Movement.

B. Reduction of local entropy.

C. Ability to cause local energy form changes.

D. Reproduction.

A. **Movement.**

There are many definitions of "life," but in all cases, a living organism reduces local entropy, changes chemical energy into other forms, and reproduces. Not all living things move, however, so the correct **answer is (A)**.

35. **Identify the correct sequence of organization of living things from lower to higher order: (Skill 7.6)(Average Rigor)**

A.   Cell, Organelle, Organ, Tissue, System, Organism.

B.   Cell, Tissue, Organ, Organelle, System, Organism.

C.   Organelle, Cell, Tissue, Organ, System, Organism.

D.   Organelle, Tissue, Cell, Organ, System, Organism.

C.   Organelle, Cell, Tissue, Organ, System, Organism.

Organelles are parts of the cell; cells make up tissue, which makes up organs. Organs work together in systems (e.g. the respiratory system), and the organism is the living thing as a whole. Therefore, the **answer must be (C)**.

36.   Amino acids are carried to the ribosome in protein synthesis by: (Skill 8.1)(Average Rigor)

A.   transfer RNA (tRNA).

B.   messenger RNA (mRNA).

C.   ribosomal RNA (rRNA).

D.   transformation RNA (trRNA).

A.   Transfer RNA (tRNA).

The job of tRNA is to carry and position amino acids to/on the ribosomes. mRNA copies DNA code and brings it to the ribosomes; rRNA is in the ribosome itself. There is no such thing as trRNA. Thus, the **answer is (A)**.

37.   **Which of the following is not a nucleotide?(Skill 8.1)(Average Rigor)**

A.   Adenine.

B.   Alanine.

C.   Cytosine.

D.   Guanine.

B.   Alanine.

Alanine is an amino acid. Adenine, cytosine, guanine, thymine, and uracil are nucleotides. The correct **answer is (B).**

38.   **What is not a type of RNA? (Skill 8.1)(Average Rigor)**

A.   Ribosomal

B.   Transfer

C.   Transcriptional

D.   Messenger

Answer is C: Types of RNA include ribosomal RNA, transfer RNA and messenger RNA. Each of these serves a different function within the cell.

39.   **A child has type O blood. Her father has type A blood, and her mother has type B blood. What are the genotypes of the father and mother, respectively?(Skill 8.2)(Average Rigor)**

A.   AO and BO.

B.   AA and AB.

C.   OO and BO.

D.   AO and BB.

A.   AO and BO.

Because O blood is recessive, the child must have inherited two O's—one from each of her parents. Since her father has type A blood, his genotype must be AO; likewise her mother's blood must be BO. Therefore, only **answer (A)** can be correct.

40.   A white flower is crossed with a red flower. Which of the following is a sign of incomplete dominance?(Skill 8.2)(Average Rigor)

A.   Pink flowers.

B.   Red flowers.

C.   White flowers.

D.   No flowers.

A.   **Pink flowers.**

Incomplete dominance means that neither the red nor the white gene is strong enough to suppress the other. Therefore both are expressed, leading in this case to the formation of pink flowers. Therefore, the **answer is (A)**.

41.   The first stage of mitosis is called _____(Skill 8.3)(Rigorous)

A.   telophase.

B.   anaphase.

C.   prophase.

D.   mitophase.

C.   **Prophase.**

In mitosis, the division of somatic cells, prophase is the stage where the cell enters mitosis. The four stages of mitosis, in order, are: prophase, metaphase, anaphase, and telophase. ("Mitophase" is not one of the steps.) During prophase, the cell begins the nonstop process of division. Its chromatin condenses, its nucleolus disappears, the nuclear membrane breaks apart, mitotic spindles form, its cytoskeleton breaks down, and centrioles push the spindles apart. Note that interphase, the stage where chromatin is loose, chromosomes are replicated, and cell metabolism is occurring, is technically not a stage of mitosis; it is a precursor to cell division.

42. A series of experiments on pea plants formed by _____ showed that two invisible markers existed for each trait, and one marker dominated the other. (Skill 8.4)(Easy Rigor)

A. Pasteur.

B. Watson and Crick.

C. Mendel.

D. Mendeleev.

C. **Mendel.**

Gregor Mendel was a ninteenth-century Austrian botanist, who derived "laws" governing inherited traits. His work led to the understanding of dominant and recessive traits, carried by biological markers. Mendel cross-bred different kinds of pea plants with varying features and observed the resulting new plants. He showed that genetic characteristics are not passed identically from one generation to the next. (Pasteur, Watson, Crick, and Mendeleev were other scientists with different specialties.) This is consistent only with **answer (C)**.

43. Which process(es) result(s) in a haploid chromosome number? (Skill 8.4)(Average Rigor)

A. Mitosis.

B. Meiosis.

C. Both mitosis and meiosis.

D. Neither mitosis nor meiosis.

B. **Meiosis.**

Meiosis is the division of sex cells. The resulting chromosome number is half the number of parent cells, i.e. a 'haploid chromosome number'. Mitosis, however, is the division of other cells, in which the chromosome number is the same as the parent cell chromosome number. Therefore, the **answer is (B)**.

44.   The duplication of genetic material into another cell is called: (Skill 8.6)(Rigorous)

A.   Replicating

B.   Cell duplication

C.   Cloning

D.   Genetic restructuring

Answer is C. Cloning is the duplication of genetic material into another cell.

45.   Gel electrophoresis: (Skill 8.6)(Rigorous)

A.   Isolates fragments of DNA for scientific purposes

B.   Cannot be used in proteins

C.   Requires the polymerase chain reaction

D.   Only separates DNA by size

Answer is A. Gel electrophoresis separates DNA by size and charge. It can be used in proteins as well and is not dependent on the polymerase chain reaction.

46.   What is not true of decomposers? (Skill 9.1)(Rigorous)

A.   Decomposers recycle the carbon accumulated in durable organic material

B.   Ammonification is the decomposition of organic nitrogen back to ammonia.

C.   Decomposers add phosphorous back to the soil

D.   Decomposers belong to the Genus Escherichia.

Answer is D. Decomposers recycle phosphorus and carbon and undergo ammonification.

47.   **What eats secondary consumers? (Skill 9.1)(Easy Rigor)**

A.   Producers

B.   Tertiary consumers

C.   Primary consumers

D.   Decomposers

Answer is B. The tertiary consumers eat the secondary consumers and the secondary consumers eat the primary consumers.

48.   **Which of the following is found in the least abundance in organic molecules? (Skill 9.2)(Rigorous)**

A.   Phosphorus.

B.   Potassium.

C.   Carbon.

D.   Oxygen.

B.   Potassium.

Organic molecules consist mainly of Carbon, Hydrogen, and Oxygen, with significant amounts of Nitrogen, Phosphorus, and often Sulfur. Other elements, such as Potassium, are present in much smaller quantities. Therefore, the **answer is (B)**. If you were not aware of this ranking, you might have been able to eliminate Carbon and Oxygen because of their prevalence, in any case.

49.   **What is not true of the carbon cycle? (Skill 9.2)(Average Rigor)**

A. Ten percent of all available carbon is in the air.

B. Carbon dioxide is fixed by glycosylation.

C. Plants fix carbon in the form of glucose.

D. Animals release carbon through respiration.

Answer is B. Ten percent of all available carbon is in the air. Plants fix carbon via photosynthesis to make glucose and animals release carbon through respiration.

50.   **A wrasse (fish) cleans the teeth of other fish by eating away plaque. This is an example of _____ between the fish. (Skill 9.4)(Rigorous)**

A.   parasitism.

B.   symbiosis (mutualism).

C.   competition.

D.   predation.

B.   Symbiosis (mutualism).

When both species benefit from their interaction in their habitat, this is called 'symbiosis', or 'mutualism'. In this example, the wrasse benefits from having a source of food, and the other fish benefit by having healthier teeth. Note that 'parasitism' is when one species benefits at the expense of the other, 'competition' is when two species compete with one another for the same habitat or food, and 'predation' is when one species feeds on another. Therefore, the **answer is (B)**.

51.   **Which of the following does not result in the detriment of one species and the advancement of another? (Skill 9.4)(Rigorous)**

A.   Parasitism

B.   Mutualism

C.   Predation

D.   Herbivory

Answer is B. Parasitism, Herbivory and Predation all result in the detriment of one species.

52.   **Viruses are responsible for many human diseases including all of the following *except:* (Skill 9.5)(Average Rigor)**

A.   influenza.

B.   A.I.D.S.

C.   the common cold.

D.   strep throat.

D.   **Strep throat.**

Influenza, A.I.D.S., and the "common cold" (rhinovirus infection), are all caused by viruses. (This is the reason that doctors should not be pressured to prescribe antibiotics for colds or 'flu—i.e. they will not be effective since the infections are not bacterial.) Strep throat (properly called 'streptococcal throat' and caused by streptococcus bacteria) is not a virus, but a bacterial infection. Thus, the **answer is (D)**.

53.   Darwin supported the evolutionary theory of: (Skill 10.1)(Rigorous)

A.   Punctualism

B.   Gradualism

C.   Equilibrium

D.   Convergency

Answer is B. Darwin's book is based upon gradualism.

54.   **Which of the following is a correct explanation for scientific 'evolution'? (Skill 10.1)(Rigorous)**

A.   Giraffes need to reach higher for leaves to eat, so their necks stretch. The giraffe babies are then born with longer necks. Eventually, there are more long-necked giraffes in the population.

B.   Giraffes with longer necks are able to reach more leaves, so they eat more and have more babies than other giraffes. Eventually, there are more long-necked giraffes in the population.

C.   Giraffes want to reach higher for leaves to eat, so they release enzymes into their bloodstream, which in turn causes fetal development of longer-necked giraffes. Eventually, there are more long-necked giraffes in the population.

D.   Giraffes with long necks are more attractive to other giraffes, so they get the best mating partners and have more babies. Eventually, there are more long-necked giraffes in the population.

B.   **Giraffes with longer necks are able to reach more leaves, so they eat more and have more babies than other giraffes. Eventually, there are more long-necked giraffes in the population.**

Although evolution is often misunderstood, it occurs via natural selection. Organisms with a life/reproductive advantage will produce more offspring. Over many generations, this changes the proportions of the population. In any case, it is impossible for a stretched neck (A) or a fervent desire (C) to result in a biologically mutated baby. Although there are traits that are naturally selected because of mate attractiveness and fitness (D), this is not the primary situation here, **so answer (B) is the best choice.**

55. **What is true about natural selection? (Skill 10.1)(Average Rigor)**

A. It acts on an individual genotype

B. It does not happen currently

C. It is a phenomenon of animals only

D. It acts on the individual phenotype

Answer is D. Natural selection is going on all the time in all living things and acts on the individual phenotype.

56. **Members of the same animal species _____(Skill 10.2)(Average Rigor)**

A. look identical.

B. never adapt differently.

C. are able to reproduce with one another.

D. are found in the same location.

C. Are able to reproduce with one another.

Although members of the same animal species may look alike (A), adapt alike (B), or be found near one another (D), the only requirement is that they be able to reproduce with one another. This ability to reproduce within the group is considered the hallmark of a species. Therefore, the **answer is (C)**.

57.   **A duck's webbed feet are examples of: (Skill 10.3)(Average Rigor)**

A.   mimicry.

B.   structural adaptation.

C.   protective resemblance.

D.   protective coloration.

B.   Structural adaptation.

Ducks (and other aquatic birds) have webbed feet, which makes them more efficient swimmers. This is most likely due to evolutionary patterns where webbed-footed-birds were more successful at feeding and reproducing, and eventually became the majority of aquatic birds. Because the structure of the duck adapted to its environment over generations, this is termed 'structural adaptation'. Mimicry, protective resemblance, and protective coloration refer to other evolutionary mechanisms for survival. The answer to this question is **therefore (B)**.

58.   **What is not true about reproductive isolation? (Skill 10.4)(Rigorous)**

A.   It prevents populations from exchanging genes

B.   It can occur by preventing fertilization.

C.   It can result in speciation

D.   It is not a phenomenon of islands.

Answer is D. Reproductive isolation can result in speciation, can occur by preventing fertilization and prevents populations from exchanging genes. It is a common phenomenon of islands.

59.   Vinegar is an example of a _____(Skill 11.1)(Easy Rigor)

A.   strong acid.

B.   strong base.

C.   weak acid.

D.   weak base.

C.   Weak acid.

The main ingredient in vinegar is acetic acid, a weak acid. Vinegar is a useful acid in science classes, because it makes a frothy reaction with bases such as baking soda (e.g. in the quintessential volcano model). Vinegar is not a strong acid, such as hydrochloric acid, because it does not dissociate as fully or cause as much corrosion. It is not a base. Therefore, the **answer is (C)**.

60.   Which of the following will not change in a chemical reaction?(Skill 11.2)(Average Rigor)

A.   Number of moles of products.

B.   Atomic number of one of the reactants.

C.   Mass (in grams) of one of the reactants.

D.   Rate of reaction.

B.   Atomic number of one of the reactants.

Atomic number, i.e. the number of protons in a given element, is constant unless involved in a nuclear reaction. Meanwhile, the amounts (measured in moles (A) or in grams(C)) of reactants and products change over the course of a chemical reaction, and the rate of a chemical reaction (D) may change due to internal or external processes. Therefore, the **answer is (B)**.

61.   Carbon bonds with hydrogen by: (Skill 11.4)(Rigorous)

A.   ionic bonding.

B.   non-polar covalent bonding.

C.   polar covalent bonding.

D.   strong nuclear force.

C.   Polar covalent bonding.

Each carbon atom contains four valence electrons, while each hydrogen atom contains one valence electron. A carbon atom can bond with one or more hydrogen atoms, such that two electrons are shared in each bond. This is covalent bonding, because the electrons are shared. (In ionic bonding, atoms must gain or lose electrons to form ions. The ions are then electrically attracted in oppositely-charged pairs.) Covalent bonds are always polar when between two non-identical atoms, so this bond must be polar. ("Polar" means that the electrons are shared unequally, forming a pair of partial charges, i.e. poles.) In any case, the strong nuclear force is not relevant to this problem. The answer to this question is **therefore (C).**

62.   What is necessary for ion diffusion to occur spontaneously?(Skill 11.4)(Average Rigor)

A.   Carrier proteins.

B.   Energy from an outside source.

C.   A concentration gradient.

D.   Cell flagellae.

C.   A concentration gradient.

Spontaneous diffusion occurs when random motion leads particles to increase entropy by equalizing concentrations. Particles tend to move into places of lower concentration. Therefore, a concentration gradient is required, and the **answer is (C)**. No proteins (A), outside energy (B), or flagellae (D) are required for this process.

63.   Which of the following is *not* a property of metalloids?(Skill 11.5)(Rigorous)

A.   Metalloids are solids at standard temperature and pressure.

B.   Metalloids can conduct electricity to a limited extent.

C.   Metalloids are found in groups 13 through 17.

D.   Metalloids all favor ionic bonding.

D.   Metalloids all favor ionic bonding.

Metalloids are substances that have characteristics of both metals and nonmetals, including limited conduction of electricity and solid phase at standard temperature and pressure. Metalloids are found in a 'stair-step' pattern from Boron in group 13 through Astatine in group 17. Some metalloids, e.g. Silicon, favor covalent bonding. Others, e.g. Astatine, can bond ionically. Therefore, **the answer is (D)**. Recall that metals/nonmetals/metalloids are not strictly defined by Periodic Table group, so their bonding is unlikely to be consistent with one another.

64.   The elements in the modern Periodic Table are arranged: (Skill 11.5)(Average Rigor)

A.   in numerical order by atomic number.

B.   randomly.

C.   in alphabetical order by chemical symbol.

D.   in numerical order by atomic mass.

A.   In numerical order by atomic number.

Although the first periodic tables were arranged by atomic mass, the modern table is arranged by atomic number, i.e. the number of protons in each element. (This allows the element list to be complete and unique.) The elements are not arranged either randomly or in alphabetical order. The answer to this question is **therefore (A)**.

65. **Which of the following is a correct definition for 'chemical equilibrium'?**
(Skill 11.6)(Rigorous)

A. The reaction may continue to proceed forward and backward.

B. Chemical equilibrium is when the forward and backward reaction rates are equal, and equal to zero. The reaction does not continue.

C. Chemical equilibrium is when there are equal quantities of reactants and products.

D. Chemical equilibrium is when acids and bases neutralize each other fully.

A. **Chemical equilibrium is when the forward and backward reaction rates are equal. The reaction may continue to proceed forward and backward.**

Chemical equilibrium is defined as when the quantities of reactants and products are at a 'steady state' and are no longer shifting, but the reaction may still proceed forward and backward. The rate of forward reaction must equal the rate of backward reaction. Note that there may or may not be equal amounts of chemicals, and that this is not restricted to a completed reaction or to an acid-base reaction. Therefore, the **answer is (A)**.

66. **The chemical equation for water formation is: $2H_2 + O_2 \rightarrow 2H_2O$. Which of the following is an *incorrect* interpretation of this equation?(Skill 11.6)(Rigorous)**

A. Two moles of hydrogen gas and one mole of oxygen gas combine to make two moles of water.

B. Two grams of hydrogen gas and one gram of oxygen gas combine to make two grams of water.

C. Two molecules of hydrogen gas and one molecule of oxygen gas combine to make two molecules of water.

D. Four atoms of hydrogen (combined as a diatomic gas) and two atoms of oxygen (combined as a diatomic gas) combine to make two molecules of water.

B. **Two grams of hydrogen gas and one gram of oxygen gas combine to make two grams of water.**

In any chemical equation, the coefficients indicate the relative proportions of molecules (or atoms), or of moles of molecules. They do not refer to mass, because chemicals combine in repeatable combinations of molar ratio (i.e. number of moles), but vary in mass per mole of material. Therefore, the answer must be the only choice that does not refer to numbers of particles, i.e. **answer (B)**, which refers to grams, a unit of mass.

67. **The measure of the pull of Earth's gravity on an object is called: (Skill 12.1)(Average Rigor)**

A. mass number.

B. atomic number.

C. mass.

D. weight.

D. **Weight.**

To answer this question, recall that mass number is the total number of protons and neutrons in an atom, atomic number is the number of protons in an atom, and mass is the amount of matter in an object. The only remaining **choice is (D)**, weight, which is correct because weight is the force of gravity on an object.

68. **What is the main obstacle to using nuclear fusion for obtaining electricity?(Skill 12.1)(Rigorous)**

A. Nuclear fusion produces much more pollution than nuclear fission.

B. There is no obstacle; most power plants us nuclear fusion today.

C. Nuclear fusion requires very high temperature and activation energy.

D. The fuel for nuclear fusion is extremely expensive.

C. **Nuclear fusion requires very high temperature and activation energy.**

Nuclear fission is the usual process for power generation in nuclear power plants. This is carried out by splitting nuclei to release energy. The sun's energy is generated by nuclear fusion, i.e. combination of smaller nuclei into a larger nucleus. Fusion creates much less radioactive waste, but it requires extremely high temperature and activation energy, so it is not yet feasible for electricity generation. Therefore, the **answer is (C)**.

69. **Which reaction below is a decomposition reaction?(Skill 12.2)(Rigorous)**

A. $HCl + NaOH \rightarrow NaCl + H_2O$

B. $C + O_2 \rightarrow CO_2$

C. $2H_2O \rightarrow 2H_2 + O_2$

D. $CuSO_4 + Fe \rightarrow FeSO_4 + Cu$

C. $2H_2O \rightarrow 2H_2 + O_2$

To answer this question, recall that a decomposition reaction is one in which there are fewer reactants (on the left) than products (on the right). This is consistent only with **answer (C).** Meanwhile, note that answer (A) shows a double-replacement reaction (in which two sets of ions switch bonds), answer (B) shows a synthesis reaction (in which there are fewer products than reactants), and answer (D) shows a single-replacement reaction (in which one substance replaces another in its bond, but the other does not get a new bond).

70. **Which of the following is a correct explanation for astronaut 'weightlessness'?(Skill 12.3)(Rigorous)**

A. Astronauts continue to feel the pull of gravity in space, but they are so far from planets that the force is small.

B. Astronauts continue to feel the pull of gravity in space, but spacecraft have such powerful engines that those forces dominate, reducing effective weight.

C. Astronauts do not feel the pull of gravity in space, because space is a vacuum.

D. Astronauts do not feel the pull of gravity in space, because black hole forces dominate the force field, reducing their masses.

A. **Astronauts continue to feel the pull of gravity in space, but they are so far from planets that the force is small.**

Gravity acts over tremendous distances in space (theoretically, infinite distance, though certainly at least as far as any astronaut has traveled). However, gravitational force is inversely proportional to distance squared from a massive body. This means that when an astronaut is in space, s/he is far enough from the center of mass of any planet that the gravitational force is very small, and s/he feels 'weightless'. Space is mostly empty (i.e. vacuum), and there are some black holes, and spacecraft do have powerful engines. However, none of these has the effect attributed to it in the incorrect answer choices (B), (C), or (D). The answer to this question must **therefore be (A).**

71. **What is specific gravity?(Skill 12.3)(Average Rigor)**

A. The mass of an object.

B. The ratio of the density of a substance to the density of water.

C. Density.

D. The pull of the earth's gravity on an object.

B. **The ratio of the density of a substance to the density of water.**

Mass is a measure of the amount of matter in an object. Density is the mass of a substance contained per unit of volume. Weight is the measure of the earth's pull of gravity on an object. The only option here is the ratio of the density of a substance to the density of water, **answer (B).**

72.   **Enzymes speed up reactions by _____(Skill 12.5)(Average Rigor)**

A.   utilizing ATP.

B.   lowering pH, allowing reaction speed to increase.

C.   increasing volume of substrate.

D.   lowering energy of activation.

D.   Lowering energy of activation.

Because enzymes are catalysts, they work the same way—they cause the formation of activated chemical complexes, which require a lower activation energy. Therefore, the **answer is (D).** ATP is an energy source for cells, and pH or volume changes may or may not affect reaction rate, so these answers can be eliminated.

73.   **Catalysts assist reactions by _____(Skill 12.5)(Rigorous)**

A.   lowering effective activation energy.

B.   maintaining precise pH levels.

C.   keeping systems at equilibrium.

D.   adjusting reaction speed.

A.   Lowering effective activation energy.

Chemical reactions can be enhanced or accelerated by catalysts, which are present both with reactants and with products. They induce the formation of activated complexes, thereby lowering the effective activation energy—so that less energy is necessary for the reaction to begin. Although this often makes reactions faster, answer (D) is not as good a choice as the more generally applicable **answer (A)**, which is correct.

74. **All of the following measure energy *except* for _____(Skill 13.1)(Easy Rigor)**

A.   joules.

B.   calories.

C.   watts.

D.   ergs.

C.   Watts.

Energy units must be dimensionally equivalent to (force)x(length), which equals (mass)x(length squared)/(time squared). Joules, Calories, and Ergs are all metric measures of energy. Joules are the SI units of energy, while Calories are used to allow water to have a Specific Heat of one unit. Ergs are used in the 'cgs' (centimeter-gram-second) system, for smaller quantities. Watts, however, are units of power, i.e. Joules per Second. Therefore, the **answer is (C)**.

75. **Energy is measured with the same units as _____(Skill 13.1)(Easy Rigor)**

A.   force.

B.   momentum.

C.   work.

D.   power.

C.   Work.

In SI units, energy is measured in Joules, i.e. (mass)(length squared)/(time squared). This is the same unit as is used for work. You can verify this by calculating that since work is force times distance, the units work out to be the same. Force is measured in Newtons in SI; momentum is measured in (mass)(length)/(time); power is measured in Watts (which equal Joules/second). Therefore, the **answer must be (C)**.

76.   **The Law of Conservation of Energy states that: (Skill 13.2)(Rigorous)**

A.   there must be the same number of products and reactants in any chemical equation.

B.   objects always fall toward large masses such as planets.

C.   energy is neither created nor destroyed, but may change form.

D.   lights must be turned off when not in use, by state regulation.

C.   **Energy is neither created nor destroyed, but may change form.**

Answer (C) is a summary of the Law of Conservation of Energy (for non-nuclear reactions). In other words, energy can be transformed into various forms such as kinetic, potential, electric, or heat energy, but the total amount of energy remains constant. Answer (A) is untrue, as demonstrated by many synthesis and decomposition reactions. Answers (B) and (D) may be sensible, but they are not relevant in this case. Therefore, the **answer is (C).**

77. **A ball rolls down a smooth hill. You may ignore air resistance. Which of the following is a true statement?(Skill 13.3)(Rigorous)**

A.   The ball has more energy at the start of its descent than just before it hits the bottom of the hill, because it is higher up at the beginning.

B.   The ball has less energy at the start of its descent than just before it hits the bottom of the hill, because it is moving more quickly at the end.

C.   The ball has the same energy throughout its descent, because positional energy is converted to energy of motion.

D.   The ball has the same energy throughout its descent, because a single object (such as a ball) cannot gain or lose energy.

C.   **The ball has the same energy throughout its descent, because positional energy is converted to energy of motion.**

The principle of Conservation of Energy states that (except in cases of nuclear reaction, when energy may be created or destroyed by conversion to mass), "Energy is neither created nor destroyed, but may be transformed." Answers (A) and (B) give you a hint in this question—it is true that the ball has more Potential Energy when it is higher, and that it has more Kinetic Energy when it is moving quickly at the bottom of its descent. However, the total sum of all kinds of energy in the ball remains constant, if we neglect 'losses' to heat/friction. Note that a single object can and does gain or lose energy when the energy is transferred to or from a different object. Conservation of Energy applies to systems, not to individual objects unless they are isolated. Therefore, the **answer must be (C)**.

78.   A long silver bar has a temperature of 50 degrees Celsius at one end and 0 degrees Celsius at the other end. The bar will reach thermal equilibrium (barring outside influence) by the process of heat _____.
(Skill 13.4)(Rigorous)

A.   conduction.

B.   convection.

C.   radiation.

D.   phase change.

A.   **conduction.**

Heat conduction is the process of heat transfer via solid contact. The molecules in a warmer region vibrate more rapidly, jostling neighboring molecules and accelerating them. This is the dominant heat transfer process in a solid with no outside influences. Recall, also, that convection is heat transfer by way of fluid currents; radiation is heat transfer via electromagnetic waves; phase change can account for heat transfer in the form of shifts in matter phase. The answer to this question must **therefore be (A)**.

79.   **Which of the following is a true statement about radiation exposure and air travel?(Skill 13.4)(Rigorous)**

A.   Air travel exposes humans to radiation, but the level is not significant for most people.

B.   Air travel exposes humans to so much radiation that it is recommended as a method of cancer treatment.

C.   Air travel does not expose humans to radiation.

D.   Air travel may or may not expose humans to radiation, but it has not yet been determined.

A. Air travel exposes humans to radiation, but the level is not significant for most people.

Humans are exposed to background radiation from the ground and in the atmosphere, but these levels are not considered hazardous under most circumstances, and these levels have been studied extensively. Air travel does create more exposure to atmospheric radiation, though this is much less than people usually experience through dental X-rays or other medical treatment. People whose jobs or lifestyles include a great deal of air flight may be at increased risk for certain cancers from excessive radiation exposure. Therefore, the **answer is (A)**.

80. **When you step out of the shower, the floor feels colder on your feet than the bathmat. Which of the following is the correct explanation for this phenomenon?(Skill 13.4(Rigorous)**

A. The floor is colder than the bathmat.

B. Your feet have a chemical reaction with the floor, but not the bathmat.

C. Heat is conducted more easily into the floor.

D. Water is absorbed from your feet into the bathmat.

C. **Heat is conducted more easily into the floor.**

When you step out of the shower and onto a surface, the surface is most likely at room temperature, regardless of its composition (eliminating answer (A)). Your feet feel cold when heat is transferred from them to the surface, which happens more easily on a hard floor than a soft bathmat. This is because of differences in specific heat (the energy required to change temperature, which varies by material). Therefore, the **answer must be (C)**, i.e. heat is conducted more easily into the floor from your feet.

81. **The transfer of heat by electromagnetic waves is called _____ (Skill 13.4)(Skill Average Rigor)**

A. conduction.

B. convection.

C. phase change.

D. radiation.

D. **Radiation.**

Heat transfer via electromagnetic waves (which can occur even in a vacuum) is called radiation. (Heat can also be transferred by direct contact (conduction), by fluid current (convection), and by matter changing phase, but these are not relevant here.) The answer to this question is **therefore (D)**.

82. **When heat is added to most solids, they expand. Why is this the case?**
    (Skill 13.4)(Average Rigor)

A.   The molecules get bigger.

B.   The faster molecular motion leads to greater distance between the molecules.

C.   The molecules develop greater repelling electric forces.

D.   The molecules form a more rigid structure.

B.   **The faster molecular motion leads to greater distance between the molecules.**

The atomic theory of matter states that matter is made up of tiny, rapidly moving particles. These particles move more quickly when warmer, because temperature is a measure of average kinetic energy of the particles. Warmer molecules therefore move further away from each other, with enough energy to separate from each other more often and for greater distances. The individual molecules do not get bigger, by conservation of mass, eliminating answer (A). The molecules do not develop greater repelling electric forces, eliminating answer (C). Occasionally, molecules form a more rigid structure when becoming colder and freezing (such as water)—but this gives rise to the exceptions to heat expansion, so it is not relevant here, eliminating answer (D). Therefore, the **answer is (B)**.

83.   **If the volume of a confined gas is increased, what happens to the pressure of the gas? You may assume that the gas behaves ideally, and that temperature and number of gas molecules remain constant.(Skill 13.6)(Average Rigor)**

A.   The pressure increases.

B.   The pressure decreases.

C.   The pressure stays the same.

D.   There is not enough information given to answer this question.

B.   **The pressure decreases.**

Because we are told that the gas behaves ideally, you may assume that it follows the Ideal Gas Law, i.e. PV = nRT. This means that an increase in volume must be associated with a decrease in pressure (i.e. higher T means lower P), because we are also given that all the components of the right side of the equation remain constant. Therefore, the **answer must be (B)**.

84.   **Which of the following is most accurate?(Skill 14.1)(Average Rigor)**

A.   Mass is always constant; Weight may vary by location.

B.   Mass and Weight are both always constant.

C.   Weight is always constant; Mass may vary by location.

D.   Mass and Weight may both vary by location.

A.   **Mass is always constant; Weight may vary by location.**

When considering situations exclusive of nuclear reactions, mass is constant (mass, the amount of matter in a system, is conserved). Weight, on the other hand, is the force of gravity on an object, which is subject to change due to changes in the gravitational field and/or the location of the object. Thus, the **best answer is (A)**.

85.   **A Newton is fundamentally a measure of _____.(Skill 14.1)(Easy Rigor)**

A.   force.

B.   momentum.

C.   energy.

D.   gravity.

A.   Force.

In SI units, force is measured in Newtons. Momentum and energy each have different units, without equivalent dimensions. A Newton is one (kilogram)(meter)/(second squared), while momentum is measured in (kilgram)(meter)/(second) and energy, in Joules, is (kilogram)(meter squared)/(second squared). Although "gravity" can be interpreted as the force of gravity, i.e. measured in Newtons, fundamentally it is not required. Therefore, the **answer is (A)**.

86.   **The force of gravity on earth causes all bodies in free fall to _____ (Skill 14.2)(Easy Rigor)**

A.   fall at the same speed.

B.   accelerate at the same rate.

C.   reach the same terminal velocity.

D.   move in the same direction.

B.   Accelerate at the same rate.

Gravity causes approximately the same acceleration on all falling bodies close to earth's surface. (It is only "approximately" because there are very small variations in the strength of earth's gravitational field.) More massive bodies continue to accelerate at this rate for longer, before their air resistance is great enough to cause terminal velocity, so answers (A) and (C) are eliminated. Bodies on different parts of the planet move in different directions (always toward the center of mass of earth), so answer (D) is eliminated. Thus, the **answer is (B)**.

87.   **All of the following are considered Newton's Laws *except* for:(Skill 14.5)(Rigorous)**

A.   An object in motion will continue in motion unless acted upon by an outside force.

B.   For every action force, there is an equal and opposite reaction force.

C.   Nature abhors a vacuum.

D.   Mass can be considered the ratio of force to acceleration.

C.   Nature abhors a vacuum.

Newton's Laws include his law of inertia (an object in motion (or at rest) will stay in motion (or at rest) until acted upon by an outside force) (A), his law that (Force)=(Mass)(Acceleration) (D), and his equal and opposite reaction force law (B). Therefore, the **answer to this question is (C)**, because "Nature abhors a vacuum" is not one of these.

88.   **Sound can be transmitted in all of the following *except:* (Skill 15.1)(Average Rigor)**

A.   air.

B.   water.

C.   diamond.

D.   a vacuum.

D.   A vacuum.

Sound, a longitudinal wave, is transmitted by vibrations of molecules. Therefore, it can be transmitted through any gas, liquid, or solid. However, it cannot be transmitted through a vacuum, because there are no particles present to vibrate and bump into their adjacent particles to transmit the waves. This is consistent only with **answer (D)**. (It is interesting also to note that sound is actually faster in solids and liquids than in air.)

89. **The electromagnetic radiation with the longest wave length is _____. (Skill 15.1)(Average Rigor)**

A. radio waves.

B. red light.

C. X-rays.

D. ultraviolet light.

A.   Radio waves.

As one can see on a diagram of the electromagnetic spectrum, radio waves have longer wave lengths (and smaller frequencies) than visible light, which in turn has longer wave lengths than ultraviolet or X-ray radiation. If you did not remember this sequence, you might recall that wave length is inversely proportional to frequency, and that radio waves are considered much less harmful (less energetic, i.e. lower frequency) than ultraviolet or X-ray radiation. The correct answer is **therefore (A)**.

90. **Sound waves are produced by _____(Skill 15.1)(Easy Rigor)**

A. pitch.

B. noise.

C. vibrations.

D. sonar.

C.   Vibrations.

Sound waves are produced by a vibrating body. The vibrating object moves forward and compresses the air in front of it, then reverses direction so that the pressure on the air is lessened and expansion of the air molecules occurs. The vibrating air molecules move back and forth parallel to the direction of motion of the wave as they pass the energy from adjacent air molecules closer to the source to air molecules farther away from the source. Therefore, the **answer is (C)**.

91.   The Doppler Effect is associated most closely with which property of waves?(Skill 15.2)(Rigorous)

A.   Amplitude.

B.   Wavelength.

C.   Frequency.

D.   Intensity.

C.   Frequency.

The Doppler Effect accounts for an apparent increase in frequency when a wave source moves toward a wave receiver or apparent decrease in frequency when a wave source moves away from a wave receiver. (Note that the receiver could also be moving toward or away from the source.) As the wave fronts are released, motion toward the receiver mimics more frequent wave fronts, while motion away from the receiver mimics less frequent wave fronts. Meanwhile, the amplitude, wavelength, and intensity of the wave are not as relevant to this process (although moving closer to a wave source makes it seem more intense). The **answer to this question is therefore (C)**.

92.   As a train approaches, the whistle sounds (Skill 15.2)(Rigorous)

A.   higher, because it has a higher apparent frequency.

B.   lower, because it has a lower apparent frequency.

C.   higher, because it has a lower apparent frequency.

D.   lower, because it has a higher apparent frequency.

A.   Higher, because it has a higher apparent frequency.

By the Doppler effect, when a source of sound is moving toward an observer, the wave fronts are released closer together, i.e. with a greater apparent frequency. Higher frequency sounds are higher in pitch. This is consistent only with **answer (A)**.

93.   **The speed of light is different in different materials. This is responsible for _____(Skill 15.3)(Rigorous)**

A.   interference.

B.   refraction.

C.   reflection.

D.   relativity.

B.   Refraction.

Refraction (B) is the bending of light because it hits a material at an angle wherein it has a different speed. (This is analogous to a cart rolling on a smooth road. If it hits a rough patch at an angle, the wheel on the rough patch slows down first, leading to a change in direction.) Interference (A) is when light waves interfere with each other to form brighter or dimmer patterns; reflection (C) is when light bounces off a surface; relativity (D) is a general topic related to light speed and its implications, but not specifically indicated here. Therefore, the **answer is (B)**.

94.   **A converging lens produces a real image _____(Skill 15.5)(Rigorous)**

A.   always.

B.   never.

C.   when the object is within one focal length of the lens.

D.   when the object is further than one focal length from the lens.

D.   When the object is further than one focal length from the lens.

A converging lens produces a real image whenever the object is far enough from the lens (outside one focal length) so that the rays of light from the object can hit the lens and be focused into a real image on the other side of the lens. When the object is closer than one focal length from the lens, rays of light do not converge on the other side; they diverge. This means that only a virtual image can be formed, i.e. the theoretical place where those diverging rays would have converged if they had originated behind the object. Thus, the correct **answer is (D)**.

95. **Resistance is measured in units called: (Skill 16.2)(Average Rigor)**

A.   watts.

B.   volts.

C.   ohms.

D.   current.

C.   Ohms.

A watt is a unit of energy. Potential difference is measured in a unit called the volt. Current is the number of electrons per second that flow past a point in a circuit. An ohm is the unit for resistance. The correct **answer is (C).**

96. **Rough endoplasmic reticulum contains: (Skill 7.1)(Average Rigor)**

A.   Vacuoles

B.   Mitochondria

C.   Microfilaments

D.   Ribosomes

Answer is D. Rough endoplasmic reticulum is defined as such because of the occurrence of ribosomes on its surface.

97.   **What is the scientific method?(Skill 17.1)(Rigorous)**

A.   It is the process of doing an experiment and writing a laboratory report.

B.   It is the process of using open inquiry and repeatable results to establish theories.

C.   It is the process of reinforcing scientific principles by confirming results.

D.   It is the process of recording data and observations.

B.   **It is the process of using open inquiry and repeatable results to establish theories.**

Scientific research often includes elements from answers (A), (C), and (D), but the basic underlying principle of the scientific method is that people ask questions and do repeatable experiments to answer those questions and develop informed theories of why and how things happen. Therefore, the best **answer is (B).**

98.   **After an experiment, the scientist states that s/he believes a change in color is due to a change in pH. This is an example of: (Skill 17.2)(Easy Rigor)**

A.   observing.

B.   inferring.

C.   measuring.

D.   classifying.

B.   **Inferring.**

To answer this question, note that the scientist has observed a change in color, and has then made a guess as to its reason. This is an example of inferring. The scientist has not measured or classified in this case. Although s/he has observed [the color change], the explanation of this observation is **inferring (B).**

99.   When is a hypothesis formed? (Skill 17.3)(Easy Rigor)

A.   Before the data is taken.

B.   After the data is taken.

C.   After the data is analyzed.

D.   While the data is being graphed.

A.   **Before the data is taken.**

A hypothesis is an educated guess, made before undertaking an experiment. The hypothesis is then evaluated based on the observed data. Therefore, the hypothesis must be formed before the data is taken, not during or after the experiment. This is consistent only with **answer (A).**

100.   **Identify the control in the following experiment: A student had four corn plants and was measuring photosynthetic rate (by measuring growth mass). Half of the plants were exposed to full (constant) sunlight, and the other half were kept in 50% (constant) sunlight.(.Skill 17.3)(Rigorous)**

A.   The control is a set of plants grown in full (constant) sunlight.

B.   The control is a set of plants grown in 50% (constant) sunlight.

C.   The control is a set of plants grown in the dark.

D.   The control is a set of plants grown in a mixture of natural levels of sunlight.

A. **The control is a set of plants grown in full (constant) sunlight.**

In this experiment, the goal was to measure how two different amounts of sunlight affected plant growth. The control in any experiment is the 'base case,' or the usual situation without a change in variable. Because the control must be studied alongside the variable, answers (C) and (D) are omitted (because they were not in the experiment). The **better answer of (A) and (B) is (A)**, because usually plants are assumed to have the best growth and their usual growing circumstances in full sunlight. This is particularly true for crops like the corn plants in this question.

101. Which is the correct order of methodology?(Skill 17.3)(Rigorous)

1. collecting data
2. planning a controlled experiment
3. drawing a conclusion
4. hypothesizing a result
5. re-visiting a hypothesis to answer a question

A.   1,2,3,4,5

B.   4,2,1,3,5

C.   4,5,1,3,2

D.   1,3,4,5,2

B.   4,2,1,3,5

The correct methodology for the scientific method is first to make a meaningful hypothesis (educated guess), then plan and execute a controlled experiment to test that hypothesis. Using the data collected in that experiment, the scientist then draws conclusions and attempts to answer the original question related to the hypothesis. This is consistent only with **answer (B)**.

102. Who determines the laws regarding the use of safety glasses in the classroom? (Skill 18.1)(Average Rigor)

A.   The state government.

B.   The school site.

C.   The federal government.

D.   The local district.

A.   The state government.

Health and safety regulations are set by the state government, and apply to all school districts. Federal regulations may accompany specific federal grants, and local districts or school sites may enact local guidelines that are stricter than the state standards. All schools, however, must abide by safety precautions as set by state government. This is consistent only with **answer (A)**.

103. **When measuring the volume of water in a graduated cylinder, where does one read the measurement?(Skill 18.1)(Easy Rigor)**

A. At the highest point of the liquid.

B. At the bottom of the meniscus curve.

C. At the closest mark to the top of the liquid.

D. At the top of the plastic safety ring.

B. **At the bottom of the meniscus curve.**

To measure water in glass, you must look at the top surface at eye-level, and ascertain the location of the bottom of the meniscus (the curved surface at the top of the water). The meniscus forms because water molecules adhere to the sides of the glass, which is a slightly stronger force than their cohesion to each other. This leads to a U-shaped top of the liquid column, the bottom of which gives the most accurate volume measurement. (Other liquids have different forces, e.g. mercury in glass, which has a convex meniscus.) This is consistent only with **answer (B).**

104. **Under a 440 power microscope, an object with diameter 0.1 millimeter appears to have a diameter of _____(Skill 18.1)(Rigorous)**

A. 4.4 millimeters.

B. 44 millimeters.

C. 440 millimeters.

D. 4400 millimeters.

B. **44 millimeters.**

To answer this question, recall that to calculate a new length, you multiply the original length by the magnification power of the instrument. Therefore, the 0.1 millimeter diameter is multiplied by 440. This equals 44, so the image appears to be 44 millimeters in diameter. You could also reason that since a 440 power microscope is considered a "high power" microscope, you would expect a 0.1 millimeter object to appear a few centimeters long. Therefore, the correct **answer is (B)**.

105. **Which is the most desirable tool to use to heat substances in a middle school laboratory? (Skill 18.1)(Easy Rigor)**

A.   Alcohol burner.

B.   Freestanding gas burner.

C.   Bunsen burner.

D.   Hot plate.

D.   Hot plate.

Due to safety considerations, the use of open flame should be minimized, so a hot plate is the best choice. Any kind of burner may be used with proper precautions, but it is difficult to maintain a completely safe middle school environment. Therefore, the best **answer is (D)**.

106. **Chemicals should be stored _____(Skill 18.1)(Easy Rigor)**

A.   in the principal's office.

B.   in a dark room.

C.   in an off-site research facility.

D.   according to their reactivity with other substances.

D.   According to their reactivity with other substances.

Chemicals should be stored with other chemicals of similar properties (e.g. acids with other acids), to reduce the potential for either hazardous reactions in the store-room, or mistakes in reagent use. Certainly, chemicals should not be stored in anyone's office, and the light intensity of the room is not very important because light-sensitive chemicals are usually stored in dark containers. In fact, good lighting is desirable in a store-room, so that labels can be read easily. Chemicals may be stored off-site, but that makes their use inconvenient. Therefore, the best **answer is (D)**.

107. **Which item should always be used when handling glassware?(Skill 18.1)(Easy Rigor)**

A. Tongs.

B. Safety goggles.

C. Gloves.

D. Buret stand.

B. **Safety goggles.**

Safety goggles are the single most important piece of safety equipment in the laboratory, and should be used any time a scientist is using glassware, heat, or chemicals. Other equipment (e.g. tongs, gloves, or even a buret stand) has its place for various applications. However, the most important is safety goggles. Therefore, the **answer is (B)**.

108. **In a science experiment, a student needs to dispense very small measured amounts of liquid into a well-mixed solution. Which of the following is the \best choice for his/her equipment to use?(Skill 18.1)(Easy Rigor)**

A. Buret with Buret Stand, Stir-plate, Stirring Rod, Beaker.

B. Buret with Buret Stand, Stir-plate, Beaker.

C. Volumetric Flask, Dropper, Graduated Cylinder, Stirring Rod.

D. Beaker, Graduated Cylinder, Stir-plate.

B. **Buret with Buret Stand, Stir-plate, Beaker**.

The most accurate and convenient way to dispense small measured amounts of liquid in the laboratory is with a buret, on a buret stand. To keep a solution well-mixed, a magnetic stir-plate is the most sensible choice, and the solution will usually be mixed in a beaker. Although other combinations of materials could be used for this experiment, **choice (B)** is thus the simplest and best.

109. **A laboratory balance is most appropriately used to measure the mass of which of the following?(Skill 18.1)(Easy Rigor)**

A.   Seven paper clips.

B.   Three oranges.

C.   Two hundred cells.

D.   One student's elbow.

A.   Seven paper clips.

Usually, laboratory/classroom balances can measure masses between approximately 0.01 gram and 1 kilogram. Therefore, answer (B) is too heavy and answer (C) is too light. Answer (D) is silly, but it is a reminder to instruct students not to lean on the balances or put their things near them. **Answer (A)**, which is likely to have a mass of a few grams, is correct in this case.

110. **All of the following are measured in units of length, *except* for: (Skill 18.2)(Easy Rigor)**

A.   Perimeter.

B.   Distance.

C.   Radius.

D.   Area.

D.   Area.

Perimeter is the distance around a shape; distance is equivalent to length; radius is the distance from the center (e.g. in a circle) to the edge. Area, however, is the squared-length-units measure of the size of a two-dimensional surface. Therefore, **the answer is (D)**.

111. **If one inch equals 2.54 centimeters, how many millimeters are in 1.5 feet (Approximately)?**
(Skill 18.2)(Rigorous)

A. 18

B. 1800

C. 460

D. 4600

C. 460

To solve this problem, note that if one inch is 2.54 centimeters, then 1.5 feet (which is 18 inches), must be (18)(2.54) centimeters, i.e. approximately 46 centimeters. Because there are ten millimeters in a centimeter, this is approximately 460 millimeters:

(1.5 ft) (12 in/ft) (2.54 cm/in) (10 mm/cm) = (1.5) (12) (2.54) (10) mm = 457.2 mm

This is consistent only with **answer (C).**

112. **Which of the following is the worst choice for a school laboratory activity?(Skill 18.4)(Average Rigor)**

A. A genetics experiment tracking the fur color of mice.

B. Dissection of a preserved fetal pig.

C. Measurement of goldfish respiration rate at different temperatures.

D. Pithing a frog to watch the circulatory system.

D. Pithing a frog to watch the circulatory system.

While any use of animals (alive or dead) must be done with care to respect ethics and laws, it is possible to perform choices (A), (B), or (C) with due care. (Note that students will need significant assistance and maturity to perform these experiments.) However, modern practice precludes pithing animals (causing partial brain death while allowing some systems to function), as inhumane. Therefore, the answer to this **question is (D)**.

113. Who should be notified in the case of a serious chemical spill?(Skill 18.5)(Rigorous)

A.   The custodian.

B.   The fire department or other municipal authority.

C.   The science department chair.

D.   The School Board.

B.   The fire department or other municipal authority.

Although the custodian may help to clean up laboratory messes, and the science department chair should be involved in discussions of ways to avoid spills, a serious chemical spill may require action by the fire department or other trained emergency personnel. It is best to be safe by notifying them in case of a serious chemical accident. Therefore, the **best answer is (B)**.

114. In which situation would a science teacher be legally liable? (Skill 18.5)(Rigorous)

A.   The teacher leaves the classroom for a telephone call and a student slips and injures him/herself.

B.   A student removes his/her goggles and gets acid in his/her eye.

C.   A faulty gas line in the classroom causes a fire.

D.   A student cuts him/herself with a dissection scalpel.

A.   The teacher leaves the classroom for a telephone call and a student slips and injures him/herself.

Teachers are required to exercise a "reasonable duty of care" for their students. Accidents may happen (e.g. (D)), or students may make poor decisions (e.g. (B)), or facilities may break down (e.g. (C)). However, the teacher has the responsibility to be present and to do his/her best to create a safe and effective learning environment. Therefore, the **answer is (A)**.

115. **Which of these is the best example of 'negligence'? (Skill 18.5)(Rigorous)**

A.   A teacher fails to give oral instructions to those with reading disabilities.

B.   A teacher fails to exercise ordinary care to ensure safety in the classroom.

C.   A teacher displays inability to supervise a large group of students.

D.   A teacher reasonably anticipates that an event may occur, and plans accordingly.

B.   A teacher fails to exercise ordinary care to ensure safety in the classroom.

'Negligence' is the failure to "exercise ordinary care" to ensure an appropriate and safe classroom environment. It is best for a teacher to meet all special requirements for disabled students, and to be good at supervising large groups. However, if a teacher can prove that s/he has done a reasonable job to ensure a safe and effective learning environment, then it is unlikely that she/he would be found negligent. Therefore, **the answer is (B)**.

116. **For her first project of the year, a student is designing a science experiment to test the effects of light and water on plant growth. You should recommend that she _____(Skill 18.3)(Easy Rigor)**

A.   manipulate the temperature also.

B.   manipulate the water pH also.

C.   determine the relationship between light and water unrelated to plant growth.

D.   omit either water or light as a variable.

D.   Omit either water or light as a variable.

As a science teacher for middle-school-aged kids, it is important to reinforce the idea of 'constant' vs. 'variable' in science experiments. At this level, it is wisest to have only one variable examined in each science experiment. (Later, students can hold different variables constant while investigating others.) Therefore it is counterproductive to add in other variables (answers (A)or (B)). It is also irrelevant to determine the light-water interactions aside from plant growth (C). So the only possible **answer is (D)**.

117. Formaldehyde should not be used in school laboratories for the following reason: (Skill 18.4)(Easy Rigor)

A.   it smells unpleasant.

B.   it is a known carcinogen.

C.   it is expensive to obtain.

D.   it is an explosive.

B.   It is a known carcinogen.

Formaldehyde is a known carcinogen, so it is too dangerous for use in schools. In general, teachers should not use carcinogens in school laboratories. Although formaldehyde also smells unpleasant, a smell alone is not a definitive marker of danger. For example, many people find the smell of vinegar to be unpleasant, but vinegar is considered a very safe classroom/laboratory chemical. Furthermore, some odorless materials are toxic. Formaldehyde is neither particularly expensive nor explosive. Thus, the **answer is (B)**.

118.   Experiments may be done with any of the following animals except: (Skill 18.4)(Easy Rigor)

A.   birds.

B.   invertebrates.

C.   lower order life.

D.   frogs.

A.   Birds.

No dissections may be performed on living mammalian vertebrates or birds. Lower order life and invertebrates may be used. Biological experiments may be done with all animals except mammalian vertebrates or birds. Therefore the **answer is (A).**

119. **In an experiment measuring the growth of bacteria at different temperatures, what is the independent variable?(Skill 19.2)(Rigorous)**

A. Number of bacteria.

B. Growth rate of bacteria.

C. Temperature.

D. Light intensity.

C. **Temperature.**

To answer this question, recall that the independent variable in an experiment is the entity that is changed by the scientist, in order to observe the effects (the dependent variable(s)). In this experiment, temperature is changed in order to measure growth of bacteria, so **(C) is the answer**. Note that answer (A) is the dependent variable, and neither (B) nor (D) is directly relevant to the question.

120. **When designing a scientific experiment, a student considers all the factors that may influence the results. The process goal is to _____(Skill 19.2)(Average Rigor)**

A. recognize and manipulate independent variables.

B. recognize and record independent variables.

C. recognize and manipulate dependent variables.

D. recognize and record dependent variables.

A. **Recognize and manipulate independent variables.**

When a student designs a scientific experiment, s/he must decide what to measure, and what independent variables will play a role in the experiment. S/he must determine how to manipulate these independent variables to refine his/her procedure and to prepare for meaningful observations. Although s/he will eventually record dependent variables (D), this does not take place during the experimental design phase. Although the student will likely recognize and record the independent variables (B), this is not the process goal, but a helpful step in manipulating the variables. It is unlikely that the student will manipulate dependent variables directly in his/her experiment (C), or the data would be suspect. Thus, the **answer is (A)**.

121. **Which of the following data sets is properly represented by a bar graph?(Skill 19.3)(Average Rigor)**

A.   Number of people choosing to buy cars, vs. Color of car bought.

B.   Number of people choosing to buy cars, vs. Age of car customer.

C.   Number of people choosing to buy cars, vs. Distance from car lot to customer home.

D.   Number of people choosing to buy cars, vs. Time since last car purchase.

A.   **Number of people choosing to buy cars, vs. Color of car bought.**

A bar graph should be used only for data sets in which the independent variable is non-continuous (discrete), e.g. gender, color, etc. Any continuous independent variable (age, distance, time, etc.) should yield a scatter-plot when the dependent variable is plotted. Therefore, the **answer must be (A)**.

122. **A scientific law _____(Skill 19.8)(Average Rigor)**

A.   proves scientific accuracy.

B.   may never be broken.

C.   may be revised in light of new data.

D.   is the result of one excellent experiment.

C.   **May be revised in light of new data.**

A scientific law is the same as a scientific theory, except that it has lasted for longer, and has been supported by more extensive data. Therefore, such a law may be revised in light of new data, and may be broken by that new data. Furthermore, a scientific law is always the result of many experiments, and never 'proves' anything but rather is implied or supported by various results. Therefore, the **answer must be (C)**.

123. **In a laboratory report, what is the abstract?(Skill 19.8)(Easy Rigor)**

A. The abstract is a summary of the report, and is the first section of the report.

B. The abstract is a summary of the report, and is the last section of the report.

C. The abstract is predictions for future experiments, and is the first section of the report.

D. The abstract is predictions for future experiments, and is the last section of the report.

A. **The abstract is a summary of the report, and is the first section of the report.**

In a laboratory report, the abstract is the section that summarizes the entire report (often containing one representative sentence from each section). It appears at the very beginning of the report, even before the introduction, often on its own page (instead of a title page). This format is consistent with articles in scientific journals. Therefore, the **answer is (A).**

124. **Newton's Laws are taught in science classes because _____. (Skill 20.3)(Average Rigor)**

A. they are the correct analysis of inertia, gravity, and forces.

B. they are a close approximation to correct physics, for usual Earth conditions.

C. they accurately incorporate Relativity into studies of forces.

D. Newton was a well-respected scientist in his time.

B. **They are a close approximation to correct physics, for usual Earth conditions.**

Although Newton's Laws are often taught as fully correct for inertia, gravity, and forces, it is important to realize that Einstein's work (and that of others) has indicated that Newton's Laws are reliable only at speeds much lower than that of light. This is reasonable, though, for most middle- and high-school applications. At speeds close to the speed of light, Relativity considerations must be used. Therefore, the only correct **answer is (B).**

125. **The theory of 'continental drift' is supported by which of the following?(Skill 20.3)(Average Rigor)**

A.   The way the shapes of South America and Europe fit together.

B.   The way the shapes of Europe and Asia fit together.

C.   The way the shapes of South America and Africa fit together.

D.   The way the shapes of North America and Antarctica fit together.

C.   **The way the shapes of South America and Africa fit together.**

The theory of 'continental drift' states that many years ago, there was one land mass on the earth ('pangea'). This land mass broke apart via earth crust motion, and the continents drifted apart as separate pieces. This is supported by the shapes of South America and Africa, which seem to fit together like puzzle pieces if you look at a globe. Note that answer choices (A), (B), and (D) give either land masses that do not fit together, or those that are still attached to each other. Therefore, the **answer must be (C)**.

CPSIA information can be obtained
at www.ICGtesting.com
Printed in the USA
BVHW011600181119
564177BV00015B/1066/P